SHE HATH DONE WHAT SHE COULD

SHE HATH DONE WHAT SHE COULD

A History of Women's Participation
in the Church of the Brethren

PAMELA BRUBAKER
Foreword by Ruby Rhoades

BRETHREN PRESS
Elgin, Illinois

She Hath Done What She Could

Brethren Press, 1451 Dundee Avenue, Elgin, IL 60120

Edited by Fred W. Swartz

Library of Congress Cataloging in Publication Data

Brubaker, Pamela, 1946-
　　She hath done what she could.

　　Bibliography: p.
　　Includes index.
　　1. Women in church work—Church of the Brethren—History.　2. Church of the Brethren—History.　I. Title.
BX7815.B79　1985　　286′.5　　　　85-6622
ISBN 0-87178-942-6

to my mother and father
Helen Kiracofe Brubaker and Elbert D. Brubaker

my sister
Beverly Ann Brubaker

my grandmothers
Lucy Eby Kiracofe and Lona Apple Brubaker

and all those women
who have faithfully shared their gifts and vision
and thus enlarged the place of women within the church

Contents

List of Illustrations

Unless otherwise noted, photographs are from the Brethren Historical Library and Archives or *Messenger* files. Used with permission.

FOREWORD

This is the courageous story of women's participation in the life of the church, from just being admitted to the Lord's Supper to "having the same privilege of breaking bread and passing the cup the Brethren now enjoy"; from preparing the food for Annual Meeting to becoming voting delegates to that body; from serving as "deaconess" only when their husbands were elected deacon to being elected to serve in their own right; from sitting quietly together on one side of the church to standing in the pulpit, ordained to preach God's word.

Such accomplishments have been slow in coming, and the pain of struggle is visible in these pages. Julia Gilbert's valiant efforts, repeated defeats, her daring speech on the floor of Annual Meeting stand before us all as courageous symbols that what is right and just is possible. Sara Righter Major, after being denied official permission to preach by an Annual Meeting appointed committee, continued quietly in her preaching ministry, opening doors for other women to enter. And through those doors dedicated women have eagerly entered the life and leadership of the church.

I found myself developing a love/hate relationship with the scripture which is the theme of this book—"She hath done what she could." The church's response to Jesus' affirmation of the act of a devoted woman has both affirmed and limited our participation in church life. I remember using this scripture in women's meetings to encourage those who felt they had little or nothing to offer in the life of the church. (I doubt if it has ever been the rallying cry for a men's meeting.) It was a second-class yardstick, but it served as encouragement when many of us were seeking just that.

How ironic that this bold woman is to be remembered "wherever the gospel is preached in the whole world," yet no one bothered to record her name. The timing also interests me. Surely she could have found a less conspicuous moment to carry out her act—not at a dinner party for the Pharisees. As I read of our sisters' actions later, I find some of that intuitive timing has caused us to be remembered throughout our church history.

A certain generation of us who read this book will know "we have done what we could" within the limits of another measuring stick. We were nudged gently into several vocational directions— teaching, nursing, secretarial positions, Christian education, and pastors' wives. Business and financial management, personnel and career development skills, these were for our brothers who could aspire to executive positions in the church, to college and university presidencies, to hospital or retirement home management, to seminary posts or ecumenical positions. And then we were told, "She hath done what she could."

Yet a later generation who read this book will have grown up under the leadership of a woman pastor, will have heard women speak at Annual Conference, and will read with disbelief that such waiting, pain, and insult ever took place in the church family. To them it will seem ludicrous that the following reasoning could ever have been uttered and accepted by Standing Committee: "I would have no objection to their voting, but it would be deviating from the order of our meeting, which I do not like."

Pam Brubaker has done us a great favor in pulling this story together so we can celebrate our history with realism. She has carefully researched every name, place, and happening and can be quoted with confidence. She recognizes the values for which women have stood firmly down through the centuries.

But our story does not end here, impressive as it is. It goes on in the dreams and aspirations of women around the world as we take our rightful place in the leadership of the church. Now we can say with new meaning, "She hath done what she could."

Ruby Rhoades
World Ministries Commission
Church of the Brethren General Board

PREFACE

The Church of the Brethren is celebrating one hundred years of organized women's work in 1985. My own research into the involvement of women in the Church of the Brethren began when Fran Nyce requested that I co-author (with Jack Lowe) a historical article for a special issue of *Brethren Life and Thought* (Summer 1977) which she was editing. I became fascinated with what I was discovering about the sustained debate over the proper place for women within the church. I was moved when I read about the many women who faithfully responded to their call, even when that call was questioned. It seemed to me imperative that the church be made aware of the historical precedents to the contemporary debate over the role and status of women.

After the completion of this article I produced a multimedia presentation—"Journey of the Sisters Among the Brethren"—to share with the church more of the story I was uncovering. "Journey" was presented by a cast of women and men from the District of Southern Ohio to the Gathering of Church of the Brethren Women in 1978 and then at the 1979 Annual Conference in Seattle.

Somewhat prior to this I had suggested to the Womaen's Caucus steering committee, of which I was then a member, that we propose publication of an anthology about the history of women in the church for the one hundredth anniversary of women's organizations. Karen Hoover, who was Womaen's Caucus worker, and I prepared a proposal which was presented to the Historical Committee and General Services Commission of the denomination. They supported the idea, but with some modification. As a result I was commissioned by Brethren Press early in 1980 to write a narrative history of women in the church, with both Womaen's Caucus and the Parish Ministries Commission agreeing to help fund its publication.

Research began in the summer of 1980. Since then I have spent several weeks working at the Brethren Historical Library and Archives in Elgin, Illinois. I am deeply grateful to James Lynch and the staff there for their patient and thorough response to my many requests and for their suggestions as to other resources with which I was not familiar. Edith Bonsack Barnes and Mildred Etter Heckert were most helpful in leading me to the materials from the women's organizations which are housed in the archives. I also am appreciative of the use of the Juniata College Archives, the Southern Ohio District Historical Library, the Burke Library of Union Theological Seminary, and the Bridgewater College Brethren Room where I was privileged to examine a Bible thought to have been used by Alexander Mack.

I am indebted to all those throughout the denomination who sent me sketches of women they wished to be remembered in this volume. Through them I learned of women I would not otherwise have known. I have included many of those sketches in this volume. The vignettes of these and other individual women are crucial in illustrating the goals, values, and vision of Brethren women and their organizations. I am also grateful to Jack Lowe and Dave Eller for sharing their historical expertise and resources with me and to Fred Swartz for his editorial assistance.

The foreword to this volume was the last gift of Ruby Frantz Rhoades to the Church of the Brethren before her death, January 8, 1985. I am deeply grateful that Ruby was able to write this profound and moving foreword. Ruby will be sorely missed by many of us. For as Bonnie Kline Smeltzer said in her tribute to Ruby at her memorial service:

> I think Ruby's life bridged two eras. In her early adult years, it was the time when women were respected most for being ladies, wives, and good mothers. And from mid-life on, Ruby experienced a time when women were still respected as ladies, wives, and mothers, but in addition felt the challenge and call to leadership in many walks of life. . . .
>
> The life and death of Ruby Rhoades bridged these two generations. She moved in and out of each one with ease. As the gracious lady and courageous church leader whose life we celebrate today, we know "she hath done what she could . . . "

The support of the steering committee of Womaen's Caucus through the years has been irreplaceable to me, both in my own personal growth and in completion of this project—which they co-sponsored with Brethren Press. I also am grateful for the research assistance given me by "caucus workers" Karen Woody Hoover, Andrea Warnke, and Shirley Kirkwood. The support, companionship, and encouragement of the sisters in Elgin who housed and fed me during my research trips there is fondly remembered: "thank you" to Von James, Mary Cline Detrick, Harriet Ziegler, Joyce Stoltzfus, Nancy Lamia, and Connie Andes. I am also grateful for my participation in the women's organizations of the Gratis, Drexel Hill, Green Tree, Chambersburg, and Springfield (Ohio) congregations where I first learned about the faithful participation of women in the life and work of the church.

I also wish to thank those friends from other faith traditions whose encouragement and presence were invaluable during long periods of writing in New York City: Elizabeth Bounds, Marilyn Legge, Linda Marshall Manuel, William Mengot, David Wildman, and Jeanne Wilson. I am deeply indebted to my sons John and Cory Lowe for their patient and understanding love for me even as I spent many hours researching and writing and also to their father, grandparents, aunts, uncles, and cousins who helped care for them and also encouraged me.

As I present this volume for the 100th Anniversary celebration, I am aware that there are areas of women's participation in the church which have not been treated. I apologize for oversight and also those instances in which I lacked adequate insight. Yet I hope that the legacy recorded here will enrich our celebration.

Representatives of current women's organizations within the denomination have been appointed by the Parish Ministries Commission to plan for the celebration. These women represent a wide spectrum of the concerns and involvements of contemporary Brethren women. Martha Dubble and Lucille West Rupel represent Women's Fellowship. Martha, from Pennsylvania, is active in local and district Women's Fellowship in Atlantic Northeast District. Lucy, from California, was a member of the National Concil of Women's Work and is active in Women's Fellowship in the Pacific Southwest District. Mary Eikenberry, of Ohio, represents missionary activity. She recently returned with her husband Ivan after 37 years in Nigeria. Shirley Kirkwood, from Virginia, represents Womaen's Caucus. She is the caucus worker and was instrumental in organizing the Caucus's "Feminism and Nonviolence Conference" in May of

1984. Fran Clemens Nyce, from Maryland, represents district Person Awareness team and the Global Women's Project. Fran is also a member of the General Board. Anna Warstler, from Indiana, represents former staff for women's organizations. Mary Cline Detrick, from Illinois, was staff consultant for the celebration through 1984. Melanie May joined the committee in early 1985 and assumed staff responsibilities for the celebration. I serve as the committee's historian.

We have chosen the theme *Empowered by Our Birthright* for the 100th Anniversary. The theme is a call to each of us to accept the gifts and privileges that come from being a child of God and to use the empowerment that comes from this acceptance on behalf of others. Although the primary source of our empowerment is the Holy Spirit, the legacy of women who came together to participate more fully in the mission and ministry of the church can also empower us. As we remember their commitment and vision, may our own commitment and vision be strengthened.

Pamela Brubaker
New York City

PROLOGUE

SHE HATH DONE WHAT SHE COULD

And while he.[Jesus] was at Bethany in the house of Simon the leper, as he sat at table, a woman came with an alabaster flask of ointment of pure nard, very costly, and she broke the flask and poured it over his head. But there were some who said to themselves indignantly, "Why was the ointment thus wasted? For this ointment might have been sold for more than three hundred denarii, and given to the poor." And they reproached her. But Jesus said, "Let her alone, why do you trouble her? She has done a beautiful thing to me. For you always have the poor with you, and whenever you will, you can do good to them; but you will not always have me. *She has done what she could*; she has anointed my body beforehand for burying. And truly I say to you, wherever the gospel is preached in the whole world, what she has done will be told in memory of her" (Mark 14: 3-9, RSV, with emphasis added).

She had slipped quietly to the table in the house of Simon the leper where Jesus was eating. She brought with her an alabaster flask of costly ointment. She took the flask to the place where Jesus was reclining, broke it open, and poured it over his head. A simple act of ministry, yet one that was questioned. Some of Simon's guests thought that the ointment had been wasted. Wouldn't it have been better to sell the ointment and give the money to the poor? So they reproached this unnamed woman.

Jesus rebuked them. He asked why they troubled her. For she had done "a beautiful thing" to him. Whenever they would, they could do good for the poor. But Jesus would soon be gone. And this woman had done for him what she could—she had anointed him for burial before his death. The story of her act would be told wherever the gospel spread throughout the world "in memory of her."

Her story has been retold. It appears with variations in all four Gospels. As the gospel has spread throughout the world, so has this story of her act of ministry to Jesus. At times the story has been misunderstood. It has been used to justify the fact of poverty by quoting Jesus' statement about the poor "being with you always."

But others have found a larger and more constructive meaning in the passage. They hear Jesus saying "and whenever you will, you can do good to them." They know that Jesus is no longer with them in bodily form. He does not need the ministry which this unnamed but remembered woman provided for him. But there are still those who are poor, and consequently much opportunity to minister to them in Jesus' name.

Many women have understood this story in such a way. They have ministered in whatever ways they could to the poor near them. Some began to organize themselves early in the nineteenth century to increase their effectiveness in this ministry. A few boldly advocated this work from platform and pulpit. They envisioned reaching out not only to those in need near them, but also to those in need throughout the world.

Women in the Church of the Brethren shared this vision. In 1885 they began a denominational organization to support the domestic and foreign mission movement of the church. Local organizations also were formed at this time. These would continue the ministry of caring for those in need within their communities as well as supporting national and global outreach. The women's group in Huntingdon, Pennsylvania, chose as the motto for their organization, "She hath done what she could."

These beginnings were not easy, however, for any such activity in which women visibly displayed leadership or public initiative represented a departure from the tradition of the church. Just as the woman who ministered to Jesus in Simon's home was criticized for her unorthodox act, so too the initiative of these early Brethren women to lead out in faith and mission was considered contrary to the appropriate role for women. Within a year after the effort to begin a women's organization, the Church of the Brethren Annual Meeting passed a paper forbidding "Sisters' Mission Bands."

But the vision still lingered in the minds of many women, and through the efforts of local groups the outreach ministry of women persisted until ten years later (1895) Annual Meeting officially recognized the right of women to organize. This opened the way for women to demonstrate their God-given abilities to contribute to the advancement and ministry of the church. As organized women's activity increased and this contribution was recognized as valuable, many of the limitations on women's participation in the church were lifted.

This anniversary volume, commemorating the 100th year of organized women's work in the Church of the Brethren, focuses upon the legacy of these pioneering efforts and the vital role in the church which that heritage has provided for women today.

1

BRETHREN BEGINNINGS

> . . . in the year 1708, eight persons agreed together to establish a
> covenant of a good conscience with God, to accept all ordinances
> of Jesus Christ as an easy yoke, and thus to follow after their Lord
> Jesus—their good and loyal shepherd—as true sheep in joy or
> sorrow until the blessed end. (Alexander Mack, Jr.[1])

EUROPEAN ORIGINS

Early in the eighteenth century a small group gathered in the
home of Alexander and Anna Margaret Mack in what is now
southwestern Germany to pray and study scripture. These men and
women were a part of the Pietist movement which was sweeping
through the established churches of parts of Europe. Discontented
with the emphasis on a mechanical, emotionless religion present in
these churches, Pietists turned to a form of practical Christianity
grounded in a personal experience of spiritual renewal.

Alexander Mack was attracted to Pietism around 1702. He and
Anna became friends with Ernst Christoph Hochmann von Hoch-
enau, a radical Pietist leader. In 1704 Mack withdrew from participation in the Reformed Church, in which he had been baptized and
reared. He identified himself with the Pietist Separatists, a branch of
Pietism which separated from the established churches rather than
working to renew them from within.

Mack joined Hochmann in preaching missions in 1706. That
same year Anna, Alexander, and their children moved from Schries-
heim in the Palatinate area of Germany to Schwarzenau, where
greater freedom of conscience was promised. Each German state
was to be aligned with one of the three established churches—the
Reformed, the Lutheran, or the Roman Catholic—according to the

provisions of the Peace of Westphalia of 1648. Usually the sovereign of each state determined the religion of his subjects. Schwarzenau was in the area of the Wittgenstein province of Germany ruled by Count Henry Albert. There was religious toleration in Count Henry's province because he welcomed the skilled artisans who were among the religious refugees.

In Schwarzenau a group of Pietists met together in a large room in the Mack home on Sunday afternoons or weekday evenings. Families, widows, and single persons searched to discern the truth of the teachings of Jesus. Their services began with the singing of Pietist hymns and praying in unison the Lord's Prayer. If Hochmann was present, he would "explain the word"; if not, Mack interpreted the scripture for the group. They then knelt together for prayer following this period of scriptural exposition. The meeting concluded with a hymn and closing prayer.

Through their study of scripture, Mack and some others of the group came to believe that baptism of adult believers by immersion was a teaching of Jesus. Most Pietists were opposed to infant baptism, which was the practice of the established churches. But they did not believe an outer form of baptism was necessary as they believed repentant Christians received a spiritual baptism during their experience of conversion. Mack thought that Jesus' own example, as well as his teaching in Matthew 28 to baptize disciples, required water baptism. Mack also researched church history for more information about baptism and its forms.[2] He was convinced from his study that baptism by immersion was the practice of the early Christian church. Mack and another Pietist corresponded with Hochmann, their spiritual leader who was at that time imprisoned in Nürnberg for his preaching and teaching, requesting his counsel concerning baptism of adults. He responded, affirming that baptism was a teaching of Jesus but cautioning the group to carefully consider whether this was God's will as the consequences of rebaptism could be costly. At that time, rebaptism of anyone who previously had been baptized into an established church was illegal.

Some of the Schwarzenau group were willing to risk the cost of rebaptism. They were concerned to be obedient to the example and teaching of Jesus not only in regard to baptism, but also in regard to love feast and communion and church discipline. For this, a "gemeinde"—a congregation or community—of baptized believers was necessary.

A letter was sent from this group in the summer of 1708 to Pietists in the Palatinate. The author, drawn by lot from the group, explained why baptism was necessary for an obedient Christian and invited others to participate in beginning "this high act of baptism."[3] Sometime in late summer, eight believers came together to be baptized in the river Eder which ran through Schwarzenau. They were Alexander Mack; Anna Margaret Mack; Andrew Boni, from Basel; Joanna Nothiger Boni, a widow married to Andrew for less than a year; George Grebe, who, along with his wife, had fled from Kassel to Schwarzenau; Luke Vetter, who with his wife had fled from Hesse; and Joanna and John Kipping from Wurttemberg. Coming together early in the morning, they first sang several hymns and read from Luke 14 on "counting the cost" of discipleship. Then Mack was baptized by a brother drawn by lot. He then baptized the other seven. Each person was totally immersed three times in the flowing water, being baptized in "the name of the Father, and of the Son, and of the Holy Spirit." The group then sang another hymn and received a benediction.

These eight were now a congregation. They called themselves the "Schwarzenau Baptists" or the "New Baptists."[4] Their life and practice were to be based on the model of the New Testament church, as it was known to them through scripture and church history.

The congregation grew and began to expand into other areas. Women were involved in every area of expansion.[5] Both married and single women appear to have taken part in this early organization of the church. Some couples were both Brethren, but in some instances women of non-Brethren husbands participated in the new movement. The latter relationship at times produced tension in the home as well as in the community.[6]

Essential to the congregational life of these first Brethren was the celebration of the Lord's Supper, also called the "love feast." In this as in other areas of their life together, they wanted to be faithful to New Testament teaching and to the practice of the early church. Through a study of scripture, the Brethren developed a form for this celebration which is still practiced today.

The congregation would gather for love feast in the Macks' large room with the men around one table and the women around another. They began with a service of examination and praise. Only those who had been baptized by immersion were eligible to participate. Even these were to examine themselves to see if they were worthy to partake; if not, they would withdraw from participation.

Feetwashing followed the examination service. First the story of Jesus washing the disciples' feet was read from John 13. Then each woman would gird herself with a towel and kneel to wash the feet of the sister next to her. The men did likewise. Hymns were sung, some of which had been composed by members of the congregation. A simple meal followed. Prayers of gratitude were then offered.

The Eucharist (the bread and cup) concluded the love feast. After a reading of scriptures telling of Jesus' crucifixion, the bread and cup were passed among the participants. Again prayers of gratitude were offered. A closing hymn was followed by a benediction. [7]

The congregation was strengthened in their love for each other and in their commitment to following Christ through this celebration. Exclusion from participation in love feast was a means of enforcing church discipline. Following the teaching of Matthew 18, the Brethren would put "in avoidance" any member who was not faithful to the commands of the New Testament as understood by the congregation. Other members were not to associate with a member who was put in avoidance until that member repented and was restored to fellowship. If repentance did not come, the sinful member was to be separated from the congregation. This was to assure the salvation of individual members and the faithfulness of the congregation as a body of believers. [8]

With their insistence on believer's baptism and church discipline, the Brethren shared the convictions of the group of Separatists, known as Anabaptists, with whom the Mennonites also were identified. The Brethren were familiar with various Mennonite groups in the Palatinate area. But they had chosen not to be baptized into Mennonite congregations, as the Mennonites baptized by sprinkling or pouring. The Brethren believed trine immersion to be the New Testament command as well as early church practice.

Some Pietists challenged the Brethren on their Anabaptist view of the church. Among them was Hochmann, to whom the first Brethren had looked for spiritual leadership. He was concerned that they not develop a "sectarian spirit" toward others who did not share their views on baptism. Others accused the Brethren of emphasizing outward forms, rather than the experience of the spirit, in their practice of baptism, love feast, and avoidance.

The Brethren were also challenged by the established churches and sovereigns of some territories. Rebaptism of anyone baptized into an established church was illegal. As the law required that children be baptized into the established church of their state, those who came to the Brethren for baptism had been previously baptized. Count Henry Albert of Wittgenstein did not arrest the Brethren as they preached and baptized in the Schwarzenau area. But he was challenged for his tolerance by his brother-in-law, Count Charles Louis of Sayn-Wittgenstein. Charles Louis wrote to various officials, including the imperial solictor of the Holy Roman Empire, calling on them to force Henry Albert to banish the dissenters.

Henry Albert defended his right to tolerate Anabaptists in a letter to Charles Louis. The sisters of Henry Albert, who had Pietist sympathies, published this defense. But Charles Louis continued his efforts to get the imperial solicitor to take action against Henry Albert's religious toleration. In a report he sent to the solicitor to be used in court proceedings, he made the following charges against "the pack of fanatics, the so-called Pietists and Anabaptists" in Wittgenstein:

(1) They organize private meetings where males and females are permitted to teach whatever the Spirit moves them.
(2) They deny their own infant baptism, refuse to baptize their children, and engage in notorious re-baptism.
(3) Rather than going to church for the sacraments of communion, they engage in the *Agape* (love feast) in their secret meetings.
(4) They discard considerations of social rank, honors, positions, respect for parents, respect of wives for husbands, obedience to authorities. They also reject oaths, courts, and court proceedings.[9]

The first three charges seem to be a rather accurate description of the practice of the Brethren. Their views on baptism and love feast were not hidden. Mack's son later wrote that the original eight "witnessed publicly."[10] He also recorded a woman elder in the congregation at Schwarzenau: the wife of Jacob Schneider, who "after her husband's death . . . lived and served the congregation seven years."[11]

Although the Brethren would not take oaths or go to court, the remainder of the fourth charge seems questionable. In responding to this document, Count Henry Albert claimed that the Brethren "have led quiet lives to this date, out of a pure desire to lead lives pleasing to God." He reminded his peers that it was his right as a prince to tolerate "one or more subjects who do not agree with the authorities of other counties on this or that point in matters of conscience, but are otherwise leading quiet lives."[12] He was able to maintain his policy of religious toleration for a while longer.

As the Brethren expanded into other territories, they faced punishment for their disobedience. One such instance occurred in the Marienborn area in 1711. Mack had been invited to do evangelistic work there by some Brethren families. While there he baptized the daughter of the widow Eva Elizabeth Hoffman, whom Mack had already baptized. When the court councilors of Count Charles August heard about this, they withdrew the count's protection from Widow Hoffman and ordered her to leave the Marienborn area. Mack was also ordered to leave the area. Mack unsuccessfully appealed to the count on behalf of Widow Hoffman.

Not realizing that his ban from Marienborn was permanent, Mack returned a month later and baptized four more converts. The council then issued orders that no more baptisms were to be performed, that Mack must leave the area within twenty-four hours, and that those baptized and those who attended the baptism must leave Marienborn within eight days. Some rejoined the established church; others left Marienborn for more tolerant areas. Yet, a congregation did develop in the Marienborn area. Those desiring baptism came to Schwarzenau to be baptized and then returned to Marienborn. In 1712 the consistory of the Reformed Church there recommended to the count that religious protection not be revoked from the Brethren in that area. But in 1714 religious dissenters were forced to confine their religious practices to their own homes or leave the territory. Most Brethren moved to Krefeld, a German city on the Rhine River that granted religious freedom.

The congregation at Krefeld prospered at first, winning converts from Mennonites in the area. But a controversy that arose a few years later over church discipline was said to have caused the loss of the support of one hundred persons who "had been convinced in favor of the new baptism."[13] At issue were marriage outside the Brethren faith and the severity of the discipline administered in response.

In 1719 twenty families from Krefeld migrated to Pennsylvania. The following year some two hundred Brethren migrated from Schwarzenau to Holland, under the leadership of Alexander Mack.

Their economic survival and freedom of conscience had become threatened because of a change in state policy in Wittgenstein.

In Holland they enjoyed a measure of religious toleration and the support of other Anabaptist groups. Mack experienced personal sorrow there with the deaths of his wife, Anna Margaret, and their six-year old daughter, both in the fall of 1720. Anna Margaret had been a source of strength to Alexander. Together they shared a life centered in their faith. When Alexander was gone on preaching missions to share this faith, Anna Margaret cared for their daughter and three sons and managed their household. Her support helped make possible his ministry.[14] Now Mack needed to continue his ministry without her support, as well as caring for their three sons.

In time, the economic situation of the Brethren in Holland became more tenuous. They were drawn to migrate to Pennsylvania where religious freedom was guaranteed and economic prosperity was reported to abound. Some thirty families left Holland with Mack in 1729 for Pennsylvania, where they were warmly welcomed by the Brethren already there.

COLONIAL AMERICA

The first Brethren families who had migrated from Krefeld in 1719 had settled in Germantown, a center for German settlement established in the late seventeenth century by German Mennonite-Quaker immigrants. Some families dispersed into nearby areas where land was available. In 1722 Peter Becker, leader of the Krefeld migration, attempted to bring together the scattered Brethren for congregational fellowship. Meetings were held alternately in the Becker and Gumre homes.

The first baptisms into the Germantown congregation were on Christmas Day of 1723. Seventeen members of the congregation gathered in the Becker home to celebrate the baptism of Martin and Catherine Urner, Henry Landis and his wife, Frederick Lang, and John Mayle. The group journeyed from here to a spot along the Wissahickon Creek, owned by Gumre and the "congregation of the Brethren."[15] There Becker immersed these six into the icy water. Then all the congregation gathered in the Gumre home to celebrate a love feast together.

This event marked the beginning of a period of growth and expansion as well as controversy and schism. The first new congregation established was Coventry. Nine people were baptized there in

1724. Later that year a congregation was established at Conestoga in what would soon become Lancaster County, Pennsylvania. Among those baptized was Conrad Beissel, a radical Pietist immigrant from Germany. He was placed in charge of the Conestoga congregation by Becker.

Beissel began celebrating the Sabbath on the seventh day of the week, or Saturday. This became a source of controversy among the Brethren, as did his views on celibacy. Beissel taught that celibacy was a higher spiritual state than marriage, a belief which some other radical Pietists shared. The Schwarzenau Brethren at first practiced celibacy but later affirmed that "the state of marriage of two persons who are one in the fear of God and in faith in God is ordained and blessed by God . . ."[16]

A division occurred in the Conestoga congregation in 1728, with one group following Beissel and another remaining loyal to the Germantown congregation's leadership. Beissel "gave back" his baptism to the Brethren and withdrew to live as a religious hermit on Mill Creek near Conestoga.[17] Two single women and three men joined him there, placing themselves under Beissel's leadership. The women were Anna and Maria Eicher, both baptized by Beissel in 1726. Their parents had been among the first baptized into the Coventry congregation. Some question was raised as to the propriety of two single women living in such close proximity to Beissel and his male followers. The arrival of two married women at Mill Creek in 1730 was even more controversial, as they had left their husbands to follow Beissel.

One of these women was Maria Sauer. She had migrated with her husband, Christopher, and young son from Germany to Philadelphia in 1724. The family at first settled in Germantown but moved in 1726 to the Conestoga area where they had purchased some farmland. Her husband and son returned to Germantown the year after her departure, possibly because of the difficulty of homesteading without a housewife.

Beissel and his followers moved to the Cocalico region of Pennsylvania in 1732. There he was to organize the Ephrata community, also known as the Ephrata Cloister. Four of the women vowed together in 1735 to lead a common life. An order of celibate sisters grew from this beginning. These Spiritual Virgins, as they were sometimes called, "acknowledged no headship but that of Christ, and no guardianship but that of the Christian Church."[18] Beissel appointed Maria Eicher prioress of the order and Maria Sauer sub-prioress. An order of celibate brothers also was organized.

At times, the entire community came together for love feast and communion. During these services, the sisters would be seated in a balcony out of sight of the brothers and the householders. Beissel usually gave the bread and cup to all participants. Occasionally he held love feasts with the women of the community with no other men present. According to the *Chronicles*, the sisters served as deacons at these services and "officiated in all things."[19]

Contact between Ephrata and the Brethren continued. Alexander Mack tried unsuccessfully to reconcile the two groups shortly after his arrival in Germantown. A few years later he again attempted a reconciliation. But before his death in 1735, he seemed to realize that the differences between the two groups would not be bridged.

Members from Ephrata went on preaching missions in the surrounding area, as did the Brethren. Although the Amwell, New Jersey, congregation (organized in 1734) would not permit a night watch to be held there, some of its members were persuaded to follow Beissel.

Communication was continued with the Germantown congregation. A few members from Ephrata stayed in Germantown to supervise Sauer's printing of their first hymnal. In 1738 about twenty members left Germantown to join the Ephrata community. Among them were Valentine Mack, oldest son of Alexander and Anna Margaret; his wife, Maria Hildebrand Mack; and Alexander Mack, Jr., who joined the order of brothers.

Shortly after the arrival of the Mack brothers, both orders at Ephrata took a vow of perpetual virginity and had their hair tonsured as a symbol of their vow. The householders, who lived nearby and looked to Beissel for leadership, then decided to dedicate themselves to a life of celibacy within the orders. Leaving their homes and farms, they built a convent at Ephrata, with one section for "housefathers" and one for "housemothers." One of the housefathers was installed as steward to manage the household. He soon met difficulty:

> But, when the house was to be inhabited, the house-mothers objected and said: They had . . . again to be on a free footing, and this must be done by divorce; for although they had thus far lived a life of continence, they still stood under the will of their husbands, and lived at their mercy. The superintendent [Beissel] granted their request, to which the care for their eternal salvation had ac-

tivated them. Consequently one of the Brethren had to write the letters of separation, which afterwards, being sealed, one part handed to the other.[20]

Although this action created controversy in the surrounding area, the household continued some time in their ordered life. They took in several poor widows whom they supported from their own means.

But dissension soon arose within the household. One cause was the concern of the mothers for their children who had not followed them to Ephrata but remained on the farms "in a neglected state." Another was the departure of three Eckerlin brothers after a confrontation with Beissel over their business enterprises. After a brief period of disorder and financial uncertainty within the community, Beissel released the householders from their vows and encouraged "every house-father to again receive his helpmate, which they did, and then all letters of separation were burnt on one pile."[21] The householders then returned to their farms.

Several sisters and brothers left their orders during this period of dissension. Maria Sauer left in late fall of 1744 to move in with her son, Christopher II, who had often asked her to rejoin her family. The next year she rejoined her husband in Germantown. Alexander Mack, Jr., left with the Eckerlin brothers in 1745. They traveled together to Virginia, where they attempted to establish a sabbatarian community.

But Mack decided to rejoin the Germantown congregation and was welcomed back into the community. He and Christopher Sauer II were elected to the ministry in 1748. Mack, who earned his living as a weaver, was married in 1749 to Elizabeth Nice, who also had belonged to the Ephrata community. Sauer performed the wedding. In turn, Mack officiated when Sauer, a printer, married Catharine Scharpnack in 1751. Then in 1753 both Mack and Sauer were installed as full elders of the Germantown congregation. Under their leadership the church prospered.

Care of the poor was an important part of the ministry of the congregation. Poorbook accounts record regular contributions of food, clothing, and money to widows in need. Deacons were elected to supervise this work. At least one deaconess also was elected by the Germantown congregation, as indicated in their church records: "Anno 1769, the 20th of August. According to the Council of the Holy Ghost (1 Tim. 5:9, 10) in the community of Brethren and Sisters of Germantown, and according to the manner and regulations of the Apostolic congregation of the first Christians, was elected by vote as a ministress [deaconess] the Sister Margaretha Bayerin."[22] This same woman is listed as an elder in a register of deaths kept by Alexander Mack, Jr., as is sister Philipine Hertzback.[23]

Prior to 1760 the congregation met in members' homes. Then in 1760 one of the families offered a house for the congregation to use for meetings. One room and the kitchen were used for free housing for widows. Later, when a meetinghouse was built in 1770, the entire house was converted to housing for widows.[24]

The congregation kept in touch with other Brethren congregations through correspondence, visitation, and Annual Meetings. Congregations encouraged each other and held each other accountable to Brethren beliefs and practices. Before the organization of Annual Meeting in 1742, this support was given through visits and correspondence. But after its organization, Annual Meeting increasingly became the means for reunion, inspiration, exhortation, and discipline among Brethren. A description of Annual Meeting as it was conducted prior to mid-nineteenth century was given by Henry Kurtz, Brethren editor, historian, and elder.

> Brethren met on Friday morning before Pentecost, and opened as usual by singing, exhortation, prayer, and perhaps, reading the Scriptures. Having met in the fear of the Lord and invited him to preside over the meeting, and prayed for the Holy Spirit to guide and direct all hearts, they considered the meeting ready for business. Cases were presented and decided, questions asked and answered, all by word of mouth, as in ordinary Council meetings . . .[25]

Saturday was given over to public worship and a love feast in the evening. The meeting ended after Sunday morning worship, and participants returned to their homes.

Brethren continued to strive to be faithful to the teachings of Jesus in their daily lives. Those who were judged by the congregation to be disobedient were disciplined, much in the same way that the European Brethren practiced avoidance. At times they faced issues different from those confronted by the European Brethren. If there was no direct New Testament teaching on a particular issue, they sought for "the mind of Christ" in reaching a decision.

One such issue was that of slavery. The Brethren from their early days in America opposed this institution and would not permit members to own slaves. Annual Meeting in 1782 instructed a brother who owned "a negro woman" and the four children born to her to free her before some Brethren witnesses. He was also to free each of the four children at age twenty-one, with new outfits of clothing. In the meantime, he was to feed, shelter, clothe, and school the children, "as it is just and proper."[26]

Another issue confronting the church was the visions which believers at times experienced. A controversial instance of this among the colonial Brethren was the visions of Catherine Hummer. She experienced "heavenly visitations" over a short period of years. Her father, who was a Brethren minister in what was to become the White Oak congregation, had her testify about these visions in meetings he conducted. A spiritual awakening at times was experienced by those who heard her testimony. The Ephrata community, which highly valued such experiences, recorded her accounts of these visions.

Her first vision occurred late one evening in October, 1762, when an angel visited her in her father's home. This visitor spoke to her of the hearts grown cold among the Brethren. A conversation ensued in which Catherine wanted to bring her friends to the angel but the angel insisted they were asleep, in body and heart. Catherine wept when she thought of her sins, but was assured by the angel of her Savior's forgiveness. They sang together until the angel returned to heaven. Then Catherine entered into a trance "for the greater part of seven days and nights." During this time she felt her spirit transported to "the heavenly principalities," where she experienced "a bliss that is inexpressible and indescribable."[27]

Some Brethren were concerned about such manifestations. Catherine Hummer's case was brought to the 1763 Annual Meeting. The minutes of that meeting indicate a concern for mutual respect of individual conscience and for the unity of the church. The decision included both counsel in regard to this specific case and counsel as to principles by which Brethren should live. Such counsel is typical of Annual Meeting decisions.

> First, we believe and find indeed, that Brother Hummer has brought too much of his human nature into these doings, out of which various fruits of disunity have grown. In the second place, we also believe that both sides have gone too far against each other in words and judgments. Hence it is our brotherly advice that Brother Peter Hummer [Catherine's father] should make acknowledgment where he might have transgressed in regard to

brotherly obedience. And then, when there is acknowledgment on both sides, we advise out of brotherly love that on both sides all rumors and harsh expression be entirely renounced.

Although we have no consensus about the occurence in question, those who believe in it are not to judge those who do not. Likewise, we shall not look down on those who derive some lesson and benefit from it. In general, we admonish you, beloved brethren, to receive one another as Christ has received us, and to forgive one another as Christ has forgiven us also. Let us altogether hold the opinion that all dispute, judging, and contempt has been and will remain completely laid aside. Let everyone leave to the other his own opinion in the fear of the Lord, that we might all spare our consciences. Moreover, it is our advice that . . . we practice truth and honesty in all things in order that truth may free us from everything that might still keep us in captivity and prevent us from attaining a unity of mind in Christ Jesus according to the will of God.[28]

Evidently Alexander Mack, Jr., wrote to Catherine Hummer sharing these concerns with her, for Catherine wrote a response to a letter she had received from Mack.

In this letter she says that she "is not only persecuted by the world but also hated by those who call themselves believers." She attributes this to their lack of understanding and asks that they not be punished by God for this offense. Her letter shows both a strong faith and a willingness to be corrected if she has erred. It is one of the earliest writings still extant by a Brethren woman. Selections from this letter are quoted below.

Glory to God in the highest for His great love, kindness and mercy, for He is continually merciful, kind, and full of love, and does not forsake those who believe in Him, but awakens them from the indolence of the world and their lusts and desires. I wish from all my heart and soul that I, too, may be lifted up to God's honor together with all of His faithful and may join in crying: "Glory to God in the highest, peace on earth and good will toward men." Peace has been taken from the earth, from the entire world, and from most of those who call themselves believers and each one acts according to his own pleasure.

Dear Brother Sander Mack! I thank you warmly for your love and loving admonitions and for your warm greeting. I, Catherine Hummer, your lowliest fellow-sister, my heart and my soul wish you health and happiness of body and soul. I will be patient in the paths of tribulation, for the dear Savior has said that one must pass through many tribulations in entering the Kingdom of God. Therefore I will prepare myself for it as far as the Lord provides grace that I might be found worthy to enter into the Kingdom of God, for the winter of persecution is here . . . .

O God, fill all our hearts with Thy Holy Spirit so that we might pray from our whole hearts for divine peace, that it might be planted in all hearts who call themselves believers, that peace might be planted in this time of grace, that we might be as one heart and soul in eternity.

Dear Brother, I am writing this in great meekness and imperfection. I hope, however, you will not reject it but rather consider and read it in love. When and wherever I may have erred I will be gladly reminded of it by you and accept it from you in love.[29]

Catherine Hummer's visions ended after she married the man who was the only person present with her during these experiences. For some this called into question the validity of her visionary experiences. But perhaps others continued to follow the Annual Meeting admonition to refrain from judging and to receive one another in Christian forgiveness and love.

This spirit of forbearance and love combined with a commitment to faithfulness to New Testament teaching was characteristic of Alexander Mack, Jr. Under his leadership, the Germantown congregation recovered from its earlier losses and became a flourishing congregation. Brethren congregations spread beyond Pennsylvania to New Jersey, Maryland, Virginia, and the Carolinas.[30] Although there were still occasional losses to the Ephrata movement, the Brethren were firmly established as a growing, vital movement when the former colonies became a newly independent nation.

CONCLUSION

The desire to be members of obedient, disciplined congregations, grounded in love of each other and of God, was at the heart of Brethren faith. It brought together the first eight in Schwarzenau, and it spread with them in Europe and then in America. Although the Brethren were sometimes accused of being dogmatic in their insistence on trine immersion, they strove to be open to new understandings of the will of God. As their growth continued in the coming centuries, the Brethren were challenged by changing social conditions and by their own faith to test and redefine what Brethren life should be.

THE ORDER OF THE BRETHREN

. . . all who call themselves Christians should live as children of one household. The good Householder has given them rules and laws which they are to keep and respect well and prudently. Along with it, He has promised them life eternal, if they will obey Him in all things—insignificant as well as important ones (Alexander Mack, Sr., *Rights and Ordinances*).

The principles which shaped Brethren life were well established soon after the first baptisms in Schwarzenau in 1708. Mack issued "the outward . . . yet sacred RIGHTS AND ORDINANCES of the House of God" in his 1715 publication by that name. In this work he sought to establish that the church—the household of God—was to be a faithful, disciplined community obedient to the commands of God made known through Jesus Christ in the New Testament.[1]

Yet, the Brethren recognized that there could be new understandings of just what these commands meant for them. Sometimes new understanding came through experience, as when the Schwarzenau Brethren abandoned the practice of celibacy. Sometimes different translations or interpretations of scripture brought new understanding. A different interpretation caused the Brethren to wash feet before the meal during love feast rather than afterwards.

Alexander Mack, Jr. wrote an open letter (1774) giving the scriptural basis for the Brethren practice of feetwashing. He was careful to state that this practice would be changed "if a brother or some other person can in love and humility demonstrate by the word of the Lord something other than what is now done, we are willing to accept it . . . . we do not intend to rest upon old practice but the word of the Lord alone is to be our rule and guideline."[2] Mack concluded his letter with guidelines for the proper interpretation of scripture.

> Therefore the Scriptures require spiritual eyes, mind, and under-
> standing, for otherwise, through the letter, one would achieve but
> misery and division, if without true enlightenment one intended to
> cling to the letter in one place and act against it and disregard it in
> another. Therefore, dear brethren, let us watch and be careful,
> and above all preserve love, for thus one preserves light . . . . The
> good God, who is the pure impartial love, can and will supply
> gradually where insight is lacking here or there.[3]

This approach to discernment and decision making characterized the
Brethren at their best. Yet there were instances in which they seemed
to "cling to the letter in one place" while acting against it in another.
This seemed to happen especially as they faced controversial issues.
The ordering of relations between women and men and the position
of women in the church were such instances.

Among the accusations against the Schwarzenau Brethren were
charges that their women taught publicly and that wives were not
respectful to their husbands, serious breaches of contemporary
customs. Such charges also were made against earlier Anabaptists
and Pietists. Women in these movements did enjoy a greater degree
of participation than women in the established churches, but it did
not seem to be a true equality with men.[4] Women might speak
publicly, but they usually were not ordained ministers—at least to the
same degree as men. Wives normally were expected to submit to
their husbands. Alexander Mack, Sr., wrote in 1715 that after marriage "the wife . . . must be obedient to her husband."[5]

The Brethren in America also faced the questions of the role of
women in the church and authority in marriage, especially in relation
to the Ephrata community. The pain and disruption experienced by
a family when the wife chose to leave was evident in the Sauer family. Martin Urner, one of the first group baptized in Germantown,
pleaded publicly with his wife, Catherine, also baptized at Germantown, not to leave him and follow Beissel.[6] One husband not known
to be Brethren commanded his wife not to participate in meetings at
Ephrata, removed her by force from such meetings, and tied her to a
chair to prevent her going again.[7]

The author of the *Chronicles* recognized the problem this
caused the Christian community.

> At this time also two married women ran away from their

husbands and betook themselves under the Superintendent's [Beissel's] leading, who also received them, notwithstanding it was against the canons of the New Covenant; for at that time the Pentecostal winds still blew so strongly that they dissolved all associations and relations save those entered into directly under the cross of Jesus. The Apostles themselves experienced the same, wherefore they early introduced again the order of nature, and taught that wives should love their husbands.[8]

But the Apostle also taught the oneness of male and female in Christ, suggesting that there is an equality of worth.

The Brethren concept of the church as a covenantal community lent itself to this understanding of women and men standing together in Christ, rather than the superiority of man over woman. Alexander Mack, Jr., defended such an interpretation in his *Apologia*, published in 1788. In this passage, he answers the charge that there are no scriptural grounds for administering communion to women: "Therefore faithful disciples of Christ had no doubts whether faithful sisters of Christ (who together with them wished to do the will of the heavenly Father) should be admitted to the Last Supper or not. For they had preached to them the gospel of Christ and had baptized them (Acts 16:14-15). And now they were commanded to teach them to keep not only several things according to their own wishes, but rather all things, that is, all that He had commanded them."[9]

The Brethren would continue to struggle with ordering relations between women and men as they lived out their commitment to be faithful to the commands of scripture in their lives. Some believed that scripture commanded the submission of women in marriage and the church. Others believed that scripture encouraged full participation of women in the church by teaching the oneness of male and female in Christ. Still others believed it possible to order relations so that both these teachings were honored. Annual Meeting was to spend many hours attempting to discern the mind of Christ in regard to these questions (see chapter 4 for a fuller discussion).

CHURCH POLITY

Decisions about church order among the Brethren are made by an annual meeting of representatives of all congregations. Prior to the organization of Annual Meeting in the mid-eighteenth century, congregations conferred with each other as needed. Church discipline primarily was maintained at the congregational level through local council meetings. Each congregation elected an elder who presided over these meetings.[10] When attending to church discipline, the elder was called the housekeeper, housefather, or householder. Members of the church from the beginning were called "brothers" and "sisters." Elders from neighboring congregations were invited to these meetings, as well as to congregational love feasts. They also were present when a congregation held elections for its ministers.

Sisters participated in elections of ministers and in congregational council meetings. Their participation seemed to be unquestionable, as indicated by Annual Meeting minutes: "Can a person be reinstated into the church after having been excluded for immoral conduct, when he holds the opinion that the sisters have no voice in church-council? Considered, better not receive such, as long as they entertain views contrary to the order of the church" (1854, Article 7).

Matters which could not be settled at the local level were sent to Annual Meeting. A "Standing Committee" of elders organized the queries (questions) which came and then recommended answers to the assembled Brethren. Congregations were then to see that these decisions were enforced at the local level. If there was dissatisfaction with the policy set by Annual Meeting, queries would again be brought for discussion.[11]

The participation of sisters in Annual Meeting definitely was constrained. Originally any church member in attendance was permitted to vote. But it is not clear from the minutes whether many sisters attended the business meetings of Annual Meeting and if those present voted. Women of the host congregation may have been too busy with food preparation to participate in the Meeting program. The wives of Brethren from other congregations often may have remained at home to care for children and farms. Women could not serve on Standing Committee, as it was made up of elders. Ministerial offices in the church until mid-twentieth century were only open to men. This leads us to conclude that recommendations on policies which affected both women and men were made by an all-male group.

This limited role for the sisters began to be questioned. Henry Kurtz, editor of the 1867 *Brethren's Encyclopedia*, made this comment when discussing the church's policy on headcoverings for sisters: "In cases like the present, which concern the female portion of the church, would it be out of the way or contrary to the gospel to appoint a committee of elderly sisters (perhaps with an aged brother elder), to consider such questions and report thereupon? It would seem to be consistent with the principles of equality, see Gal. 3:28, and their verdict would perhaps have more weight with their younger sisters."[12] Committees appointed by Annual Meeting continued to include only men until the twentieth century.

In mid-nineteenth century, congregations were instructed to send one or two delegates to Annual Meeting, depending on their size. Then in 1877 it was decided that if a decision could not be reached by consensus, only delegates and Standing Committee members would vote on that action. As women did not serve as delegates, they thus could not vote in such instances. This practice was first questioned during an 1881 Annual Meeting debate on sisters wearing hats.

> I feel that our sisters have not an equal right with their brethren, and their liberties are greatly circumscribed in this matter. [They] are often censured if they dare to offer the slightest protest. They are not allowed to vote on any matter. But we, their lords, assume the authority to make rules to bind them, and they dare not open their mouths in helping to decide these rules . . . . I will not ask any more for our sisters than we have ourselves, and I think that they ought to have.[13]

The following day a brother rose during business session to move "that the sisters be allowed the privilege of the brethren, giving them permission to vote." Annual Meeting adopted the answer of a Standing Committee member: "I would have no objection to their voting, but it would be deviating from the order of our meetings, which I do not like."[14]

This question was not yet settled. A request was made in 1882 that "Annual Meeting grant the same liberality to sisters to vote on questions . . . that Brethren have." The moderator then made what seemed a rather surprising announcement: "I am informed that it has always been their privilege, but it has lain dormant and they were never called on particularly to carry out their privilege. If that is so, this [request] simply asks whether they be allowed to use the privilege already granted to them"[15]

Annual Meeting granted the request. Moderator Enoch Eby then gave these instructions: "The sisters will now remember that when a vote is called for, they should be as active as the brethren, and I wish to have no neutrality in the meetings but be active in expressing your sentiments one way or the other."[16]

The following year rules were proposed which would limit all voting to delegates. J. H. Moore, editor of the *Gospel Messenger*, saw the implications of this for women: "If that rule should be adopted, then our sisters cannot have any voice whatever in the proceedings of this meeting, that is, so far as opposition to passing a motion is concerned, because they are not delegates."[17] The rules were accepted by Annual Meeting, and the sisters lost their recently won franchise.

A query came in 1889 requesting that sisters be eligible to be elected delegates to Annual Meeting. The request was not granted. Then in 1899 women began appearing on the list of Annual Meeting delegates. That year Bertha Ryan, a missionary, represented India. Most likely, the 1899 decision permitting women to be delegates to district meetings was interpreted as permitting them to be delegates to Annual Meeting as well. In 1901 there were seven women delegates representing congregations in Indiana, Kansas, and Nebraska. By 1915, twenty-four of the forty-two district delegations included women. Women thus began to have a voice in shaping the polity and practice of the church.

Major changes in polity and practice came in the latter nineteenth and early twentieth centuries. These changes were not made without struggle. Disagreements and divisions led to a schism of the Brethren into three separate denominations in the early 1880s.[18] Among the differences was disagreement over the role of women in the church. The traditionalists, while believing in spiritual equality in the salvation of women and men, held that scripture intended women to be under the headship of men in church and home life. The progressives supported full participation of women in the church. The moderate main body was unsettled on the issue and willing to debate these and other issues yet awhile longer.

FAMILY RELATIONS

In Alexander Mack's *Rights and Ordinances*, the Brethren leader affirms marriage as being ordained by God. The early Brethren understood scripture to teach that marriage was to be between believers and to endure for life. Sexual relations were only permitted within marriage. Obedience to these teachings became "tests of fellowship" for the Brethren. Disobedient members were put into avoidance. In cases which were seen as "private offenses and minor faults" partial avoidance was the norm. This included withdrawal of the kiss of charity[19] and barring from admission to church council or communion. For more serious cases or when a member in partial avoidance refused to repent, full avoidance was practiced. There was to be no relations with the person at all, although they were to be aided if in distress or need.[20]

When a person was put in avoidance by the congregational meeting, family members were also expected to avoid the errant member. A letter from Alexander Mack, Jr., to a friend indicated that two of his and Elizabeth's daughters were disciplined for disobedience to Brethren teachings on marriage.

> I can therefore not very well avoid telling you a bit about the present situation of my children. It is true, my Hannah had thought at first that her sin was not so great because they had been engaged never to leave each other, and both she and her husband indeed intend to prove this. However, she realizes her error and recognizes her misdeed . . . .
>
> My Sarah thinks that she has done quite well, because she has rejected many and finally accepted the one she loves. She has indeed been spared the kind of shame my Hannah bears . . . . She has been excluded from the kiss and the communion for three reasons. First, because she married outside of the brotherhood; secondly, because [the marriage] was performed without a license; and thirdly, because her husband had not quite completed [his apprenticeship] and his master knew nothing about [the marriage]. My Hannah, however, has been disciplined even more severely, so that we do not even eat with her. Yet most of the members said that they would be more willing to accept her again if she returned in repentance, in fact they would be more willing to accept her again than they were ready to expel her.[21]

Avoidance was discussed during many Annual Meetings in the nineteenth century. Cases which could not be resolved locally were sent to Annual Meeting. Questions arose regarding the correct practice of avoidance. A query came in 1843 asking how a congregation was to relate to the family of one put in avoidance and whether there should be a distinction between the spouse and children under lawful age. In answering the question, Annual Meeting stressed the purpose of the practice.

> Considered, though we are always truly sorry when such a case occurs, where we must put a member into avoidance, and feel sincere compassion for those that suffer immediately under it. Yet we can not set aside this apostolic ordinance, and do really believe

that the more strictly it is observed by all the members, and especially by the nearest relations, the more powerful it would operate to the salvation of the fallen member. But in case a wife would not withdraw fellowship with the husband to be avoided, it was always considered that such a member could not break the bread of communion while so doing. We do conceive that children are in the same predicament, either to withdraw fellowship with the parent in avoidance or not to break bread . . .[22]

A family member's first obligation was clearly to the teachings of scripture as interpreted by the church.

Marriage was not to be entered into lightly. Annual Meeting expected church members to confer with the congregation before marriage: "We know that all who have entered into the covenant of grace, have promised also to receive counsel, and it seems to us, in such an important matter as marriage is, we should by all means seek counsel of our fellow believers" (1819, Article 5). In the nineteenth century the banns announcing an upcoming marriage were to be published three times before the wedding (1804, Article 2). Marriages were to be performed by a Brethren minister (1819, Article 4), with the consent of the parents (1850, Article 16).

Couples were expected to live together "agreeably." At times, this was a test of fellowship: "Whether we can hold, as members, man and wife, that live together in strife, that have been parted on that account, and now live together, but not as man and wife should? Considered, that we could not hold such as members" (1850, Article 10). In some cases brought to Annual Meeting, congregations were told to make a careful investigation and then "judge according to the gospel and the circumstances or facts in the case, in fear of the Lord" (1856, Article 18).

Adultery normally was given as the only acceptable reason for divorce between church members. But the Brethren also permitted divorce in the case of abuse by a spouse. Alexander Mack was progressive in this regard. In writing that a converted person could remain married to an unbelieving spouse, Mack added:

By this we understand that the unbelieving partner must not be a wolf or brute, as some men who are like dogs, lions, or wild beasts. They quarrel, blaspheme, and continually try to destroy and ruin with violence all that is good. If the unbeliever were to break out into all kinds of outrage and adultery, so that the believing partner were only a cloak for his scandals, the believer should definitely not be bound to remain with such a vicious person.[23]

Annual Meeting never encouraged women with abusive husbands to leave them. But, in decisions made in 1850 and 1880, it did not expel women who divorced for those reasons as long as they did not remarry.

Divorced persons were not permitted to remarry, as remarriage while the first spouse was still living was considered adultery (1867, Article 16). Some of the cases which came to Annual Meeting in this regard for resolution were complicated.

> A man goes to the army, and when he comes home his wife was married to another man, and she continues to be the second man's wife. Some time after he marries a widow, and they live together agreeably for some years. They both then make application to be received into the church by baptism, manifesting fruits of repentance to the satisfaction of the church, his first wife, in the meanwhile, still living in adultery. The church examines him concerning separation, and finds him innocent. They examine the Scriptures, and the advice of the Annual Meeting of 1857, Art. 8; also minutes of 1856, Art. 24, in the fear of the Lord, and in the presence of the applicants, and according to the best judgment the church receives them. Can they be held as members of the church? Answer. They can not while they live together (1870, Article 16).

As indicated in this last query, some Brethren had interpreted the teaching that adultery was an acceptable reason for divorce as annulling the marriage contract, thus permitting remarriage. Annual Meeting long refused to accept this interpretation. One district meeting had even accepted this interpretation but was then overruled by Annual Meeting.

The 1870 Annual Meeting reiterated the teaching of the church on marriage and divorce: " . . . viewing the difference of sentiment among us, and the majority believing that fornication [adultery] only suspends the marriage contract, and as the tendency of the practice of the age is toward too great a looseness of the binding power of the marriage vow, we think it most advisable, for the present, to act in the church as if the marriage contract is only broken by death" (1870, Article 14). This remained the teaching of the church for many years. Any person divorced—for whatever reason—and remarried while the first spouse was still living was not received or continued in church membership.

Church members who committed fornication or adultery were removed from fellowship for a period of time. This was seen as necessary to maintain church order and be faithful to the teaching of scripture, as the minutes indicate:

> In case a young sister, being deceived by promises of marriage, and is left afterward in shame and distress by her deceiver, can she be retained as a member if she shows repentance, etc.? This question might be answered with a question of the apostle (1 Cor. 5: 6) "Know ye not that a little leaven leaveneth the whole lump?" It was considered that such a sister should be expelled until she comes and makes a humble and public acknowledgment of her error before the church, and affords ample proof of sincere penitence (1855, Article 18).

The 1863 Annual Meeting clearly asserted that there could be no exceptions to this practice, even with confession and repentance. A period of expulsion was necessary.

This decision of 1863 was questioned in 1879 but retained. Then in 1915 two queries came asking that the 1863 decision be overruled. One query offered further interpretation of 1 Corinthians 5:

> Whereas, our churches forgive, without expulsion, members who are guilty of some of the sins named in 1 Cor. 5:11, when they are repentant, and whereas, the culprit named in 1 Cor. 5:1-5, that was expelled, was unrepentant, and whereas, the teaching of the Scriptures is forgiveness on repentance and confession, therefore we ask that the decision of Conference on this question be reconsidered without relieving of membership all who bring forth fruits meet for repentance, and make public confession for any of the sins named in 1 Cor. 5:11.

Elder J. Calvin Bright, the author of this query, spoke during the conference debate of experiences that led him to bring this query.

> Take all those statements made in the query. . . They are all statements of facts that every one must accept. That is the rule of heaven, that members of the church, when they repent and plead for mercy, should have mercy. It has been one of my delicate tasks, as I have had some experience in overseeing a number of churches. It has been a very difficult task for me, when members come and make confession, to say, "We will have to relieve you of your membership." I have done that for a number of years, and I have always had trouble to get such members to understand, when they have repented.[24]

Annual Meeting granted this request: "If the penitence and confessions are satisfactory to the church, such may be retained."

The 1933 Annual Conference adopted a statement on "Divorce and Remarriage" which reasserted that although divorce was permitted because of fornication, remarriage was not. However, a divorced person who had remarried when their former spouse was still living could be received or continued in church membership "if there seems to be evidence of repentence and a desire to live as nearly right as possible thereafter." But such persons were not eligible for the office of deacon or minister.

Comparatively little was said by Annual Meeting about relations between parents and children prior to the twentieth century. The one article specifically addressing this was adopted quite early (1789) and illustrates the interweaving of home and congregational life characteristic of the Brethren.

> Article 2. Inasmuch as many of our children and young people fall into a coarse life and a great occasion of it seems to be a want that there is not sufficient diligence used in instructing the children according to the word of the Lord. . . . it is opinion (and advice) that there should be used more diligence to instruct our dear youth and children in the word of truth to their salvation, and that it is the special duty of the dear parents, as well as of the pastors and teachers, to be engaged herein that they would use all possible diligence that our dear youth might be provoked to love God, and to appreciate his word from their childhood. Do not spare any labor and toil to convince them by our teaching and by our life, not after the manner which is almost too common nowadays, where the young are made to learn something by heart and then to rehearse it in a light, thoughtless manner, and then are permitted to go on in a life as thoughtless as before—but that they may give themselves up to God in an earnest life.

Further instruction on relations within the family were given in the Brethren periodicals which began publishing in mid-nineteenth century (a sampling of these is in Appendix B).

Then in 1915 Annual Meeting appointed a committee to study "Saving our Children to the Church." Two women—Eva Trostle and Eva Lichty—were among its five members. The committee brought a report in 1917, which was accepted by Annual Meeting. It recommended action in the church, Sunday school, and school, as well as the home. Its counsel for parents was similar to that of 1789: "Real, vital Christian life and living are the most imperative need of fathers and mothers in home-making and rearing children. Only this condition gives the homes the right atmosphere and outlook, where the child is welcome and the rights of childhood are provided, and where the child can develop under the influence of prayer and religious instruction." For Brethren, faith is expressed in daily living.

LIFE STYLE

Life in the home also was regulated in relation to what today we would call lifestyle—dress, home furnishings, social activities, and livelihood. Nonconformity to the world, as commanded in Romans 12, has always been a central principle of Brethren life. During the nineteenth century, Annual Meeting attempted to define, in response to specific queries, just what this meant.

Dress did not become an issue for the Brethren until the nineteenth century. During the colonial period the dress of most women and men differed little from their European forebears. Women usually wore "a one- or two-piece dress with fitted bodice, long sleeves, and ankle-length gathered skirt" and a neckerchief and apron. Married women wore white caps over their hair. This cap had both a social and a religious significance, as scripture also required that women cover their heads.[25]

When trade embargoes were lifted following the Revolutionary War, new fabrics and styles from Europe flowed in abundance into the newly independent nation. In 1804 Annual Meeting urged both parents and ministers to avoid these new fashions and to discourage the youth from adopting them. Their manner of dress was an area in which Brethren should practice nonconformity to the world.

Queries about dress began to appear frequently at Annual Meetings. In 1848 Annual Meeting declared that both married and unmarried women must cover their heads when praying or prophesying, thus breaking with the custom of a cap signifying marriage. When queried in 1856 as to what the proper covering was, Annual Meeting answered: "We are satisfied, with our ancient Brethren, that the plain cap, worn by our dear aged sisters, is a covering, as required by the scripture according to Paul" (Article 26). In 1866 Annual Meeting made dress a test of fellowship, and certain fashions were forbidden.

> Article 27. Inasmuch as pride and an inclination to follow the fashions of the world are still increasing among us, in wearing fine apparel, frock and sack coats, dusters, shawls, etc., with the hair parted off to one side, or shingled and roached, moustaches, etc.;

and, as admonition, in some cases, has not effected anything, can not this Yearly Meeting propose some plan by which this growing evil may be arrested? Answer: We think members of the church, conforming to the fashions of the world as stated above, should be admonished again and again, and if they will not hear the church, the Savior has given directions in Matt. 18 how to deal with them.

In 1870 Annual Meeting decided that sisters who were unwilling to cover their heads during worship should be dealt with "mildly, but strictly." Sisters who wore hats, rather than bonnets, to the communion table were not to be served communion (1876, Article 21).

In 1880 a query came to Annual Meeting calling for the "gospel authority" forbidding women to wear modest hats and requiring them to wear bonnets instead. The answer referred to scriptures commanding nonconformity to the world and avoiding appearances of evil. A brother pointed out during debate that the Brethren seemed to require stricter nonconformity of the sisters than of themselves, but the 1870 ruling stood.

Appropriate dress continued to be an issue into the twentieth century. At the 1911 Annual Conference a comprehensive statement on dress was adopted. It included scriptural teachings on dress and nonconformity, early church tradition, and previous Brethren statements on dress. One section described appropriate dress for the sisters: "That the sisters attire themselves in plainly-made garments, free from ornaments and unnecessary appendages. That plain bonnets and hoods be the headdress, and the hair be worn in a becoming Christian manner. That the veil be worn in time of prayer and prophesying. The plain cap is regarded as meeting the requirements of scriptural teaching on the subject. That gold for ornament, and jewelry of all kinds, shall not be worn."

Sisters and brothers who did not observe this order of dress were not permitted to serve as delegates to district or Annual Conferences or to sit on discipline committees. But full conformity to the order of dress was no longer a test of fellowship.

The 1913 Annual Meeting appointed a committee to organize the work of dress reform. This committee included two women among its five members. These women—Florence H. Myers and Mary Teeter—were the first known women to serve on an Annual Meeting committee. This committee recommended in 1914 that a permanent committee on dress reform be appointed to "maintain an aggressive campaign of education on the subject of dress, presenting it in the aesthetic, economic, social, moral, and religious aspects." The committee was to consist of three sisters and two brothers. Annual Meeting accepted this recommendation.

A query came to the 1925 Annual Meeting asking for "a plain interpretation of the doctrine of the prayer veil." A committee of three was appointed. Bertha Miller Neher, a licensed preacher who had served on the Dress Reform Committee, was one of its members. They brought a report in 1926 which reaffirmed the necessity of sisters covering their heads, as Paul's teachings on this were not "local in their application, but are general and apply to the churches throughout all Christendom." The committee's interpretation of the need for this teaching spelled out the place of women in church order. This teaching was seen to be a response to the disorder in the church at Corinth. A divine order of headship was laid down to counter disorder: "God as the Head of Christ, Christ the Head of man, and man the head of woman."[26] This interpretation, which was adopted by Conference, seems to regard the covering as a symbol of the subordination of woman—rather than as a sign of her redeemed status and her authority to pray and prophesy, as some unofficial interpretations claimed. The committee's interpretation did mention the "angel ministry" of women, yet man stands between woman and Christ.[27] Although this teaching still stands, many sisters no longer cover their heads.[28]

The doctrine of nonconformity to the world also applied to household furnishings. Carpets were forbidden in the early nineteenth century, and toward the end of the century, when the ban was lifted, only plain carpets were permitted.[29] Flowered wallpaper also was forbidden in members' homes. Even instrumental music was considered worldly. Members were not to have instruments in their homes or to give their children music lessons, although this was not to be a test of fellowship.

Nor were Brethren to participate in any forms of worldly entertainment. Two queries brought to the 1871 Annual Meeting indicate what the Brethren then thought of as worldly: "dinners or feasts on Sundays, or on other days, spending much time in baking and cooking and setting their tables with many luxuries, and then inviting other members, and such as are not members, to come and feast with them; and then, while eating, be engaged in vain conversation, such as jesting and joking, and perhaps eating to excess" (Article 18) and "places of merriment, such as state and county fairs, celebrations, circus shows, mass-meetings, and political conventions" (Article 24). Annual Meeting decided that it was "utterly wrong" for Brethren to participate in such activities. Those who persisted in going to "places of merriment" were to be disciplined.

The 1874 Annual Meeting forbade members joining "any organized body of the world" (Article 22). This included labor unions and farmers clubs as well as organizations such as temperance societies, with whose purpose the Brethren agreed. This stance was not modified until early in the twentieth century. Members were then permitted to join unions, if necessary for their work. Participation in peace and temperance societies was also permitted.

The means of earning one's livelihood also was subject to regulation of the church. Seldom did these statements refer to women, perhaps assuming that women were financially supported by men. An exception is the 1804 ruling prohibiting the keeping of a tavern. The statement indicates a sensitivity to the lack of legal status of women during this period.

> Whether it should or would be allowed to a brother or sister to keep public tavern by or with a license; it was unanimously considered that it could not be allowed, because we are convinced that it could not be done without disorder, and is rather a hindrance to a godly life and quietness of spirit. . . If a brother or sister would not hear, accept or obey such counsel or admonition in regard to keeping a tavern, then we would have to consider such as disobedient, and could not have fellowship with them. Yet the sisters, who are bound in such matter by the urging of their husbands, and would gladly be relieved from it, but can not without the consent of their husbands, they should be held less guilty (1804, Article 1).

Earning one's livelihood often was difficult for divorced and widowed women. We know from church records that, since their European beginnings, Brethren congregations have provided for members who were in financial distress. Annual Meeting instructed churches to provide for widows in need: "Concerning a woman whose husband is dead; and having several children and no property, and her hands too weak to provide for them; it was considered that the church should provide for her, and at the proper time to put out the children in good places, and thus supply their wants" (1812, Article 3).

A widow was permitted to receive her full legal share of her husband's estate, even if the remainder of the property would not cover his debts (1846, Article 12). Widows were also permitted to receive government pensions from their husband's service as soldiers, although the Brethren forbade participation in war (1866, Article 42).

CONCLUSION

Brethren life has been shaped in some detail by the interpretations of scriptural commands made by Annual Meeting. It would be interesting to know the stories of the women who were the subjects of some of these queries. Unfortunately, their stories have not been preserved for us. They are some of the many nameless women who are a part of the story of the Church of the Brethren. We can only imagine from these queries the grief of wives who were abused or deserted, the daring or desperation of a wife who would leave her husband, the plight of the young woman "deceived," the independence of those sisters who would not fully conform to the order of dress, or the financial insecurity of many widows.

But some stories of women in the Church of the Brethren have been preserved for us. These illustrate the vital contribution women have made in the establishment and preservation of both homes and congregations. Some of their stories are told in the next chapter.

3

WOMEN IN HOME AND CONGREGATION

Brethren women have always worked with Brethren men as builders. Part of the time they were building houses for homes, and part of the time, houses for schools and churches occupied their hands and minds. Always, in all ways they *builded together*. Then, upon the completion, there have been dedications, house-warmings—periods of rejoicing together (From the 75th Anniversary Program Guide for 1960-61).

Church participation and family life were more closely related when most Brethren were rural people. "Going to meeting" (Sunday services) was a high point of Brethren family life. Families within a congregation more often visited with each other and aided each other in time of need.

The work of building homes and congregations was foremost in the lives of many women during the period of Brethren geographic expansion following the colonial period. With the dawn of the nineteenth century Brethren moved into western Pennsylvania, Virginia, the Carolinas, Kentucky, Ohio, Illinois, and Missouri. Courage and patience were required to cope with the poor travel conditions of that time. Establishing a homestead was backbreaking work for both women and men.

These were people of stout hearts who chopped down the virgin timber and burned the logs following the "log rolling" to make way for fields and gardens. On these fields and gardens they depended for their livelihood. A crop failure was a serious matter. They made most of their household furniture and many of their kitchen utensils. Nearly every farm had a blacksmith shop in which many of their rude farming implements were made. Flax and hemp were raised and spun into cloth by busy housewives and daughters. Wool from their sheep was likewise processed.[1]

Keeping contact with the relatives and friends left behind also could be arduous. There are stories from the Shenandoah Valley of folk walking miles to visit their former communities. Among them was Barbara Garber, who more than once walked the nearly four hundred mile round trip back to Pennsylvania and Maryland to visit.

At times there were dangers to be faced on the frontier. A story from the Brumbaugh family of Pennsylvania provides a vivid illustration. Mary Brumbaugh settled with her family in Morrison's Cove, Pennsylvania, in the late eighteenth century. While going for the cows one evening, she became lost in the woods. Wolves approached as night fell. She climbed a tree to escape them and spent the night there. The next morning she found her way home to her family, which included a nursing baby.[2]

In some areas, Brethren pioneers had contact with the American Indians who already inhabited areas in which the Brethren were settling. The Brethren strove for friendly relations with them. A story from Ohio tells of the efforts of one family. Margaret Younce moved with her husband and two children from North Carolina to Miami County, Ohio, in 1813. The following summer three or four thousand Indians were camped nearby while the second Treaty of Greenville was being negotiated. Margaret baked a large basket of cakes, which she shared with the Indian women.[3]

Another story from Ohio tells of a young woman's contribution to the growth of the church. This "nameless sister" was the wife of Isaac Karns, who came to Ohio from Pennsylvania some time prior to 1817. Isaac was Lutheran who married into a Brethren family in Ohio. When the first child came to the Karnses' home, a disagreement arose between Isaac and his wife as to whether Jacob should be baptized. Isaac insisted he must be baptized. His wife insisted that he would not be, as infant baptism was not scriptural. Soon thereafter, the wife's father visited the Karns family. He advised his daughter to permit the baptism, as it would please her husband and not harm the baby—even if it were not scriptural. When Isaac failed to find a scripture supporting infant baptism, he suggested a meeting with his minister and his father-in-law. During this meeting, the minister admitted that the Lutheran practice was policy not based on "direct" scripture. Isaac was surprised to hear this. He began searching scripture, and soon after both he and his wife were baptized into the

Brethren church. Later both Isaac and Jacob were elected to the ministry in their congregation.[4]

Brethren parents were to instruct their children in the faith. This responsibility was especially important in frontier areas where other Brethren families or a congregation might not be nearby. A biographical sketch (written in the 1860s) of Joseph Hostetler, a frontier evangelist, recounts the care his parents took "to bring up their children in the nurture and admonition of the Lord." The Hostetlers had migrated to Kentucky in 1795. Joseph was born there in 1797. His mother, Agnes Hardman Hostetler, "spared no pains in teaching her little ones to pray." She also taught them what she understood to be the basic doctrines of Christian faith. Joseph was moved by her teaching to read the Biblical stories of the patriarchs and the prophets. He prayed that he might be like "little Samuel or . . . faithful Abraham."[5]

Other Brethren also spread their faith as they traveled across country. The Wolfe family is a noted illustration. Catherine and George Wolfe first migrated (1787) with their three children from Lancaster County to the western frontier of Pennsylvania. Then in 1800 they traveled by flatboat to establish a homestead in Logan County, Kentucky. Their son George II was soon of marriageable age. He married Anna Hunsaker, who was of Brethren background, in 1803. She also had been sought after by a lawyer, who threatened to "thrash" any man who married her. George pointed out that Anna had made her choice freely, and that they were now married. No fight ensued, perhaps because George was a larger built man than the lawyer.[6] George and Anna moved with George's brother Jacob and his wife, Barbara, to Illinois in 1808-10. There George would become a prominent community and church leader. George and Anna's children were also leaders: John was a deacon, and David was a state legislator before becoming a Brethren minister.

By mid-nineteenth century Brethren crossed the plains to the Oregon Territory. Women and men together made this journey. Jacob Wigle, a nephew of George Wolfe II, was among the first group to make the long, dangerous trip. Wigle wrote two letters to the *Monthly Gospel-Visitor*, the first Brethren church paper, telling of the journey of the group he traveled with and their efforts to establish a congregation in the Oregon Territory.

> But in the spring of 1852 . . . I and two of my brothers set out for Oregon Territory. I was told before I started by father Wolf, that

our crossing the plains was a denial of the faith, because we would
have to travel under military form. Which we did not do; for we
found no need of it, but the Indians were no hindrance to us. . . .
We are 7 in number, 3 brothers and 4 sisters; there were 3 more
crossed the plains, but settled about one hundred miles from us.[7]

His second letter indicated the importance of hospitality among the
pioneer Brethren. He and William Carey, who had migrated to
Oregon from Indiana in 1850 with eight other Brethren, traveled in
various areas to see how many Brethren they might find to hopefully
begin a meeting.

The next morning we started for Marion Co. to visit brother
Peebler; we found where he lived, but he was not at home, yet his
wife was at home, and we were happily entertained there again
one night. Here we found 4 members, and in the morning we
started for home.[8]

Eventually a meeting was organized when Daniel Leedy, who had
been authorized to preach, arrived in the Oregon Territory. A love
feast was not held until the "mother church" authorized the Oregon
Brethren to advance brother Leedy to the second degree of the
ministry, which authorized him to conduct communion.

Brethren in other frontier settlements also missed congregational fellowship. A letter from Catherine and Joseph Brubaker, who
had migrated to Iowa in 1853, shared both the bounty and the
loneliness of pioneer life.

This is one of the most fertile and beautiful countries in the
world. Our corn fields and wheat fields show what strong, rich
land this is. We have the best garden that we ever had since we
kept house. . . . Our melons weigh from 20 to 50 pounds here
and [are] the best kind. We have a large patch of melons. I want to
make some watermelon butter if I can. We have wild fruit here in
abundance. . . . I have eaten more good pie this spring and summer than I ever did in that length of time before. We are highly
pleased with the country and our home. . . .

We are quite by ourselves and we have not that blessing that
we can hear our dear beloved Brethren preach the gospel in its
purity. But we hope that the time will come when some of our
dear Brethren will move here and some preachers that will teach
the gospel the right way. . . . But we have a civil neighborhood
and clever, friendly people here. . . . some wish very much to
hear the Brethren preach. . . . There are so many preachers living
in Franklin County that one or the other ought to come out here
and build up a church.[9]

Nancy Caudill first migrated from Kentucky to Illinois, where she joined the Brethren church (ca. 1831). Sometime after 1850 Nancy, herself a widow, married a widower, Alfred Thompson, who was a member of the Disciples' church. She and Alfred and one of her daughters settled in California where to their knowledge Nancy and her daughter were the only Brethren. Alfred wrote to *The Monthly Gospel-Visiter* in 1856 asking for help in organizing a congregation, as his wife and her daugher were "very anxious to have a church formed and enjoy the blessed privilege of meeting with the brethren to worship God once more."[10] Alfred expressed his willingness to become a member of the church, also. He asked that they be notified if any Brethren preachers were to come to California.

That same year George Wolfe III, a son of Jacob and Barbara Wolfe, traveled by steamer through the Panama Canal to California. As the first Brethren elder to settle on the Pacific slope, Wolfe was active in preaching and organizing congregations.[11]

When the Brethren settled in pioneer areas of Idaho near the end of the nineteenth century, they were able to organize a congregation soon after their arrival. As this sketch indicates, the contribution of Lizzie Johnson—the elder's wife—was invaluable to the life of the congregation. Elder Johnson began preaching in Nezperce soon after their arrival in 1897. Another Brethren had arrived the year before and also preached in Nezperce. With the arrival of other Brethren, seventeen members formed a congregation in November 1897. A full program of congregational life soon was established. The first service of the Wednesday evening prayer meeting was led by Lizzie Johnson early in 1898. Then in April she was elected superintendent of the newly organized Sunday school.[12]

Women in settled areas also contributed to the preservation of home and congregation. One such woman was Barbara Yount, of Virginia, whose story was told by her granddaughter for the *Gospel Messenger*.

> Barbara Yount was born near Broadway, Rockingham, Va., June 27, 1807. . . . She was married to Benjamin Yount. To them were born six children, two dying in infancy. She was left a widow before her youngest daughter was born. Thus she was left to struggle alone, with the care of her little children.
>
> She lived near the Linville Creek church . . . and carried water from the spring under the "old oak tree". . . . She was a close neighbor of Elder John Kline. Her home was always open for members of the church. Often at love feast she would entertain as

many as forty people. That meant much, for so many rode horseback then, and it took a great deal of feed for the horses; yet she did it willingly, even if she did have to support her family by weaving. She died April 8, 1893, aged almost eighty-seven years. She was familiarly known all over the valley of Virginia as "Aunt Barbara Yount."[13]

Mary Sayler Herring was the daughter of Daniel Sayler, a prominent Maryland elder. The Sayler family had migrated from Pennsylvania to Maryland in 1772. Mary was born soon after (ca. 1774). During her sixteenth year, she joined the Beaver Dam congregation of the Brethren. She married Henry Herring, a non-Brethren who had come to America from Switzerland. Marrying outside the church was at that time against church teaching. Mary was expected to acknowledge her sin before the congregation, repent, and ask for their forgiveness. This Mary would not do. She argued her case before the congregation, which decided in her favor. Disciplinary action was annulled. Soon after Henry also joined the Beaver Dam congregation. Mary and Henry bore eight children, one of whom died in childhood. Mary continued living on their homestead for several years after Henry's death. She survived two operations for cancer of the breast without anesthetics and lived an active life until her nineties. She died ca. 1872.[14]

Ann Gilbert Rowland is another woman who was active in her congregation while raising a family. Born in December of 1811, Ann lived on her parents' farm in Longmeadow, Maryland, until her marriage to Jonas Rowland. She was an influential woman in her congregation. She joined the campaign against the sale of liquor, then thought to be a necessity at harvest time. She inherited four hundred acres from her parents, and she and Jonas donated land and built the meetinghouse for the Longmeadow congregation in 1863. The building was used by General Lee for a week during the Civil War. Ann insisted that the meetinghouse and its Bible not be damaged. The general and his troops complied with her request. After her husband's death, she raised their eight children alone as well as managed the family farm. Ann shared liberally with the church and those in need.[15]

Hannah Pfouts was born in 1805. She moved with her parents from Pennsylvania to Maryland, where she married Henry Knouff, ca. 1827. Soon after, Hannah and Henry moved to southern Ohio, where they were baptized in a Brethren congregation. Hannah was a firm abolitionist. She prayed publicly for the liberation of slaves in the

1860s. Hannah also was generous in aiding those in need. She supported Sunday schools and contributed articles to the *Gospel Visitor*.[16]

Evalena Porter Blocher was born in Kansas in 1878. Her father was a Brethren minister who hired a substitute rather than fight in the Civil War. (This was permissable practice at that time for Brethren and others who refused to participate in war.) Evalena married and raised four children. She "weathered" a divorce and financial difficulties during the depression. Her "deep spirituality" was apparent in her commitment to the church and in her care for her children and those in need. Music and wisdom gained from good books were gifts Evalena shared with those near her. She sang and played the guitar, piano, and harmonica. She kept her sense of humor throughout her eighty-plus years.[17]

These women combined the responsibilities of time-consuming housekeeping chores with dedicated efforts to build up congregations. When children came, mothering was added to their responsibilities. Their stamina was remarkable. Rather than becoming preoccupied with the cares of home and family, they found time and energy to devote to both home and congregational life.

WOMEN MARRIED TO MINISTERS

Women married to deacons, ministers, and elders uniquely contributed to and established homes and congregations. Their labors in the home often included management of the family farm while their husbands attended to their ministry. As Brethren ministers were nonsalaried until the twentieth century, this was a much needed contribution. An elder's ministry could include much traveling. His wife then tended alone to the farm management and the child-rearing, and sometimes to needs in the congregation.

Being married to a minister was no easy task! Yet for some women it was gladly welcomed as another way they could contribute to the life of the congregation.

The story of Sarah Lint Berkey is representative of the role played by many nineteenth century ministers' wives. She and her husband, elder Jacob Berkey, moved with their five children from Pennsylvania to Indiana in 1848. Soon after their arrival, they helped organize the Rock Run congregation. Jacob became a prominent leader in this congregation and the surrounding area. Sarah's contributions to this work were varied.

> She was the mother of eight children [three born after their move] and tenderly cared for them. By their help she made the garden, cared for the cows, sheared the sheep, spun the yarn and made the clothes for the entire family. She could carry a baby and walk three miles to church. Later when her husband became so well known, their home became a kind of hotel where dozens and even hundreds were entertained free of charge. Being of spare build, her endurance was remarkable.[18]

Women were expected to help in the ministries of their husbands. Wives were received with their husbands when the latter were elected to the ministry, as Annual Meeting Minutes indicate: "Whether in case that brethren who are called to some ministry move from one church to another, are received with their office by the church, to which they have removed, whether the sisters, their wives, ought to be received with them, as in the case of an election? Considered, that it would be good to receive the sisters also with them" (1838, Article 12).

There was no special charge to the wives during the installation services for ministers recorded in Annual Meeting minutes during the nineteenth century. A charge to the wives was included in the services of installation adopted by the 1919 Annual Conference. The expectations most likely reflect nineteenth century practice. There were separate charges for the wives of deacons, ministers, and elders:

> Dear Sister: You are likewise called into a very definite service in the church. The church authorizes and expects you to assist in the preparation for love feasts, baptismal occasions and all other duties of your position. You should also be willing to labor for the spiritual interests of the church, in visiting the sick and giving comfort and help wherever needed. You will have especial opportunity to be an example and help the younger sisters of the congregation, to lead them to the higher spiritual life (1 Tim. 3:11).

> Dear Sister: You, with your husband, are likewise specially called into the service of God and the church. In the duties and responsibilities that fall to him, you are to be a true helpmeet and co-laborer in service. In your home you should, by your devotion and loyalty, strengthen the heart of your husband and make a good report among all for him and his family. We exhort you to sincerity and holiness in life, that you may likewise be an example to the flock. You will have large opportunity for leadership and service in the church, especially among the sisters of the church, as you help them in their special problems, strengthen them for their special

temptations and increase the spirit of holiness in their lives. Thus you will also share the rewards and joys of a faithful servant (1 Peter 3:1-6).

Dear Sister: You have likewise been faithful in service and, with your husband, share the rewards of a larger opportunity. In the new duties and responsibilities that fall to him you will share as a true helpmeet and colaborer. We exhort you to continued increase in holiness and a renewed willingness to be used in service. In a larger sense now than before you will be an example to the flock, and you will be called upon to give help in many ways. You will be entrusted with special tasks in giving help and counsel to the sisters of the church, with whom you will always labor for an increase in holiness. Thus, as you are faithful, you will also share in the joys and rewards (1 Peter 3:1-6).[19]

The statement additionally recommended that when a deacon, minister, or elder married after being installed into office or ordained, his wife should be installed into their respective office soon after the marriage. The language of these charges is in harmony with the 1891 decision of Annual Meeting which declared that sisters were not themselves installed into church office, but received only as helpmeets to their husbands.

Countless women have contributed to the church as wives of deacons, ministers, and elders. Only a few representative stories can be told here. Some of these women are known only through the stories of their husbands.

For example, Mary Summers Chapman's husband, Giles, was born in 1748 in Virginia. He moved with his parents to South Carolina where he became Brethren and eventually entered the ministry. The date of Mary's birth is unknown. She was the daughter of Joseph Summers, originally from Maryland. A friend of Giles Chapman wrote the following description of him, which makes mention of his wife—although not by name.

He began to preach in 1782. . . . He married more persons than any other clergyman; he never would have more than one dollar for this service; "that was as much as any woman was worth," was his laughing reply to the question "how much do you charge?" This was his jest. For no man ever appreciated more highly woman, good, virtuous, suffering, feeble woman, than he did, and none had ever more cause to value her; for certainly none better as wife and mother was to be found than his "ain gude wife."[20]

This description of woman as "suffering and feeble" may be prejudice, or it may reflect the author's experience of seeing many women die during or shortly after childbirth.

One is struck in reading through the stories of elders in the church by the number who lost one or more wives, for example, John Darst, an elder from Ohio. John came to Ohio in 1813. He married Rachael Williams who had just migrated from Virginia in 1815. She died in October of 1830, leaving eleven children—two of whom were two-week-old twins. In May of 1832 John married Anna Harshbarger. Anna died a year later, survived by a three-month-old son. The next year John married Mary Strasburg, who would mother his twelve children and live with him until his death.[21]

One bereaved brother—a deacon in the church—wrote to his parents to tell them of the death of his wife. Sections of the letter were published in the *Gospel Visiter* (1854).

> I have taken my pen in hand to write a few lines to you; but they are sorrowful lines for me to write, and I expect they will be sorrowful for you to read. I believe I must come to the subject at once.—It has been the will of our most kind and heavenly Father to take my most dear and tender affectionate companion home to eternal rest. . . .
>
> Her sickness was lung-fever. It took her on last Saturday week ago; she helped Anna to scrub the house in the forenoon. Then after they were done she complained that she felt chilly and some headache. We did all for her we knew till Monday morning, and then seeing she was not better we sent for the best doctor in Goshen [Indiana], who attended her regularly, till Friday morning, when three other physicians were called in. They declared that all had been done that could be done, and that we had better tell her that she must go. We did so, and the answer she made was, "Well, if it only would not go long any more." She appeared quite satisfied with the message, begged God to help her, talked a little with the children, and died the same day about half after twelve. . . . She took it very patiently from beginning to end. Her age was 31 years and 5 days.
>
> But oh when I come to think over her death, it seems to me sometimes that it cannot be, that I must be here without her. She was a true companion to me, and a true mother to her children. I do not expect ever to get it as good again, as I had it with her while we were together. Still I can comfort myself when I reflect that it has been the Lord's doing, and that it was for her good and ours too. Now if we would wish to see her again, we must prepare to meet her in the Kingdom of heaven, because I cannot believe that I can meet her at any other place.[22]

One can envision a procession of young women leaving this life, with their grief-stricken children and husbands remaining behind to rebuild their lives.

Less frequent are stories of women who outlived two husbands. Lucinda Weybright of Ohio is one such woman. She was thrice married, once to a deacon and twice to elders. She first married Henry Baker, a lifelong deacon, in 1867. Four daughters and one son were born to them. Henry died in 1885, leaving Lucinda with the responsibility of rearing their children. Then in 1898 she married elder Solomon Blickenstaff. He died in 1903. She later married elder Samuel Blocher, whom she helped in his church work.[23]

Understandably, a few women found it difficult to cope with the loss of loved ones with the responsibilities of being a minister's wife. One such woman was Anna Wampler Kline, wife of elder John Kline of Virginia. Anna and John married in 1818. They had one child who died in infancy. Anna began to suffer from severe emotional disturbances sometime in the 1840s. Her niece, Annie Zigler Bowman, described her condition in an article for the 1904 *Gospel Messenger*.

> . . . [John Kline] was deprived of much joy of the average man's homecoming because of Aunt Anna's mental condition. Sometimes she would not know him; other times she would not see him. She would convey herself away where none knew, and if we wanted to hunt her up he would say: "Let Mom alone, she will come when she gets ready." He always seemed to know what was the best thing to do, for after everything got quiet she would come in and go to her room as usual.[24]

This account raises many questions. What were the causes of Anna's condition? Was her behavior upon his homecoming perhaps an expression of resentment over his absences? Or were his trips one way in which he dealt with his grief over his wife's condition? Or was she perhaps simply ill? We cannot know the answers to these questions. But the story of Anna and John Kline prompts us to be wary of idealizing the life of an elder's family.

Nettie Stauffer brought many skills and experiences to her work as an elder's wife. Born in Ohio in 1872, she grew up on her parents' farm. After a common school education, she attended Manchester College for several years. She then taught school several terms near her home. After this she took a course in Bible at Bethany Bible School, graduating in the first class of six in 1911. The previous year she was part of a group that took a three-month tour of Europe and the Holy Lands. On this trip she and nine others, among them A. C. Wieand, founder of Bethany, and his wife, Katherine, were captured by some Arabs. They were victims of local hostilities between the Arabs and the Turks. Several days later they were rescued by another group of Arabs and their tour guide. When Nettie returned to the United States, she had many opportunities to tell congregations in several states about her travels.

In August of 1912 Nettie married elder John Calvin Bright. He had been widowed twice. Shortly after their marriage, Nettie and John moved to Troy, Ohio, to take charge of the Brethren mission work there. Sister Bright contributed significantly to this work. She was elected superintendent of the Sunday school, the Bible class, and the sisters' aid society. She canvassed the churches of southern Ohio in late 1915 to pay off the indebtedness of the Troy church. Her mission met with success—the debt was paid.[25]

Women married to deacons also helped organize congregational programs. Susan Stayer was born in Pennsylvania in 1851 and joined the church at age nineteen. The following year she married Daniel Replogle. The couple reared six children on their family farm, before moving to the town of Roaring Spring in 1897. An aid society was organized in the Replogle home in 1903. Sister Replogle was elected its first president. She and her husband helped organize a Church of the Brethren congregation in Roaring Spring in 1909. They, with Daniel's cousin George Replogle and his wife, Susan Brown Replogle, served the congregation as deacons. Among their responsibilities were visiting and caring for the sick, attending to the needs of the poor, and arranging for love feasts for the congregation. Their children have served the church as Sunday school teachers and ministers. Both women were still active in aid society in their eighties. They sat together during Sunday school and shared a pew during worship.[26]

For some women, service to the church included not only participation in its programs but at times a challenge to some of its practices. This was true of Ruth Hawkins Cayford. She and her husband, Frank Cayford, were deacons in the Glendale Church of the Brethren. Her granddaughter has shared her story.

> Ruth Viola Hawkins was born in Muncie, Indiana, in 1901. She attended McPherson College, where she got her bachelor's degree. She then spent two years at Bethany Seminary. She went

out to Emmet, Idaho, as a "pastor's assistant" in a struggling Brethren church that did not have a pastor. In 1929 she married Frank Luther Cayford and they went to Glendale, California, where she lived the rest of her life. . . . Besides singing in the choir, she was for some years treasurer of the church. . . . My grandmother was in the Women's Christian Temperance Union. She was an advocate of the right of women to participate in the church, and defied some of the conventions of dress of those days when her congregation tried exclude sincere worshippers on those grounds. She felt that the external should take second place to the internal. Of her three children, all attended LaVerne College. One son became a Brethren minister and missionary to Nigeria. . . . A daughter has been involved with several Brethren relief projects and has been a major supporter herself of the Glendale church.[27]

Because of the special responsibilities required of families of deacons and ministers, the relationship between home and church was very strong. Often it was impossible for the children to distinguish between the two spheres in their demands for loyalty and energy. For some of the children reared in such families, there has resulted a lasting commitment to the church, and they are among today's leaders. For others, a separation from the church was required to restore a healthy perspective. At any rate, the interweaving of home and congregation has been a significant characteristic of many Brethren families.

CONCLUSION

The Brethren perhaps are unique in the relationship between home and family and the character and ministry of the congregation. It is obvious that the role women have played in both home and congregation has been instrumental in establishing the family feel that Brethren have known in their faith communities. Not only have the contributions of the wives of church leaders made this possible, but the presence of every woman dedicated to her family and the church has been a sustaining force in the life of the congregation. Howard Miller paid tribute to these women as early as 1879:

There is another class, perhaps 10,000 of them who deserve mention. They are the sisters, the old sisters of the church. You can see them in the church, well up in front, dressed in black and soberly sitting in their places. They hold in their folded hands a Brethren's hymn book and a neatly folded white handkerchief and seemed relieved from waiting and watching for the hour. These be the mothers and grandmothers of the church. Nobody ever heard of **them**. They don't write for the papers, they don't give trouble at councils, they are not in the front when the fight is raging, yet for real, true Christianity I think it may be found among them purer and more of it than any place on earth . . . Some who know may wonder why I do not mention these (by name), but the tens of thousands preclude possibility. They lived and did their work well and died and were rewarded. And, my sister, that is the secret of happiness; to be content in the plane God has placed you whether to write articles, or to milk the cows in the barnyard.[28]

To be sure, the contribution of these women is irreplaceable.

Ladies Aid Society, Juniata, NE, ca. 1916

4

SISTERS AND COMMUNION

> We, the sisters of the Grundy County church, seeing we have
> made the same covenant with God in Christ Jesus that the
> brethren have made, petition Annual Meeting through District
> Meeting to repeal former petitions against us and grant us the
> same privilege in the breaking of the bread and passing the
> cup that the brethren enjoy in fulfilling the Word of the Lord
> (*Minutes of the Annual Meetings*, Query 1, 1899).

The manner in which sisters participated in the Eucharist, commonly called the communion service, was among the first challenges to the place assigned women among the Brethren. Communion was at the heart of the church. As practiced by the Brethren, it was always the climax of the love feast, a service which also included an examination service, feetwashing, and a fellowship meal.

In spite of an apparent unity, various differences in practice existed among nineteenth century Brethren in regard to the love feast. There was inconsistency in the mode of feetwashing, the time the meal should be placed on the table, the appropriate place for sermons or meditations, and the time for giving the kiss of charity and the hand of fellowship. These differences were the subject of discussion and debate at several Annual Meetings. But the practice with regard to communion was virtually the same among all Brethren. The elements of bread and cup were distributed by the administrators, the deacons and ministers under the supervision of a presiding elder. Men and women sat on different sides of the meetinghouse during the love feast. When the brothers received the bread and cup from the administrator, they distributed it among themselves. The sisters, however, were individually given the bread and cup by male administrators; they did not distribute it among themselves.

This practice was first questioned at Annual Meeting in a query brought in 1849: "Whether it would not be more consistent with the Word, if, at communion, the administrator would give the bread and cup to the sisters, and they divide it like the brethren, among themselves, and the administrator to pass along, to keep order? [Answer:] Considered, unanimously, to go on, in celebrating the communion, as heretofore" (Article 35).

This query became the subject of a letter published in the third issue of *Monthly Gospel-Visiter*, a Brethren publication begun in 1851. The letter came from a brother in southern Ohio and favored sisters breaking bread in their own right: "Will you show me wherein that the sisters have not the same privilege that the brethren have in breaking of bread and receiving the cup of the Lord. Now, dear Brother, I assert that, if the word of truth permits the brethren to break bread one to another, it admits of the sisters doing the same, and that would be unanimity indeed."[1]

A later issue of the *Gospel-Visiter* included a response to this question. This writer claimed that a different practice for women and men did not contradict the teaching of Galatians 3 on the oneness of male and female in Christ, as the earlier writer had claimed.

> Now from these words of Paul can plainly be seen and understood, that all, that are children of God by faith in Christ Jesus, have an equal share of salvation through the atonement made by Jesus upon the cross. . . . Yet reason teaches, that there is a difference between male and female, so long as we live in this earthly tabernacle, because the females often have their infants in their arms when seated at the Communion Table [and are] not able to attend in breaking of bread as the male can.[2]

The debate continued in subsequent issues of the *Gospel-Visiter*. One writer wrote about the practice of the early Brethren at communion, as he had heard it from "a great many old Brethren." He claimed that both brothers and sisters broke bread and passed the cup among themselves.[3]

A writer from the South questioned both the practice of feet-washing and communion. In regard to feetwashing, he believed that scripture called for the "single mode"—that each participant wash the feet of another—rather than the "double mode," in which the feet of several members were washed by a single administrator and wiped by another. His argument for sisters breaking bread is similar with its emphasis on the participation of each member.

> The other item is this, if it is right according to the Gospel for the brethren to break the bread of communion with and for one another, and likewise pass the cup of the Lord, it must undoubtedly be right for the sisters to observe the same rule, for all are members of that one body unto which they were all baptized by the one Spirit with water in the name of the Father, and of the Son, and of the Holy Ghost, for the remission of sins, and all are one by faith in Christ Jesus. Hence the words of Paul, "Is not the bread which we break the communion of the body of Jesus Christ?" On this subject I shall say no more until I hear what others have to say for or against the views I entertain.[4]

Several responses to this letter were published in a later issue. One writer found no scriptural support for sisters breaking bread.

> As touching the breaking of bread by the sisters, it seems to me to be hardly worth while to spend much time about it. I often thought, that if it was nearer the word of God, than the practice now is, it would of course be more convenient. But I would have to ask, where is the word or example which says, that a sister should break bread? That the Saviour himself broke it, and gave to his disciples, see Matt. xxvi, Mark xiv, Luke xxii. So if a change would be necessary, in order to observe Christ's example, we would have to change it the other way. That is, not to let even the brethren break the bread and give it to each other, but to let the administrator do it. . . . It is true, our sisters are fellow-sufferers with us in affliction, and co-heirs with us of salvation; but nowhere in scripture were they entrusted with the ministry except as deaconesses, as far as I am acquainted with the word of God, and in this may be another reason, why our ancient humble sisters never did, nor ever wished to break bread to each other.[5]

Two other responses in the same issue of the *Gospel-Visiter* also supported the practice of the administrator breaking bread to the sisters. Included in these responses were statements addressing the proper place of women. One of these was from Henry Kurtz, the editor of the *Gospel-Visiter*. In scripture he found not an equality of male and female but rather a relation of dependence and protection.

> Beneath the Cross of Christ we may learn, as well as our brethren before us undoubtedly learned, the proper distinction between the male and female part of the church, though our dear sisters stand on the same level with us. There, by the cross of Jesus, see John

xix. 25-27, you find standing the mother of Jesus, representing as we may be allowed to say, the female portion of the church, and the disciple, whom Jesus loved, representing the male portion of the church. Jesus, seeing them, gives to each a charge. . . . What these charges meant, we see in the conduct of John, of whom it is said, "And from that hour the disciple took her into his own house," undoubtedly to comfort and support her not only in her present distress, but to take care and provide for her, as long as life lasted; and she submitted willingly, and did not look to any other person for support but him, whom Jesus had appointed as her protector. There is no relation in life between the sexes, more pure, more holy and more tender, than the relation between a widowed mother and a dutiful son, and in this relation stand the two sexes to each other in the church; the sisters know and feel and are happy in their dependence on the brethren, as their natural protectors; the brethren know, and feel and are happy in performing their duty towards the sisters, whom they revere and serve as mothers and sisters in Christ, and therefore they see to it, that every one of their sisters is provided for, and actually receives the sacred emblems of Christ's sufferings and death. And how could it have been done better, but that the administrator serves them himself, and gives to each the bread and cup into her own hands.[6]

A writer from the West found no scriptural justification for women breaking their own bread. He claimed that it was "complimentary," rather than disparaging, for the sisters to be served by the administrator. Further, he had heard no objection from the sisters, and he hoped he never would: "From the high and tender regard I ever entertained towards the Female portion of Christ's inheritance I believe they always will—while the Spirit of Christ is with them—remain unassuming, humble and faithful in their holy calling, attending to their domestic concerns, the burden of their family, and at the same time "adorning themselves with a meek and quiet spirit, which in the sight of God is of great prize."[7]

Although in each of these letters respect for women is claimed by the various writers, her place in communion and in relation to men generally was seen to be subordinate. Further, this hierarchical view could not be challenged, for to do so would go against what was commonly accepted as the divinely ordained place of women. Yet, it was challenged.

A query came to the 1857 Annual Meeting to this effect. "Why do not the sisters break the bread and pass the cup to each other, in the same manner as the brethren do, at the communion?" The answer of the Meeting gives women's place and church tradition as the basis for Brethren practice: "Man, being the head of the woman, and it having been the practice of the church, from time immemorial, for the officiating brethren to break the bread to the sisters, we know of no scriptural reason for making a change in our practice (Article 9).

Yet, at least a few believed there were scriptural reasons for changing the practice so that sisters could break bread among themselves. Certainly those who brought the queries to Annual Meeting in 1849 and 1857 thought so. Unfortunately, no one recorded who those persons were. But they must have had allies enough to sustain debate on the question over a period of years.

Various explanations of the practice of bread being broken to the sisters continued to be offered in various church publications. In the *Brethren's Encyclopedia* (1867), a first compilation of Annual Meeting minutes, editor Henry Kurtz pointed to the maternal responsibilities of women.

> Observation of more than thirty years teaches the writer that a considerable number of sisters are young mothers with babes in their arms, who claim their constant attention, and employ even their hands. Hence, when such a thought as is expressed in the above query [1857] presented itself, it was always dismissed by the reflection, that it would be next to impossible to preserve order and decency, by imposing on our dear sisters this additional duty under their peculiar circumstances.[8]

Kurtz's sensitivity should be appreciated, but one wonders how these young mothers managed to eat during the fellowship meal while preserving "order and decency."

A letter in the *Christian Family Companion* (1868) gave an unusual theological rationale as to why sisters did not break bread: " . . . woman had nothing to do with breaking [Jesus'] natural body, and consequently, they need not break the *symbols* of his broken body. But man, with flinty heart put to death the Son of God, and therefore he is called upon, in memory of the maltreatment inflicted upon Christ, now to break the bread of communion."[9]

A query brought to the 1879 Annual Meeting once again raised the issue and claimed oneness in Christ as the scriptural basis for why a change was needed. "From 1 Cor. x. 16, 17, and Gal. iii. 28 would it not be more consistent with the gospel for sisters to break the bread and pass the cup of communion as the brethren do? If so, we ask the district meeting and the Annual Meeting to grant the privilege" (Article 9). The privilege was not granted. But the issue continued to be a matter of concern in church publications.

The *Brethren at Work*, for example, in 1882 published an article by D. B. Gibson on "Early Church History in Illinois." It included a discussion of love feast customs of the Far Western Brethren, a group of early congregations in Illinois, Missouri, and Iowa. Gibson, whose father was an important Far Western Brethren elder, claimed that in these churches the sisters broke bread to each other, the same as the brothers. His claim, however, contradicts a statement by George Wolfe, another leading elder of the Far Western Brethren, in the *Gospel-Visiter* (1851). Wolfe, whose letters to editor Kurtz sought to minimize the differences between the western congregations and the mainstream of the church, indicated that the administrator broke the bread to the sisters. Perhaps some of the Far Western Brethren did permit the sisters to break bread, but evidently this was not the practice among all these congregations.[10]

In 1883, *Brethren at Work* published an article by I. J. Rosenberger, a well-known evangelist. He began by observing that "sisters' rights and privileges are among the topics of controversy of the day; and among the points is that of breaking bread." Acknowledging that there was no direct scriptural teaching on this topic, he opposed sisters breaking bread because it would not be in keeping with "the spirit of the scriptures." His interpretation of this spirit gave further scriptural support to a subordinate place for women under both law and gospel.

> The Scriptures no where say whether sisters should break the bread of communion, or have it broken to them; hence it remains one of the questions that must be settled by the spirit of the gospel.
> 1. It should be remembered that under the law, women were excused from all military duty; neither did they serve in the priest's office; besides women were not allowed to go beyond the court of women, toward the holy house of the temple.
> 2. Under the gospel, woman is not "to usurp authority," but to be "in subjection." Neither Christ nor the apostles ever called woman to positions of authority in the church, hence do not administer, but are administered unto; and like under the law, they in the meantime share all the benefits of the gospel. I therefore conclude from the spirit of the above scriptures, that sisters should not break bread, but have the bread broken to them.[11]

A month later a letter from Julia Gilbert appeared in the *Gospel Messenger* questioning Rosenberger's conclusions. "If Bro. I. J.

Rosenberger's conclusion is right in the last *Brethren at Work* about sisters not breaking bread, would someone be so kind as to instruct us sisters what conclusion to come to, when we are administering the ordinance of feet-washing, and the salutation of the holy kiss to one another around the table of the Lord? I hope I am not out of place by asking this question."[12] No published answer appeared to Julia's question.

Again in 1885 a query came to the Annual Meeting, this time from Southern Illinois, requesting that sisters be given the privilege of breaking bread. Because of recent schisms in the denomination, perhaps some felt that a change could now take place.[13] Debate on the query focused on the proper place of women in the church. One brother claimed that current practice was justified because as man is the head of woman, he is the one who baptizes and was given the law by God and Christ. Another brother disagreed. "We have it very clearly stated when it says there is neither male nor female in Christ. All have equal privileges inside the church." A third brother warned against debates about inferiority and superiority: "Dearly beloved, as we, calling ourselves the lords of creation, took such a prominent part in the crucifixion of our Saviour, perhaps it would be well for us not to go on talking about inferiority and superiority, for in my judgment, we certainly would have to give superiority in this instance to our sisters.[14] Still, a decision on the query was "postponed indefinitely."

Another query requesting that sisters be permitted to break bread came to Annual Meeting in 1891, this time from Rock Creek church through the District of Northern Illinois and Wisconsin. Again Galatians 3:28 was cited as the scriptural basis for a change in practice. This query was deferred until 1892.

During the debate that year one brother warned against use of the Galatians passage in reference to this practice. He believed that the text concerned salvation and not church polity. And if applied to polity, "it would break down the division of sexes in our Church government" and hence "go too far in opposition to our practice."[15]

Also debated was whether the sisters themselves wanted this change in practice. One brother claimed that the sisters were "almost unanimously satisfied" with present practice. He asked that the sisters not be burdened with a change. As was the custom, only men spoke during debate. So a brother responded by saying that there were sisters that were asking for the same privilege as the brothers to break bread and pass the cup.

Again the privilege was not granted to the sisters. Annual Meeting decided that "our sisters occupy places of honor at our communion table. We wish our sisters to occupy that position still."

Yet, some sisters and brothers still believed that the sisters' place at the communion table was not the one intended. Among them was Julia Gilbert.[16] Gilbert was born in 1844 in Frederick County, Maryland. During her fourth year, she moved with her parents, two brothers and a young man in a covered wagon to settle in a farming community near Dayton, Ohio. Disease was one of the dangers faced by pioneers, as rural settlements often lacked adequate medical care. Both Julia's sister Anne, and brother Jonas, died on the same day in 1855 from measles and scarlet fever. Julia also suffered from these diseases. She recovered, but not without being "crippled."

Julia was baptized in the Wolf Creek congregation in Ohio when she was fourteen. She began studying scripture at an early age, but even then her interpretations were not always in keeping with traditional Brethren views. Her first love feast raised questions for her, as she later recollected.

> At that time there was no supper on the tables at the time of feet-washing. As I thought about how the Savior rose from supper, laid aside his garments and girded himself, I pondered for several days, with the testament in my hand at my work. At last I concluded I would ask my father, as he was a great lover of the Bible. I think I can almost see him yet as he sat on a low rocking chair, when I read the passage in question and asked him why the members did that way at the love feast. He gave a heavy sigh and said, "The old Brethren took the ordinance from several passages of Scripture and thought this to be the proper way it ought to be done." This explanation gave me satisfaction for a while, but then I thought of the vow that I had made to God, to walk in all his ways (and our aged Brethren used to teach that it was Christ whom we should follow), and read the Scriptures, I felt that it was my duty to see if we were doing things in the way Christ told us to do them.[17]

Julia then became involved in what she called the struggle for sisters to break bread. Her first public statement in this regard was her 1883 letter [previously quoted] in the *Gospel Messenger*. Julia was an avid reader of the various church publications and a regular participant in weekly church services and quarterly council meetings. She knew of the 1885 query and also the one which came in 1891 and was deferred. Then in 1894 she was able herself to try to bring a query. During the congregational council meeting in April of that year, the presiding elder for the first time included the sisters with the brethren in his request for any concern to be sent to district meeting. Julia submitted a query to be sent through district meeting to Annual Meeting, knowing that this was the procedure for making changes in church policy and practice. She recorded the query and its response in her diary.

> "Dear Brethren, we, the sisters of the Wolf Creek Church, seeing that we have made the same covenant with God in Christ Jesus that you made, we petition Annual Meeting through district meeting to repeal your former decisions against us and grant us the same privilege in the breaking of the bread and passing the cup as you do the brethren." My petition was not granted to be sent and now I feel I have done what I could for the present and if I was called to stand before the throne of God I would be free.[18]

Julia still hoped to bring about a change in the practice of the church. She later remembered saying in a conversation in 1894 that "if the Lord would let me live to have that experience—breaking the bread and passing the cup—he ought to take me home, as I thought I had fought enough battles. . . . It seems the Lord must have had something for me to do in this world." She brought her query again to council meeting, as reported in her diary—May 2, 1895: "Council meeting in Wolf Creek Church. My query voted down again." Still Julia did not give up.

Just a year after her parents' deaths in 1896, Julia moved to Iowa with her brother Silas's family. Silas was a minister in the Grundy County church. Julia brought her membership to this church and then brought her query to the September 1898 local council meeting. The Grundy County church accepted her query and sent it on to the district meeting of Northern Iowa, Southern Minnesota and South Dakota District on October 15, 1898. The district meeting sent the query to the Annual Meeting in 1899.

Two other queries on this subject were received by the 1899 Annual Meeting. One from the church in Lanark, Illinois, petitioned Annual Meeting "to honor the sisters by allowing them to break bread, using like words of affirmation, and pass the cup as the Brethren do, believing that a more sacred feeling would be felt among the sisters if they could share these privileges, and that such would be in harmony with the teaching of the New Testament." The other asked for a change in practice for the brothers, rather than the sisters: "Inasmuch as Jesus broke the bread of communion and gave it to his disciples and Paul delivered the same practice to the church at Corinth, would it not be well for ministers who officiate at love feasts to break the bread for the brethren as well as for the sisters, and thus secure uniformity, and restore the order of Christ and the practice of the primitive church?"[19]

The decision of Annual Meeting was to "recommend that a committee be appointed to investigate the gospel grounds and expediency of the change and report to the Annual Meeting of 1900." The committee brought the following report to the 1900 Annual Meeting.

> After a careful investigation of the question, our judgment is that Matt. 26:26-27; Mark 14:23; Luke 22: 19-20; 1 Cor. 11: 23, 24, 25, warrant us to administer the bread and cup of communion to the brethren individually, in the same manner as the practice now is to administer them to the sisters. We consider that this change would be in harmony with the teaching and example of Christ and also in harmony with the practice of the church during the apostolic period.[20]

This would be a change in practice, but not the one sought for so long by the sisters and other advocates of the privilege for women to break bread. The 1900 Annual Meeting decided to publish this report in the minutes and defer a decision for one year. In 1901, after a lengthy debate, the report was not accepted. Previous practice was continued.

During this period of the debate, claims were again made that the sisters had broken bread in the early days of the church. M. G. Brumbaugh, the most widely respected historian in the church at that time, concluded in his *History of the German Baptist Brethren* (1899): "Enough has been recorded to show that at the beginning, and at least for fifty-four years, in the early church, the sisters were treated exactly like the brethren, and each one passed the cup and broke the communion bread."[21] Brumbaugh gave no documentation for this claim. Much of his historical material came from the library of Abraham Harley Cassel, the antiquarian book collector.

Cassel was in sympathy with the traditions of the Far Western Brethren, believing that they preserved the practice of the early Brethren at Germantown. J. H. Moore claimed that Cassel's materials showed that both the practice of the single mode of feetwashing and the sisters breaking bread were carried from Germantown to Illinois by a body of Brethren who migrated from Maryland to the Carolinas and Kentucky, then Illinois. Spiritual oversight of this group was originally provided by Maryland elder Daniel Leatherman, who was supposedly ordained by Alexander Mack, Sr. (This would be the same group to which D. B. Gibson referred in his article on early churches in Illinois.)

There seem to be no documents from early Brethren history that clearly establish that sisters did break bread. But there is evidence which leaves the question open. In discussing communion in his *Rights and Ordinances* (1715), Alexander Mack, Sr., made no reference to different modes of breaking bread for sisters and brothers. He later (1730) wrote a tract about Conrad Beissel and the Ephrata community. One criticism he made was Beissel's practice of administering the bread and cup himself.[22] The Ephrata *Chronicles* (1785) recorded, in turn, that Beissel disagreed with the Brethren way of breaking bread "because they were of the mind that all must be equals; and therefore they did not wish to allow any perogative or privilege to any one person among them."[23] No mention is made of a different practice for the sisters.

But if the sisters did break bread the same as the brothers in the early days of the church, when and why did this practice change? Perhaps Alexander Mack, Jr., and Christopher Sauer II introduced such a change as they assumed leadership of the Germantown congregation in mid-eighteenth century. They may have wanted to avoid the disorder they had seen at the Ephrata community when traditional family patterns were changed (see chapter 1). A change may have been made in the practice of communion so that the sisters' bread was broken to them to symbolize the headship of man over woman.[24] This was the reason given for Brethren practice by the 1857 Annual Meeting. Or perhaps a change was made so that the administrator could be sure that women whose heads were not properly covered would not be able to receive communion, thus assuring their obedience to church authority.

Brumbaugh's statement regarding early Brethren practice was to become a matter of debate at Annual Meeting. His claim was incorporated into the next query to come from the Grundy County church (1906).

We, the sisters of the Grundy County church, knowing that the

> Brethren, at the beginning of our church, gave the sisters the same privilege that the brethren enjoyed, in acknowledging Christ as their head, in the breaking of the bread and the passing of the cup, as they were commanded, "this do in remembrance of me," Luke 22:19, and we sisters, seeing that we have made the same covenant with God, in Christ Jesus, that the brethren have made, petition Annual Meeting, through district meeting to grant us the same privilege in the breaking of bread and passing the cup, that the brethren enjoy in fulfilling the Word of the Lord. 1 Cor. 10:1-6.[25]

Another query requesting that the sisters be permitted to break bread and pass the cup also came to the 1906 Annual Meeting. This one was from the Surrey, North Dakota, congregation.

Annual Meeting gave these two queries to a study committee. The committee, made up of five elders, was to:

> investigate the matter of breaking bread by the sisters.
>   1. As to its scriptural authority.
>   2. As to its agreement with the practice of the primitive church.
>   3. As it relates to the practice of the church during the past two hundred years, and to report to the Annual Meeting.[26]

At both the 1907 and 1908 Annual Meetings the committee reported that they were investigating the matter but not ready yet to report.

The report brought by the committee to the 1909 Annual Meeting was the same as one an earlier Annual Meeting (1901) had refused. The committee recommended that "the officiating minister, or ministers, shall break the bread and pass the cup of communion to both brethren and sisters." After lengthy debate, it was decided to defer the report one year and continue the committee.

The committee's report was received for debate again in 1910. Several requests were made for an explanation from the committee. D. C. Flory responded for the committee with a detailed discussion of scripture and Christian tradition. Two portions of his speech are of significance for our discussion. The first one dealt with Christian tradition up to the Reformation.

> We, in our investigation . . . have not been able to find a single case in ecclesiastical history, from the time that Jesus Christ instituted the last supper on the night he was betrayed, —from that night until the Reformation, not one instance has been found yet . . . where the sisters, or females, broke the bread to each other. . . . Up to the time of the Reformation, the bread was always broken, as a rule, to all alike, —both men and women.[27]

Next Flory dealt with Brethren tradition, refuting claims that the sisters had ever broken bread as the brethren did.

> If you want to know the practice of the church, you must study her council. That is where her practice in everything is given. Irregularities often occur in churches without the sanction of the church. So far as we have been able to learn and investigate, there is not a syllable in all the Minutes of Annual Meeting of the Church of the Brethren, since its organization, where the sisters broke bread to each other and the church had given its sanction to it. . . . What changes there have been made in this practice, were irregular and unsanctioned.[28]

S. Z. Sharp, a noted Brethren educator, rose to respond to these remarks from the committee. He also looked to scripture and Christian tradition.

> Our attention is called to the fact that Christ broke bread for all. I wish to call attention to another fact that Christ died for all, and we claim that no one can take the place of Christ as an individual. There is a fundamental principle involved in this. . . . Christ delegated his authority to the church, and not to any one man. . . . This was offered, that, inasmuch as Christ broke the bread unto all, one individual should break the bread to all. We offer as an argument against that, if we admit that as a principle on which we introduce a practice, then, on the same principle, we must to be consistent, have the administrator wash the feet of all. Now we never placed much confidence in history, and don't yet. We make our own history, and in our history which we have made we have always taken the Word of God as our guide. In the early history of the church we washed feet after the communion. We changed that, later on, to washing feet before the communion. . . . And whenever we found we could come nearer the Gospel, we changed again, and that is why this question is here today. We want to get closer to the Gospel, and those aged Brethren,—those very Brethren contended for the double mode and afterwards practiced the single mode. So we cannot put too much stress on what they advocated earlier, for as soon as they saw the Scriptures indicated something else more plainly, they changed their minds, as we should all do.[29]

Sharp concluded by pleading that Brethren practice should regard sisters and brothers in the same way: ". . . this question has been before the Brotherhood for nearly sixty years. It has come up again and again. Why? Because so many feel that we have not come as close to the Gospel as we ought. We feel that in Christ Jesus there is neither male nor female. Why should we make it? In a sense we are different. In Christ Jesus we are one, and our practice ought to be one where the Scriptures indicate it, and I think here is one."[30]

Two other brothers then spoke. One claimed scriptural support for members breaking bread with each other. The other asked that the practice not be changed to the administrator breaking bread to all, but to brothers breaking to brothers and sisters to sisters.

At this point in the debate, Julia Gilbert rose to speak on behalf of the sisters of the Grundy County congregation. Julia had often attended Annual Meeting so she knew that sisters customarily did not speak during debate. Yet, she no longer seemed concerned about seeming "out of place."

> I feel it is my duty to give you a reason why we brought up this petition. I suppose if this decision the brother spoke about, in 1857, had always been followed, you would never be bothered by this petition before this meeting or any other meeting. I think the brethren said what they wanted to say when the question was asked. What was the reason? It was said that man is the head of the woman. He is so, naturally, but he is not the spiritual head of the woman. When I came into the church, I was young, and when I took hold of our elder's hand and he led me into the water where there was a strong stream flowing, he said, "Don't be afraid, Jesus went before." And I walked down there, and between heaven and earth I made a covenant with God to live faithful to Christ Jesus until death. And didn't I come up out of the water the same as my dear Savior did? When we came to communion, didn't I rise from the supper the same as my Savior did? Didn't I gird myself the same as he did? Didn't I wash my sister's feet and thus obey the command to wash one another's feet? When we come down to the breaking of the bread and the passing of the cup, however, then man steps in between us and our Savior. Though man never suffered, or shed a drop of blood for us, he takes his hand to break the bread for us, as if God hadn't given us any hands. We have been using our hands right along, claiming to come in the Spirit, and following him. He brake the bread and gave unto them and said, "This do in remembrance of me." Of course I have been told there was no sister there. Well, there was no sister there in feet-washing. Excuse us from that if you want to use that scripture. But Paul comes to us with the words read at every communion, "Be ye followers of me as also I am of Christ." There were certainly sisters there, and Paul could tell them to be followers of him as he was of Christ. He followed Christ in breaking the bread, and therefore I think I have the right to ask these delegates to permit us sisters to break bread one to the other. We do not ask to break it to the brethren, but we want to fulfill that command, and be in touch

with Jesus Christ. We want the letter and the spirit to go together.[31]

In claiming her right to ask to be able to obey the commands of Christ, Julia became the first woman to speak during recorded debate of Annual Meeting.

I. N. H. Beahm, Brethren educator and evangelist, followed Julia. He opposed the change called for by the committee and in its place supported extension of the privilege of breaking bread to the sisters. His speech focused on the question of what kind of church the Brethren would be.

> This is a solemn question. We are dealing with the most sacred phase of our ceremonial and doctrinal Christianity. It deals with the atonement, with the death of our Lord, by which we have life through faith in the Holy Ghost. It is the business of Annual Meeting to interpret the Scriptures to the best of her ability. . . . The paper asks for a change in our practice. That change calls for a less democratic and a more priestly or ecclesiastical form, which is not in accord with the representative democracy of the Church of the Brethren and of the New Testament. If we were to accept this report, we might easily have two ministers officiating at the love feast, and that would spoil the argument that has been advanced that the one Christ brake the bread. . . . And, again, when the Savior washed the disciples' feet every muscle and bone and fibre in his physical organism engaged in that holy ordinance. We are the representative body of Christ. And unless every brother and every sister, that is, all members in the body of Christ, wash feet, we are not representing the Christ in the upper room. And the same is true with reference to the breaking of the bread. The intrinsic idea of the Christ and now of ourselves, as the church, the representative body of Christ, is, that with every member breaking the bread and every member passing the cup, we have logical and absolute imitation of the Lord, as compared with the obligation and ordinance of feet-washing. And this interpretation of the personal Christ, the larger representative Christ, is in absolute harmony with 1 Cor. 10:16,—we bless the cup and we break the bread.[32]

After a speech by a brother who had previously held the opinion that the bread should be broken to all but now supported both sisters and brothers breaking the bread, a substitute motion was offered to the committee report. E. G. Rodabaugh moved that "we grant the sisters the same privilege of breaking the bread and passing the cup that brethren now enjoy."

The substitute motion was accepted and debate on it began. J. H. Moore, editor of the *Gospel Messenger*, supported the substitute. When the vote was taken, the substitute motion prevailed. The tally was not recorded, although it was indicated that the decision was not unanimous.

Thus the nearly sixty-year struggle for sisters to break bread and pass the cup as the brethren did came to an end. The sisters were finally granted the privilege when it was suggested that the brothers might lose it. Annual Meeting decided to retain the Brethren communal understanding of the church. Whether the early church permitted sisters to break bread or not, Annual Meeting of 1910 sanctioned their doing so.[33] Oneness in Christ Jesus ruled out man exercising headship over woman during love feast and communion. All were part of the body of Christ, and all would break bread and pass the cup.

For Julia Gilbert, this must have been a moment of deep satisfaction. She had risked being out of place to question the place assigned her at the communion table. Now she could experience what she had yearned for since her youth—to faithfully obey the command of her Savior to break bread and pass the cup "in remembrance of me."

Julia Gilbert
(1844-1934)

5

EARLY ORGANIZATIONS

One of the noble sisters who began this great work recently wrote: "We had faith that the work would grow." It was faith that began the work. It has been faith that has carried on and enlarged and improved these humble first efforts. And faith must continue to go forward with larger vision, greater efficiency and deeper consecration" (Vinnie M. Flory, "History of Sisters' Aid Society," 1928).

During the nineteenth century some Brethren began to believe that faithfulness to the command of Jesus Christ to spread the gospel required a new witness through church publications, educational institutions, and mission programs. As these endeavors were innovations, other members saw them as unscriptural and out of keeping with Brethren practice. These differences would contribute to the causes of a three-way division of the Brethren in 1881-82.[1]

Women were involved in these new endeavors. Their participation was also a matter of controversy. Some felt that women were stepping out of their God-given place in the order of creation. Others believed that the teaching of oneness of male and female in Christ meant there was no special place for women in the church. The contribution women made to these endeavors helped bring about a larger place for them within the life and work of the church. But that place did not come without struggle, just as acceptance of the innovations did not come easily.

Henry Kurtz began the *Monthly Gospel-Visiter* in 1851 to help unify the Brethren as they spread across the United States. Some welcomed this publication, but others thought it to be "worldly." Annual Meeting deliberated for two years before deciding that the

Visiter should be permitted as a private undertaking.[2] Many women wrote for its pages, as well as those other periodicals which began publication later in the century. The *Gospel Messenger*, one of whose forerunners was the *Visiter*, was made the official organ of the Church of the Brethren by the 1882 Annual Meeting.[3] Its pages carried articles by and about women and their activities in the church.

Some Brethren founded academies (for high school level work) in mid-nineteenth century. John Kline was a sponsor of the Cedar Grove Academy in Virginia (1859). Kishacoquillas Seminary in Pennsylvania was under the directorship of S. Z. Sharp from 1861 to 1864. New Vienna Academy in Ohio was operated by James Quinter from 1861 to 1864, with the support of Henry Kurtz.[4] Five women worked with Quinter and the principal, O. W. Miller: Clara Haas and her daughter Hattie, Mary Craig, and Lettie and Rachel Day. Clara wrote articles supportive of education for the *Gospel Visitor*. In one she said: "For the mind is so constituted that it never will be satisfied while there is a void to be filled; and I think we are doing just what God designed we would do in striving to fill that void with useful knowledge. The soil of the human heart is naturally barren of every doing good, though prolific of evil. If then, flowers, or trees, be not planted, and carefully cultivated, nettles and brambles will spring up; and the mind, if not cultivated and stored with useful knowledge, will become a barren desert, a thorny wilderness."[5]

Yet, some Brethren did fear higher education, believing that it might lead members from a simple faith. From 1831 until 1858, Annual Meeting opposed Brethren participation in higher education. Then in 1858 it was decided that schools conducted as private ventures and in accordance with gospel principles were not to be opposed. Even with this acceptance, Brethren were slow to support the academies established by their members.[6]

Normal schools began to be established by some Brethren in the 1870s. These schools were to prepare their graduates for teaching and for entering college. Some of these normal schools became four-year colleges as requirements for teacher certification became stiffer. A normal school was begun in Huntingdon, Pennsylvania, in the spring of 1876, by the Brumbaughs. Andrew was a physician, and John and Henry were publishers. This school would become Juniata College in the 1890s. Mount Morris College was begun by some Brethren in Illinois in 1879, under the leadership of J. H. Moore, the publisher of *Brethren at Work*. Both schools were coeducational, as were the later Brethren colleges. Women were members of the faculty from the very beginning of these educational ventures. Women were named to the board of trustees of Juniata College as early as four years after its establishment.[7]

The founders of these schools thus were leaders not only in educational and publishing endeavors, but also in expanding the place of women in the church. The story of Wealthy Clark Burkholder (1849-1933) illustrates this. Wealthy, who was reared in a non-Brethren family, joined the Brethren at age fourteen. She learned typesetting from the Brumbaugh brothers, who published the *Pilgrim*. When the Brumbaughs decided to publish a children's paper, the *Young Disciple*, in 1876, they asked Wealthy to edit it. She thus became the first woman editor among the Brethren.

Wealthy was also involved in the founding of the Huntingdon Normal School that year. She was the first woman to buy stock in the school, as well as the first woman admitted to the literary society. From 1879 to 1881 she was employed in the *Brethren at Work* office in Illinois. After her return to Huntingdon, she served on the board of trustees of the school and then managed the women's residence hall.[8]

The Huntingdon women were among the first to organize their work in support of the mission program of the church. Some of them were also leaders in the movement to organize women denominationally. The stories of the founding of these early organizations show both the commitment of these women to mission and the role church publications played in their formation.

SISTER'S MISSION BANDS

Women were among the contributors to the Danish mission that was begun by the District of Northern Illinois in 1876. The denominational Domestic and Foreign Missionary Board, organized in 1880, assumed support for this project. As support for the work of this board grew, a sister from Ohio suggested in a letter to the *Gospel Messenger* that each woman send a missionary contribution to the 1885 Annual Meeting to be held near Huntingdon, Pennsylvania.[9] The Mission Board, whose secretary was D. L. Miller, was to appoint a committee to open and read the letters and to decide how to use the sum thus collected. The editor supported the plan, commenting that: "The plan is simple and practicable. God grant it may reach the heart of many a Mary, sitting low at her Savior's feet, who, knowing that the Mission Fund has been increased by her individual effort, may be made to feel the truth of the sweet words of Jesus—'It is more blessed to give than to receive.'"[10]

Nearly one hundred letters with contributions were sent to Annual Meeting. A meeting of the sisters was called on May 27 to open the letters. An account of the meeting was published in the *Gospel Messenger.*

> At the close of the forenoon session, it was announced that the sisters would meet in the tabernacle to hold a missionary meeting. At one o'clock the tabernacle was well filled, a number of sisters occupying the stand. Several hymns were sung, and prayer was offered by one of the sisters, after which Sister Lizzie Miller stated the object of the meeting. She said "An appeal has been made through the *Messenger* by Sister Snavely of Urbana, Ohio, to the sisters to help in the missionary work of the church. About one hundred letters have been received, and we are here to open and read these letters." She then nominated Sister Ella Brumbaugh to take charge of the meeting. Sister Lizzie Howe was appointed Secretary, and Sister Fannie Quinter, Treasurer. Sister Miller then read a number of letters containing words of encouragement and also money for the work of spreading the gospel. After the reading of the letters, short talks were made by a number of the sisters, among whom we may mention Sister Moomaw of Virginia; Sister Irwin of Ohio; Sister Ella J. Brumbaugh of Pennsylvania; Sister Addie Hohf of Illinois; and Sister Clara Pittinger of Ohio. A collection was now taken up, after which the Standing Committee coming in, the meeting was dismissed.[11]

A report of this meeting organizing the first women's missionary society in the Church of the Brethren was also published in the *Mifflintown Sentinel*, the newspaper of a nearby town. This account mentioned that one of the letters contained a gold dollar that the sender had received some years before as a birthday present. The report concluded with this assessment of the meeting: "The ability displayed by the Dunker preachers was marked and beyond all expectation by people who have no acquaintance with the Brethren, but the ability of the sisters was so striking in the management of the missionary question that the like has not been witnessed among womankind in Central Pennsylvania."[12]

Four local congregational missionary societies were organized the following year—three in Pennsylvania and one in Illinois. The women of Altoona, Pennsylvania, were the first to formally organize, beginning on July 21, 1885, with twenty-five charter members. The women of Huntingdon, who had been working together in visiting the sick and assisting the poor for about four years without a formal organization, organized on September 18, 1885, into a sisters' mission band. Then in October the women of Mt. Morris, Illinois, under the leadership of Elizabeth Miller, organized a sisters' missionary band. The next group organized was in Rockton, Pennsylvania, in November.

Eliza Freet organized the women of Altoona to help pay the debts on the church property. Eliza was a single woman who ran a boardinghouse near the church, in which she housed visiting ministers. Nineteen women met on July 21, 1885, to form a sisters' aid society. They chose Galatians 6:7 for their motto: "Be not weary in well doing for in due season we shall reap if we faint not." They collected $2.60 with which to begin their work. On July 30, they met to do handwork. Ten aprons, three shirts, and two bonnets were made. Their first sale was an apron—for $.28 cents.[13]

The Huntingdon sisters adopted as their motto: "She hath done what she could." Their purpose was stated in their constitution: "To develop the missionary spirit of its members, and to aid in both home and foreign missions." This band also set up an education fund "which was intended to help worthy girls to attend the Huntingdon Normal School." The interests of these women were broad, indeed. An early report of this group indicates some of this range.

> We had our first meeting on Sept. 18, 1885, when officers were elected and the society organized. At this meeting it was agreed that each member pay a definite sum each week for the advancement of the mission work. Our meetings are held monthly when a collection is taken and such other business attended to as the needs and wants of the poor brought to our notice may suggest. Some of the work done is sewing, knitting, etc. At Christmas a number of Sunday-school papers and cards were sent out to children who usually do not have such things to enjoy. Although our experience has been short, we have had some very interesting meetings together. The money collected has been expended in different ways, and we have the assurance that some of it at least has proved a source of comfort to needy ones . . . . Let us labor to cultivate more self-denial and thus increase the means to forward the Missionary cause.[14]

Eleanor Van Dyke Brumbaugh (1854-1934), who had been in charge of the sisters meeting at Annual Meeting, was elected president of this band. Eleanor had come to Huntingdon to work on the staff of the *Pilgrim* in 1874. That same year she married John B. Brumbaugh, one of the paper's owners, and they began housekeeping in the *Pilgrim* building. They adopted a daughter, Ruth (b. 1882). Eleanor was a charter member of the Huntingdon church in 1875. In 1877 she organized and taught the first children's Sunday school class. She also helped found the Huntingdon Normal School in 1876 and in 1881 the Orphan's Home. Eleanor, who was affectionately known as "Aunt Ella," brought both commitment and experience to the organization of the sisters' mission band.[15]

The denominational Sisters' Mission also intended to continue forwarding the cause of mission through the financial contributions of its members. The secretary, Fannie Quinter, made this appeal through the *Gospel Messenger* shortly before the 1886 Annual Meeting: "Inasmuch as the envelope system introduced last year at the Annual Conference has proved to be a valuable auxiliary to the general missionary cause, it has been decided to continue its use. All sisters who will are therefore invited to send to Annual Meeting through this meeting such offering as each may desire. Wherever there is an organized band, it is requested that their contributions be sent in one letter through their secretary with a brief statement of the work done by their band.[16]. Sister Ella Snavely, who had issued the call to sisters to send an offering the previous year, also issued a call before the 1886 Conference, which concluded by asking "Is it too much to hope and expect, dear sisters, that the receipts from our efforts at Annual Meeting last year will be at least doubled this year?"[17]

The offering sent by the sisters to the 1886 Annual Meeting was nearly doubled—$432.44 was received. There were also plans calling for the organization of mission bands in every congregation. These bands were not only to raise funds for the mission program of the church, but also to engage in mission education in regard to home and foreign projects. Their work was to be "for the interests of the church and the welfare of society."[18]

Yet, there was opposition to this form of organization. A paper came to the 1886 Annual Meeting asking that there not be separate organizations of the sisters: "Inasmuch as the missionary cause is a great and noble one, and given unto the church by Christ, its Author, would it not be best for the church to labor as a united body to carry said cause into effect, and not have separate organizations, such as Sisters' Missionary Bands?"[19] Debate on the paper indicated that some opposed these bands as they believed the sisters had "made some mistakes in the work they had done in the last year." Although it was not clearly stated, the mistakes seemed to have been that some of the sisters who spoke during the 1885 meeting were wearing disapproved articles of clothing and improper headdress and that they had been too vigorous in their organizing efforts. This was seen as being detrimental to the missionary cause.

Others felt that the sisters had made an important contribution to the mission cause. Some were concerned that the sisters not be discouraged in their work. S. Z. Sharp, at that time professor at Mt. Morris College, asked that women's sphere in the church not be restricted beyond what it already was:

> If we pass this paper and place those restrictions upon them, we do it most reluctantly, and we feel it in justice to our dear sisters to say something. We have silenced them in the congregation; we have silenced them in Annual Meeting. That is, they have no longer a voice as they once had. . . . We do not allow them to preach the gospel . . . . in the name of the church, and they, feeling a desire to do something for the Master, have formed themselves into missionary bands in different places, and endeavored to do something for the Master . . . . if we pass this paper as it is, we take away from them the last opportunity that they have in laboring for the Master, as they seem to think they ought to. Inasmuch as they have no voice in this matter, as they cannot defend themselves, I feel to espouse their cause so much as to say this much on their behalf.[20]

Annual Meeting passed the paper forbidding sisters' mission bands. Women were to work through the congregation and the denominational missionary board in supporting the missionary cause.

Two queries came to the 1887 Annual Meeting requesting that this decision be "amended" to encourage the sisters in their work. A brother who supported this change spoke of the "wounded" feelings of many sisters after their bands had been forbidden. He pointed to the meaning of these bands: "These sisters who do this work tell me it is not only the sending of those little means that they send forth that is precious to them, but the coming together sometimes and talking over these matters between themselves and praying together." These papers were not accepted. Sisters were not to have separate organizations. Their work was to be under the direction of the male leaders of the church.[21]

Yet, some sisters did continue to meet quietly together, doing what they could to aid those in need. They organized sewing societies, sometimes called Dorcas societies or circles, to bring together and raise funds through sewing to aid the poor. A query came to the 1895 Conference from Northern Illinois asking "whether it is right according to the spirit of the Gospel to have sewing societies in the church?"

A representative of the district explained that "since the church itself being a society, and the only society of which Christ is the author," other societies, especially those independent of the church, should be discouraged. Standing Committee answered that "if the sisters labor in union with the church as expressed in the council, and according to the principles of the Gospel," sewing socieites could be permitted. M. J. McClure of the committee compared the societies to Sunday schools, which were in some sense separate from the church but also part of its work as the church council recognizes it and authorizes its organization. The delegate body accepted the answer of Standing Committee, thus permitting sisters to organize with the permission of their church council.[22]

SISTERS' AID SOCIETY

With this official sanction, women slowly began to organize in congregations across the country. Sometimes women would hear of the work of aid societies at Annual Meeting and return home with hopes of organizing. The aid society of the Mill Creek congregation (Virginia) was organized in this way.

> Sister Mary Shirey attended the spring of 1896 Annual Conference. After she returned from Ottawa, Kan., she called to see my mother, as was her custom after having returned from a trip. As Aunt Mary talked on in her quiet and convincing way, she told my mother of some of the most outstanding things she heard discussed at Conference. She reported that the women of some of the churches were organizing for mission work. Her great desire was that the women at Mill Creek should also organize to do mission work. In the meantime, my father, H. C. Early, came in and entered heartily into the spirit of the conversation, and they decided to call a meeting of the women at Sister Shirey's home. All of those attending this meeting were in favor of the movement, but they thought it best to defer the organization until another meeting. In the interval, seed sowing was being done. In the early fall of 1896 they met at Miss Betty Good's home near the church, and there they effected an organization known as the Sisters' Aid Society. There were twelve charter members. Mrs. Sue Landis was the first president, and Effie Showalter Long was secretary-

treasurer. The time of the meeting was set for Saturday afternoon so that the children might attend. The children were just as eager to go as the mothers were. I am glad now for that early experience.[23]

The sisters' aid society of Frederick, Maryland, which had organized in 1887 after Mrs. P. D. Fahrney visited an aid society meeting in McPherson, Kansas, attempted to organize sisters across the denomination. In 1897 they began publication of an eight-page monthly, the *Missionary Advocate*. Officers were Mrs. R. L. Rinehart, president and editor; Katie Fahrney, business manager and secretary; and Mrs. L. Sappington, treasurer. The purpose of the paper was "to send forth this little sheet, as an earnest appeal to other dear sisters in the Brotherhood, with the desire of awakening a combined and earnest effort to assist in the Missionary Cause." Sisters were asked to subscribe to the monthly at a price of $ .20 per year and to contribute an additional five cents as a membership fee. Each member would be entitled to vote on the disposition of the fund raised through these efforts. For reasons unknown, publication of the *Advocate* ceased in 1898 at the request of Standing Committee.[24]

Then in 1909 a general aid society meeting was held during Annual Conference in Harrisonburg, Virginia. Elizabeth Howe Brubaker (b. 1857) was elected president for one year. She had been previously elected secretary of both the Sisters' Mission organized at the 1885 Annual Meeting and the Huntingdon sisters' mission band, also organized in 1885. Elizabeth had studied at Juniata College and Moody Bible Institute, and taught in Pennsylvania public schools and at Juniata. She also did home mission work in Brooklyn, Chicago, and Pennsylvania before marrying John Brubaker in 1909.[25]

At the 1910 Conference, the Sisters' Aid Society was permanently organized, with a constitution adopted and officers elected. The society decided to meet annually during Annual Conference. In addition to conducting the business of the organization, the women would worship together and hear pertinent addresses. By the 1911 Conference, there were 119 local societies with a membership of 2,580. Over $5,000 was received for distribution by the General Mission Board (GMB). The 1912 Conference authorized the officers of the Sisters' Aid Society to appoint a secretary in each state district to organize and coordinate the work of local societies. The next year 244 societies were reported and over $11,000 contributed. At the 1914 meeting, it was stressed that the primary purpose of aid societies was not to raise money, but to be "an organization of help-fulness."[26]

In 1915 the Aid Society decided to support a specific mission project. The Mary N. Quinter Memorial Fund was established in honor of Mary Quinter (1863-1914), who volunteered for the India mission field at age forty. Mary died in India and was buried at Bulsar.[27] This fund was used by the GMB to build the Quinter Memorial Hospital at Bulsar. The sisters pledged to raise $13,500 for this project over a three-year period.

At their 1916 meeting, the sisters decided to revise their constitution so that they might be recognized as a "creature" of Annual Conference. The 1917 Conference did recognize the Sisters' Aid Society as an official organization of the Church of the Brethren. A report came to the 1918 meeting that Doctors Laura and Raymond Cottrell were using the Quinter Hospital. Greetings from the Dorcas Society of India were also sent to the Aid Society in the United States.

With the completion of this project, other projects were undertaken. From 1918 to 1921, $25,000 was raised for the Ping Ting Hospital in China and the Anklesvar Girls' School in India. A home mission project was supported from 1921 to 1924. Over $35,000 was raised for the Green County Industrial School in Virginia. This was a coeducational boarding school for mountain children, with a strong emphasis on industrial arts. Seventy-five elementary children were in the first session in 1923. A secondary section was added in the 1925-26 session.[28] The GMB decided in 1923 that the Sisters' Aid Society should appoint two women to the board of directors of the school. M. R. Zigler, home missions secretary, submitted three names. The society selected Mrs. J. C. Myers and Mrs. Levi Minnich.

A two-year project to raise $12,000 for construction of the Ruth Royer Kulp Hospital in Nigeria was begun in 1925. That same year the society noted that "The ultimate aim of our Aid Society work is missionary, and yet the most of our time is occupied in handwork." It was decided to emphasize the missionary phase of aid work. Nora Rhodes of Iowa was appointed as missionary secretary to coordinate this work, including the column offered to the society by the *Missionary Visitor*.

An Indian hospital fund was established in 1927. This was a three-year project to raise $15,000 for an addition and equipment for the hospital. The society also discussed asking Standing Committee to study the possibility of forming a council of women's work. The following request was brought to the 1928 Conference:

> The Women's Work in the Church of the Brethren is broadening out into various activities in our local churches. We have a General Aid Society Board approved by Conference, a Mothers and Daughters' Association under the supervision of the General Sunday School Board, as well as Women's Missionary Societies in many local churches without any Brotherhood organization as yet. In view of these conditions, and believing that there should be one General Board to supervise all the activities of the women of the church, we, the General Aid Society Board, ask Standing Committee to consider this problem, and, if they see fit, to appoint a Committee to study the whole question of the organization of Women's Work and bring a report to Conference a year hence.[29]

The request was granted and a committee appointed: Mrs. J. C. Myers, Mrs. Levi Minnich, Mrs. Eva Lichty Whisler, Mrs. J. Z. Gilbert, and Mrs. M. J. Weaver. A new plan of organization was adopted by the Aid Society in 1929, and then in 1930 the organization became a part of the newly organized Women's Work.

The Aid Society was the first officially recognized organization of women in the Church of the Brethren. It grew from 119 local societies in 1911 to nearly 700 in 1930. During this period the sisters contributed $1,378,225 to the work of the church. This is a remarkable sum for a period in which few women were employed for pay and most of the money was raised "by the use of needle and by serving meals and lunches." Schools and hospitals in India, China, and Africa had been constructed with their contributions. Each society also had contributed to meeting local needs. Clothing and food were contributed to the poor. Gifts were made to church building funds. Often aid societies furnished their churches. During World War I many societies helped the Red Cross work as well as other forms of relief.

And what of the women who were members of these societies? What difference did participation make in their lives? Vinnie Flory gave this assessment in a 1928 article on the "History of the Sisters' Aid Society":

> Have the sisters, themselves, lost in giving of their time and energy in this work? We think not. They have been immeasurably blessed spiritually. They have become efficient in organizing and conducting meetings, in rendering programs, and in making and

executing plans. They have learned the great lessons of cooperation and united effort. And above all, they have been made sen-
sitive to the needs of those around them and to the great world
needs. Without exercise we can not grow and what better way can
we find for soul development than like the Master, simply "doing
good?"[30]

In giving, these women also received. In addition to the bless-
ings named by Mrs. Flory, a larger place for women in the work of
the church was being created as their contributions came to be
recognized.

MOTHERS AND DAUGHTERS' ASSOCIATION

As early as 1893, a mothers' meeting had been organized in the
First Church of Philadelphia by Sister J. S. Thomas. Then in 1896
Catherine ("Cassie") Beery Van Dyke (1858-1929) organized a
mothers' meeting in Arkansas, where she and her husband, Dr.
George Van Dyke, had gone to do home mission work. Just a year
before their 1891 marriage, Cassie had spoken with the Brethren
Mission Board about going with the Baptists to Africa as a mis-
sionary. The Baptists did not want to send a Brethren, so Cassie and
George volunteered to serve as home missionaries. Their first assignment was in Arkansas.

In 1897 George was assigned to do medical work at the Hastings Street Mission in Chicago. The work with mothers, which was
part of the mission program, was put in Cassie's care. She organized
weekly meetings with the neighborhood mothers, most of whom
were foreign born. During these meetings, Cassie and those present
discussed the responsibilities they faced as mothers. Between 1892
and 1902, Cassie and George had seven children, six of whom survived infancy. Cassie also taught music at Bethany Bible School in
1905-06.

Cassie began mothers' meetings at the 1906 Annual Meeting at
Springfield, Illinois. As she later recalled, "I summoned courage to
ask the Committee in authority permission to hold meetings for
women in the Woman's Building on the State Fairgrounds where the
meeting was held. Consent was kindly granted and on Monday,
June 4th, at 5 pm, the first general Mothers' Meeting was called with
about two hundred women present." Cassie has hoped to hold such
a meeting and had come prepared. She brought literature with her as
well as an original address on "The Relationship of Husband and
Wife," which was used as part of the program. There was enough in-

terest that meetings were continued daily for three days.

Meetings were held yearly after this under the direction of Mrs. Van Dyke during Annual Conference. For the 1910 Conference at Winona Lake, Indiana, arrangements had been made beforehand for a regular meeting time and place. Five daily meetings were held on the following topics: the baby, the family altar, childhood, adolescence, and a mother's standard for her child.

In 1913 daughters were included in the meetings. Topics for that year's programs were: purity in the home, public health and sanitation, a health talk, and the inner circle of childhood. The Mothers and Daughters' Association was officially organized on June 4 of that year. Mrs. Van Dyke was elected president and Grace Fox of Indiana, secretary-treasurer. There were thirteen charter members. Secretaries to "represent the cause" were appointed in China, India, Sweden, and Denmark.

A kindergarten and nursery program were added to the work of the Mothers and Daughters' organization at the 1917 Conference in Wichita, Kansas. Trained young women worked with the children in activities similar to vacation Bible school, thus freeing the parents to participate in the meetings of the Conference.

Meetings of fathers and sons were begun at the 1920 Annual Conference. Seventy-five men and boys were present. These meetings continued annually. In 1926 a denominational program of men's work was organized and recognized by Annual Meeting.

In 1924, in response to a query from Middle Indiana District, the Mothers and Daughters' Association was officially recognized by Annual Conference and made part of the General Sunday School Board. Eva Whisler was to represent the Sunday school board to the association. The year before, Cassie published a brief history of the association, in which she discussed its purpose:

The object of this work and what it stands for is the uplift of the Home and it has been explained in these words: "It is not a system of religion, as such; not a passing fad; not a club for woman's wails; but a movement for cooperation in teaching women something of the care of mothers as transmitters of life and character to their offspring; to teach them something of the care of infants; to help them learn how to train their children in obedience and cooperation; teaching their children how to keep their bodies, minds and hearts pure and clear for this and succeeding generations and for God; to help them to guide their children to adolescence in ways of industry, morality and faith in God, keeping their confidence and respect.

It also aims to teach wives to love their husbands as commanded in the New Testament, to find their inheritance as the helpmeet of man and to direct her generally, in her home, social and church duties. We want to teach our daughters to be beautiful, dutiful and content, to keep their minds and bodies pure and healthful and to prepare them for their earthly crown—the crown of Motherhood."[31]

The work of the association was carried out primarily through these yearly programs at Conference and in the publication and distribution of literature on the home and family.

In 1926 Mrs. Van Dyke, who had been licensed to preach by the Chicago church, stepped down as director of the association. That year, Harriet Yoder Gilbert of California was elected director, a position she held until 1936. Harriet (Mrs. J. Z. Gilbert) had also been involved in Sisters' Aid Society, serving as district president. As a child, she had been inspired by accounts of the work of the Mt. Morris Aid Society."

When I was yet a little child I remember quite well hearing about our Aid Society in Mount Morris. My father, after his day's work was done, would read our church paper, *The Brethren at Work*, aloud and all kept quiet. Long before we smaller children were old enough to understand much of what he read, this was the family custom. We could sit and listen, play very quietly, lie down, or do whatever seemed most comfortable to us, except to make a noise, because evening was father's only study hour. Well, naturally, we heard much of the church news. Evidently some writers opposed the sisters doing active work in the church, for I recall that many times I grew anxious-hearted when some articles were read, for fear that, by the time I grew up, there would be no more active work in the church for me to do! I kept those worries to myself, but I remember they sometimes made me sad. I laugh now to think what a short-sighted little creature I was.[32]

Not only was there active work for Harriet to do when she grew up, there was also a need for the kind of innovative leadership the pioneer women's organizers had shown. Harriet was involved in such leadership as a member of the committee of five women appointed by the 1928 Conference to propose a plan for the organization of women's activities in the church. In this capacity she led the Mothers and Daughters' into a unified program of women's work.

CONCLUSION

Movement toward a more unified women's program began with the request of the Sisters' Aid Society to the 1928 Conference for a study of the organization of women's work. A committee was appointed and asked to report to the 1929 Conference.

They reported in 1929 that there were five divisions of the work of women in the church—the Aid Society, Mothers and Daughters' Association, Children's Division, Missionary Societies, and Bible Study. Each division needed a leader or secretary. These secretaries would make up the Council of Women's Work of the Church of the Brethren. The presidents of the Aid Society and Mothers and Daughters' would represent their divisions on the council. As the missionary societies and women's Bible classes had no denominational organization, their representatives would be elected by the women of the church and presented to the Conference for approval—as were the officers of the Sisters' Aid Society and Mothers and Daughters'. The secretary of Children's Work, appointed by the Board of Religious Education, would also be on the council. Yearly meetings of the council would be held for reporting and planning the work of the divisions. A meeting of the Council of Women with the Council of Boards was requested "in order to maintain a cooperative spirit with all the work of the General Brotherhood."[33]

This report was first approved by the women gathered at Conference and then by the Conference delegates. A committee of five —two to be selected from the Board of Religious Education and three by the Council of Women—was to be organized to follow through in implementing this report. The committee organized from these two groups included Florence F. Murphy (Aid Society), Harriet Gilbert (Mothers and Daughters'), Nora Rhodes (Mission director), Rufus Bowman (BRE), L. W. Schultz (BRE), and Ruth Shriver (Children's Work director). Their report on the coordination of the program for the Council of Women's Work with the general church program was adopted by the 1930 Conference. This was the beginning of a new phase of organized women's work in the Church of the Brethren.

An editorial in the *Gospel Messenger* on "Our Women of the Church" noted the beginnings of this transition in 1928. In describing the contributions which women had made, the editor referred to the woman of whom Jesus had said, "She hath done what she could." It is an apt description of the many women who, like the Huntingdon

Sisters' Mission Band, had been moved by the example of this woman.

> Throughout the history of our church the contribution of our women has been as fine and unselfish as the giving of the woman who broke the alabaster box of ointment as the measure of her appreciation. It has been as concrete and practical as the deeds of one whose busy hands ministered to the various necessities of the sick and poor. As the work of our women becomes more definitely organized, and as they gain a larger recognition, may all the wholesome qualities of their work and spirit remain. May there abide spontaneity, modesty and love, even though our women would be organized and efficient.[35]

Past Presidents of Women's Work
Left to right: Florence Murphy, Eva Bowman, Cora Fisher, and Sarah Halladay.

6

UNIFIED WOMEN'S WORK

So the united Women's Work program exists primarily and ultimately to carry on the missionary and religious educational program of the church— to give to that program the dynamic of spiritual enthusiasm which comes from a large group of women having unitedly caught a glimpse of the vision of service. (Florence F. Murphy, *Gospel Messenger*, 1930)

A new phase of women's organizations in the Church of the Brethren was entered in 1930. Rather than several organizations, each working to achieve its goals, there would be a coordinated program among women of service to the church. Further, this program would be more closely related to the general church program. Florence Murphy, president of the newly organized Council of Women, prepared an article for the *Gospel Messenger* to explain the new plan of organization and its program to the women of the church. Of especial importance was the relation of the women's programs to the general church program:

All Aid Society and missionary activities of the Women's Work will relate themselves to the program of our General and District Mission Boards. Mothers and Daughters' and Bible Class activities will more especially relate to the activities of the Board of Religious Education. And Children's Work which is now a very definite part of the religious educational program will be supported by the women through any or all of their activities. However, our General Mission Board and Board of Religious Education cooperate in every way possible, for both exist to carry on the program of the church.[1]

Additionally, the report adopted by Conference approved naming the president of the Women's Council as an additional member of the Board of Religious Education (BRE). The council the previous year had elected Florence F. Murphy its president. She thus represented the council on the BRE. Laura Swadley of Tennessee was elected vice-president and Nora Rhodes of Iowa, secretary.

The success of this cooperative endeavor was largely due to the leadership of Sara Florence Fogelsanger Murphy (1886?-1967). Florence was born in Shippensburg, Pennsylvania. As a young woman she planned on a career in educational work. She completed a teacher's training course at the local normal school. She then taught in a one-room country school from 1904 to 1908. Study at Juniata College followed. After graduating from Juniata (1912), she studied at the University of Pennsylvania (M.A., 1916 and Ph.D., 1917). She was the first woman in the Church of the Brethren to earn a doctoral degree. Florence was professor of English at Lordsburg College (La Verne), 1912-13, and Blue Ridge College, 1917-22. A student of hers at Blue Ridge remembers her as the "best teacher he ever had."

In 1918 she married Ross D. Murphy, who was president of Blue Ridge College from 1919 to 1922. In 1923 Florence and Ross moved to Philadelphia, where Ross was pastor of First Church of the Brethren. Florence assisted him in his pastoral work. She was licensed to the ministry in 1935 by this congregation, at the request of its women. The Murphys found their calling was to pastoral work rather than to educational leadership.

Florence organized the women of the Philadelphia church into a council, with a varied program, in 1925. This council received denominational recognition, and Florence was asked to prepare an article about its program for the *Gospel Messenger* in 1928. Then in 1929 she was elected national president of the Sisters' Aid Society. As president of the national Council of Women's Work from 1930 to 1941, Florence implemented a combined organization of Brethren women from the congregational to the denominational level. She also served as liaison between the Brethren Service Committee and the American Friends Service Committee from 1938 to 1945. She devoted much energy to organizing women for sending material aid to victims of war.[2]

Florence's commitment to work toward fulfilling the Christian vision of reconciliation was reflected in any activity to which she gave her creative energy. She addressed the following challenge to her sisters in 1928: "In the second quarter of the twentieth century, we, the women of the Church of the Brethren, ought to shape our every endeavor to the end of making a real and lasting contribution toward the breaking down of race and caste prejudice, toward the establishment of national and international prohibition and toward the outlawry of war. In so doing we shall be co-workers with Christ in establishing that 'peace on earth, good will toward men' which was heralded at his birth. These are the real issues of the day."[3] It was on these issues that Florence attempted to focus her own activity and the program of Women's Work for the next quarter century.

Her first project as president had been her leadership of the women's deficit campaign. Begun in late 1929, this campaign was to help pay half of the $75,000 deficit which the denominational General Mission Board had been carrying. The original goal was to pay the debt by March 1, 1930, but in the face of the depression, the date for the goal's achievement was extended indefinitely. The women's campaign began with a special Christmas offering. Weekly reports in the Gospel Messenger suggested additional ways to contribute. Ministers' wives were asked to make special gifts; many did. Various groups raised funds through special projects. Some rural women sold eggs from their laying hens to church members on Sunday and donated the proceeds. By March nearly $11,400 had been contributed. The full $37,500 eventually was reached.

The Council of Women's Work continued many of the programs of the organizations which had joined together in unified work. The work of the Mothers and Daughters' Association was continued under the direction of Harriet Gilbert (Mrs. J. Z.) until 1935 and then by Anna Gockley Hoff (Mrs. E. G.) from 1936 to 1941. At that time the name of the department was changed to Homebuilders. The objective of this work continued to be "benefiting the Christian home and family." According to the 1931 Women's Work Manual, this included popularizing homemaking, helping solve the problems of young mothers, and providing knowledge of the needs of the growing child. Regular columns discussing homemaking and parenting appeared in the Gospel Messenger. Occasionally the columns were written by men. An account of one local group's activities was published in 1938 as a way of giving suggestions for other groups. The Mothers and Daughters' Association of Denton, Maryland, wrote:

> We organized a group about seven years ago. Four years ago we felt the need of a separate organization for mothers of preschool

age. . . . At the present these mothers have outlined three lessons on the child's physical welfare, three on the mental, and three on the spiritual development. . . . They have made baby garments for the babies of Spain at some of their meetings. They have had showers for three expectant mothers this past year. . . .

This year we decided that the senior group [mothers of school-age children and up] meet on the same day the aid meets, devoting an hour in the afternoon to mothers' problems. We use the program suggestions in the Parent-Teacher magazine. . . .We have a question box in which questions which mothers would like answered may be placed.[4]

This group also sponsored a course on Christian marriage and homemaking for the high school youth of the congregation. A mother and daughter banquet was held, as was a special observance for Mother's Day. Their report indicates the role a mothers and daughters' group played in offering fellowship and support to mothers and in strengthening mother-daughter bonds. Although not every congregation had such a group, many held annual mother-daughter banquets sponsored by the Women's Work organization.

The National Council of Women's Work continued sponsoring a missionary project, as the Sisters' Aid Society had done. They chose as their five-year project (1930-35) support of the girls' schools in India, China, and Africa, with a goal of raising $60,000 by 1935. A promotional pamphlet entitled "Our Women in Service: Heralding the Dawn for Womanhood in India, China and Africa" was prepared by the council and the General Mission Board.

Support of the Girls' Schools was an "investment in the motherhood of our foreign sisters" as well as "a direct attempt to lower the illiteracy figures" among women. Illiteracy among women was reported to be 98 percent in China and India and 99 percent in Africa. A Brethren missionary claimed that "One of the greatest needs of the women of these countries is a Christian Education." The girls' schools in these countries with their combined enrollment of 1,185 attempted to provide such an education. The pamphlet described the curriculum of the schools in this regard:

There is prayer, song and memory work during the opening exercises, besides the regular school work. The schools do not try to teach them new methods and processes of work, but must help them to improve what they already have. In all the Girls' Schools, the girls are not only taught knowledge from textbooks but the many home duties, such as cleaning grain, grinding, cooking, sewing, bathing, keeping the house clean and desirable, caring for the younger children and the art of getting on with others. These schools are helping mould future motherhood. They are also educating young women as prospective wives for our Christian young men, which is very helpful. The homes must become Christianized if civilization is to progress.[5]

It was then suggested that local groups present programs on these schools, using materials available in the *Gospel Messenger* and from the council.

The women of the church undertook this project with zeal. Funds were raised through projects such as handwork and bake sales and freewill offerings. Missionary programs were held in congregations. Perhaps the objective to "Christianize" foreign homes in order to enhance the progress of civilization, which implies the equation of Western culture with Christianity, is no longer in harmony with the church's philosophy of mission. Nevertheless, the NWCC did envision a community which reached around the globe.

Women on the mission field shared this global vision. In 1934 women from Ping Ting Chow, China, contributed over $1,000 to the Women's Work project. Their "offering of love" was reported in the *Gospel Messenger:*

> Listen to the following paragraph from the letter of Brother and Sister J. Homer Bright: "The Women's Needle Society has deposited $4,000 [$1,138 in U.S. currency] for the Women's Work for 1934. At the present they are also supporting three girls in a Bible school, and plan to support two men, from next fall, in a seminary and Bible school. Besides, they care for the [evangelistic] tent, and for the school expenses for the children of the sewing women."
>
> Some of us stand amazed at this wonderful offering from China. How can we know how much this gift means! It is difficult to measure patient toil. It is hard to estimate labors of love. Those who have seen and admired the dainty, exquisite handwork of the Chinese women have some little idea of the long, patient hours required for a small group of Chinese women to make over one thousand dollars.
>
> Then they voted to have this amount credited to the Women's Work Project, where they knew it would be used to help girls and women of their own land and of other lands. Should not such an example cause each one of us, who live in this bountiful land of America, to pause and consider whether we have done anywhere nearly as well as have our Chinese sisters? Should not this gift inspire us to more consecrated living and giving?[6]

This project in support of girl's schools was continued for another five-year period (1935-40). The goal was again $15,000 per year. Anetta Mow published this call to the 53,000 women of the Church of the Brethren in her column in the *Gospel Messenger*: "Knowing that we have it within our power to make the goal, let us face this new year with the determination that every woman in our church shall be informed about the missionary project, and that every woman shall be happy to give as much as she can to bring the freedom, light and love of Christ to our sisters in other lands."[7] Although the goal was not always met during the depression years, by 1942 over $180,000 had been contributed to the project. Offerings in later years surpassed the goal and thus offset the deficit of the depression years.

Another project which helped nourish a vision of global community was the ecumenical World Day of Prayer. This project had originated in 1919 when two United States interdenominational women's mission boards—one for foreign missions and one for home missions—combined their separate prayer observances. By 1924 this day of prayer had become worldwide, as American missionaries took the practice with them to their various mission fields.[8]

Brethren women participated in this program through the Council on Women's Work, which made materials available to congregations. In calling Brethren women to observe the 1933 World Day of Prayer, using the theme "Follow Thou Me," Nora Rhodes gave a report of the 1932 observance.

> The observance of the World Day of Prayer on Feb. 12, 1932, was a demonstration of the growing world fellowship in faith and prayer. . . . From our Liao Chow, China, mission came the report that although this special day came during their evangelistic week, they decided to take the day off for prayer . . . . There were two seasons for prayer in the forenoon: first, for the deepening of their own spiritual lives; and next, for the spirit of service toward all others. In the afternoon they met at two o'clock and continuted until nearly five. During this session they prayed one by one for the leading countries of the world, beginning with China. Previous to taking up each country Sister Hutchinson showed the location of each country on a large map and also showed large pictures of the people of the different countries. . . . In India, the Khergam church sisters joined in with the world sisterhood and had their prayer meeeting. At this meeting were many non-Christian women of the community who took a deep interest in the meeting. They, too, offered just a little prayer but it certainly

meant much to all present. . . . Their efficient leader, Mrs. N. V. Solanky, wife of the Khergam elder, had a good message for these village women . . . . At Dahanu Road a meeting was held in answer to the call for world prayer. Most of their women were present and a splendid meeting was had . . .

At the Garkida leper colony they used the booklet "Hold Fast in Prayer" in connection with the school. All of the scriptures that had been translated into Bura were used; they were also read in Hausa. . . . Songs were sung in both languages and Mrs. Royer gave a talk on the meaning of the World Day of Prayer. In practically every country where Christ is known his followers met for the observance of this day.[9]

Two women, Nora Rhodes and Anetta C. Mow, were primarily responsible for the mission interpretation work of the council. Nora Rhodes (1893-1962) had begun this work in 1925 for the Sisters' Aid Society. She studied at Mt. Morris College and Bethany Bible School and then taught elementary school from 1908 to 1915. In 1925 she became editor of the women's department of the *Missionary Visitor*. As director of missions for Women's Work from 1929 to 1939 she continued writing for church periodicals as well as prepared programs for use in local groups. Then in 1937 she became the first woman to serve on the General Mission Board (GMB) of the denomination.

The GMB had recommended to the 1937 Conference that a woman be added to their membership, as "the mission cause constantly feels that sustained devotion of our good women." The response of the council was affirmative: "Inasmuch as [this] recommendation expresses our own conviction that further integration of the various departments of church activity will be helpful to the whole church program as well as to the cause of missions." The council recommended that the woman who was named should be in close touch with the Women's Work Council and its program. Nora served on the GMB for ten years.

Anetta Mow (b. 1889) was the secretary of missions education from 1933 to 1954 for the GMB. She edited missionary publications and directed the denominational program of mission education. She was also the first staff for the Council of Women's Work, serving in this position from 1933 to 1946. Anetta graduated from the University of Idaho (B.A., 1913). She had moved with her family from Indiana to Idaho in 1903. She also studied at Bethany Bible School (B.D., 1917) and University of Chicago (M.A., 1932). She taught missions at Bethany (1914-17) before serving as a missionary to India (1917-31). In India Anetta did educational and evangelistic work with women and girls. These experiences and her strong educational background well qualified her for her work in mission education.[10]

The work of the aid societies continued under the direction of Mrs. H. L. Hartsough from 1928 to 1941. The Women's Work Manual published in 1931 included a "suggestive constitution for local aid societies." The object of aid societies was stated as "serving meals, bake sales, sewing, helping the poor and overburdened, helping improve church property or any kind of Christian service." The manual additionally suggested activities that societies had found helpful in raising funds: "Sales of household articles, such as rugs, quilts, comforters, slumber-robes, pillow tops, dresser and buffet sets, tea-towels, hot pads, pot holders, dust caps, aprons, old papers and magazines, mottoes and extracts; also doughnut sales, serving meals at sales and luncheons or dinners." The manual indicated that women would give freewill offerings, and it recognized that "most Aids were organized for the specific purpose of making more money for the cause of righteousness." A social value also came from fundraising, as "when we learn to work hard together for a common good cause we seldom quarrel."[11]

Some aid societies took justified pride in the quality of their handwork, particularly their quilting. A special Women's Work Issue of the *Gospel Messenger* included an article on the quilting done by the Aid Society of First Church of Philadelphia.[12] About twenty-five women in the society quilted to pay the debt on the remodeled church kitchen as well as to earn money to support missions. Some of their quilts were displayed in Wanamaker's department store. A special quilt they did as a gift for their pastor used one of the stained glass windows of the church as the basis for its design.

At the 1938 Annual Conference there were three quilts displayed and auctioned. The quilts were sold for $12, $15, and $20, with the proceeds going to the Conference offering, Women's Work, and Brethren Young People's Department. A quilt auction is now a tradition of Annual Conference. Some of the quilts are actually made during Conference week from blocks sent in by local aid societes and women's fellowship groups.

Aid societes also continued to support relief work. A report in 1941 from Florence Murphy, Brethren Service Committee representative, indicated that Brethren had contributed over 45,000 pounds of clothing for relief, with an estimated valuation of $40,000. Clothing was sent to war-torn Europe, Central America, China, and Appalachia.[13] During World War II, women's organizations also helped supply civilian public service camps with fruits and vegetables they raised and canned. Grease was also collected to be made into soap for camps and overseas relief.

The National Council attempted to integrate women's Bible classes into a unified women's work program. Some congregations had separate Sunday school classes for women and men. These classes sometimes took on projects within the church. It was hoped that these women's classes would support Women's Work projects and programs. The programs of Bible study and children's work were primarily carried out by denominational staff and boards, with suggestions and some funding from Women's Work.

Peace and temperance were also concerns of the program of Women's Work. The National Council included representatives from the denominational Temperance and Simple Life Commission and the Peace Commission. Eva Trostle and Margaret Englar Bixler (1880-1958) represented these commissions on the early councils. Margaret was quite a crusader for peace, both nationally and in New Windsor, Maryland, where her husband (E. C. Bixler) was president of Blue Ridge College. She also campaigned for education and employment opportunities for blacks. Margaret stayed informed as to the positions of candidates for public office, and using a card campaign, she urged hundreds of likeminded people throughout the state to vote for those candidates who supported peace and social betterment. Many Women's Work leaders also were active in the Women's Christian Temperance Union. Through a campaign of telegrams to government officials the NCWW expressed opposition to the repeal of prohibition, the establishment of the draft, and the entry of the United States into World War II.

Women's Work groups combining all of the various emphases were organized locally and at district and regional levels. Regular Women's Work columns appeared in the *Gospel Messenger* to inform these groups of the plans of the National Council and to make program suggestions. Reports of their activities also were published to keep the various regions informed of each other's programs. As these organizations grew in strength, they desired more involvement in the work of the NCWW. The officers of the Central Region Women's Work requested in 1941 that the presidents of the regions be seated on the council. Beginning at the 1942 Annual Conference, regional presidents met with the National Council as ex-officio members. Periodic meetings of the council and presidents continued until 1957. At that time the membership of the council was changed to consist of the five regional presidents and three women elected in a meeting of women at Annual Conference.

Women in the Brethren mission areas of India, China, and Nigeria also were meeting for work and fellowship. A women's group was organized around 1940 in Nigeria. A pamphlet telling of this event was published by Women's Work "as a source of inspiration" for the women in the United States.

> A Christian Women's Association has been formed among our women at Lassa. The group meets twice a month. There are over thirty women and girls in the association. They are Margi, Bura, and Fulani.
>
> First a chairwoman was elected and a secretary. Also an interpreter was appointed for the Fulani women since many of them do not know the Margi dialect which is used in this district. Then we set our aims, and here they are:
>
> 1. To form a fellowship of Christian women who will meet at certain times to discuss problems common to all and consider methods to improve living conditions.
>
> 2. To help women to stand in church meetings and lead in prayer and to take part in discussions.
>
> 3. To help in times of sickness, poverty and distress both Christian and non-Christian women.
>
> 4. To make plans to keep our homes and villages in better sanitary condition and help others to do this also.
>
> 5. To visit non-Christian women and try to bring them to services and help them to become Christians.
>
> 6. To think of others in the world who are in need and in distress because of war conditions and to have a fund to help them.
>
> In order to carry out some of these aims, the women were divided into groups with the oldest member of the group acting as leader.[14]

Indian women at first organized locally under the leadership of women missionaries. Then in 1949 these local groups of women formed a national organization. Eva Bowman and Marie Brubaker from the United States were present for this event. Eva filed the following report:

> It happened at Anklesvar, March 17-19, 1949. It was the first

joint meeting that was ever held for all the women of the area. They came together with great eagerness and enthusiasm in the face of extreme difficulties of travel. . . . Twenty-two women tried to get on at Bulsar and were put off because the train was already full. But they used very wise methods and got to Anklesvar. Women came to that meeting who had never been away from their villages; who had never been on the train. Women met friends whom they had not seen since they were in boarding school at Anklesvar as long as twenty-two years before. How they all talked at once in tones of great joy!

There were eighty women present at the meeting. The program was full. Various women conducted the worship programs. Marie and I spoke at various times. Reports of work done by the women were given such as sewing, evangelistic, adult education, Bible teaching, temperance. Fellowship formed a most important part of the program. . . .

Someone suggested that they organize, so they appointed a nominating committee which brought forth the slate. The election was conducted in a most businesslike way. Officers: President, Benabai Naranji; Vice-President, Dhirajbai Thakor; Secretary, Elizabeth Waghela; Treasurer, Ratanbai Hirachar.

The organization of Women's Work in India was a high moment for them and for us who were visitors. The Brethren women in India are facing a new day. They are blossoming out into spiritual leadership. These women are products of our Girls' Schools in India and they are bearing fruit for the cause of Christ.[15]

The women in the United States understandably took pleasure in the fruit their Indian sisters were bearing, for their contributions had helped make this possible.

The end of World War II brought both challenge and hope to the church in the US. Although much reconstruction and resettlement work remained to be done, the crisis of the war years had lessened in the states. The Church of the Brethren reorganized in 1947 to meet the demands of the new day. One denominational board—the General Brotherhood Board (GBB)—replaced the several boards which had met as a Council of Boards. A unified budget was also adopted.

The officers of the national Women's Work were now to be presented as nominations to the Christian Education Commission, who would pass them to the GBB and Annual Conference for approval. Women's Work also was requested to contribute to the Brotherhood Fund, rather than to special projects. To women who had invested much time and priority to some of the projects, this change was ". . . terribly, terribly painful." It challenged their "enthusiasm, power and will."[16] But consistent with their desire to further the ministry and mission of the church, the women successfully accepted the challenge.

From the very beginning of their organization, the members of the denominational Women's Work wanted to work in cooperation with the general church program. Their intention was not to compete with or duplicate the efforts of the church as a whole. "Inasmuch as our program is the program of the church, let us be careful not to duplicate activities. Where machinery has already been set up let us bend every effort toward making it operative rather than to set up additional machinery."[17]

Yet, there was a desire to contribute their experience and perspective to the shaping of this program as well as contributing funds for its implementation. The minutes of the National Council record various instances when this desire was expressed. In 1935 they requested that a woman be appointed to the Gish Book Committee so that more books of interest to women might be made available. The council welcomed the inclusion of a woman on the General Mission Board in 1937. These concerns were reflected in a report of this event:

> Through our representation for these past eight years on the Board of Christian Education, we have become a very definite and integral part of the entire Christian education program of the church. Although we had been peculiarly and, perhaps, uniquely missionary-minded, we had not, until the present, been able to directly contribute to the shaping of our missionary policies, or to the directing of their administration. For the first time in its history a woman has functioned as a regular member of the General Mission Board. Nora Rhodes . . . is now a member of the Board, not so much to represent the women, as to help to interpret the many missionary interests and to assist, as a woman may, in the forming and in the directing of our missionary policies.[18]

The beginnings of an adult movement in the Church of the Brethren in the mid-1930s was another attempt to help unify church programs. An office of Adult Work was formulated in 1935. Then in 1939 an Adult Council was organized. This council consisted of a pastor, the secretary of mission education, and representatives from Women's Work, Men's Work, the young adult group, and the Board of Christian Education. "The Women's Work Council expressed its wish to enter the Adult Council in the spirit of cooperation with the conviction that none of the Women's Work programs suffer but rather help in the growth of adult work."[19]

Through the Adult Council the various groups looked for areas in which they could both cooperate and specialize. Temperance was an early area of such cooperation. The Council of Women's Work insisted that the area of home life should also be one of cooperation with men, rather than the responsibility of women alone.[20] There were some attempts at such cooperation through joint meetings of women and men on home life at Annual Conference. But the primary focus of Men's Work continued to be evangelism, stewardship, and temperance education as well as responsibility for church property maintenance.[21] Peace was suggested later as a possible area of cooperation between women and men.

Eva Bowman was president of the National Council of Women's Work during this period (1941-47). As the wife of a prominent Brethren leader, Eva knew firsthand the difficulties that could arise in working cooperatively with men. Her husband Rufus, in addition to pastoring, had been secretary of the Board of Religious Education before becoming president of Bethany Biblical Seminary in 1937. He was elected moderator of Annual Conference in 1940 and again in 1947.[22] Eva developed a "coat pocket" method of working with Rufus. She explained this method to a women's gathering, for use "if we can't get them to do what we feel should be done." If Eva had an idea and there was not time to talk it over with Rufus, she would write down the idea on a scrap of paper and put it in his coat pocket. Later Rufus would find the paper in his pocket. Thinking it a good idea, he would propose it, and it would be adopted.[23]

Women's Work at times needed to work in this way. The organization's minutes indicated that Women's Work was to "continue to bear in mind that it is not a board, that its work is promotional and administrative."[24] The women were willing to work in this way, but there was still a desire to have more of a voice in shaping the program they were to promote. There were only a few women on the Board of Christian Education. Nora Rhodes continued to be the only woman on the General Mission Board. When her first term ended, the National Council asked that there continue to be a woman on that board. Nora was reelected the following year.

When the General Brotherhood Board (GBB) was formed, the NCWW was concerned that women be included in its membership. The council identified twelve women whom they thought qualified for nomination to the GBB. After a selection process, the NCWW referred five of the nominees to the nominating committee. Two of those women subsequently were elected—Sarah H. Halladay and Charlotte Weaver. The council also suggested that a woman be among the Church of the Brethren delegates to the 1948 World Council of Churches Assembly in Amsterdam. This did not happen, as most of the delegation had already been selected. The council also requested that a woman be one of the speakers of the "main program" at the next Annual Conference, and suggested as well, the sponsorship of a nursery. In 1949 the Council "agreed that it would be good to have more women elected to the Standing Committee."[25]

Women's Work began to stress leadership development as one of its goals. This emphasis was a particular concern of Ruth Shriver (1899-1974), who became director of Women's Work in 1946. Prior to this she had been director of Children's Work and in that capacity worked at times with the Women's Council. Ruth attended Manchester College (B.A., 1924) after growing up in Ohio. She also studied at Boston and Northwestern universities and taught school in Ohio before going to work as Children's Work director. In this capacity she worked tirelessly and creatively to develop a grassroots network of district and regional volunteers. She emphasized leadership training through workshops and literature. Ruth also used this approach in her work with Women's Work. When she retired from this position in 1955, her services were recognized by the board. Her contribution was described by her co-workers as "great creativity, an explorer of ideas, a strong sense of purpose, insight and aggressiveness."[26]

In 1949 Ruth requested the Board of Christian Education (BCE) to study the status of women in the church, in cooperation with an emphasis recommended to member communions by the World Council of Churches in 1947. She worked with another board member to prepare a report, which was endorsed by the BCE. Ruth then worked with an Annual Conference study committee on the role of women in the church and which produced a report adopted in 1952. The committee recommended a "more extensive use of the wisdom and ability of women" by the church.

The goals adopted for the Women's Work program in the 1950s relate to this recommendation. As stated in their manual, WW aims "to include, conserve and develop the talents and interests of every woman in the congregation. It encourages the women to cooperate with the local church cabinet or governing group. It attempts to create a sense of responsibility toward the home, the church, the community, the nation, and the world, which expresses itself in active Christian service."[27] These aims were to be achieved through worship, fellowship, education and service.

During the 1950s, there was an interest in an expanded program of home and family life and a concern that there be more fellowship among the younger women of the church. The program of Women's Work shifted to accommodate these interests. Some districts were beginning weekend camps for women. The National Council was becoming "more and more an interpreter of the *total program* of Women's Work and not of specific areas such as Missions, Homebuilders, Aid-service."[28] The membership of the National Council changed, as well. No longer were directors elected nationally; rather, the five regional presidents made up the council along with three women selected at Conference.[29]

The GBB report to Conference included a section which summed up the activities and concerns of Women's Work in the fifties:

> Relief and rehabilitation, sewing and financial projects which support the local church, Bethany Hospital, Bethany Seminary, and the Brotherhood Fund are the major concerns of our organized women's work. Here and there, groups are engaged in social study and legislative and political action. The question of where women shall apply their creative energies, the relations of men's and women's work to our total program, the interests of older and younger women, the role of employed women and the problems of girls of intermediate and youth age are our major concern.[30]

Pearl Murray of Kansas was both district and Western Region president of Women's Work during the fifties. Reflecting on her experiences during this time, she remembered the all-day rallies, "where women came from near and far," for business and inspiration were important parts of their fellowship. Of course, "the women always had projects." These included sewing baby and children's clothes, making school and health kits for Church World Service, and collecting clothing for relief. When Rowena Peters, "one of our own women," was in Austria with Brethren Service, the district women contributed money for a prosthesis for a boy there who had lost his leg during the war. As regional president, Pearl corresponded with NCWW and districts, and she traveled and spoke in the fifteen districts of the region. District newsletters and a traveling library helped create interest in the work. High points of her regional years

were the women's meetings at regional conference and the presentation of Myrtle Crist Porter's pageant about Brethren women, "And
She Ministered Unto Them." Pearl is grateful for "the people, programs accomplished and spiritual enrichment of these years."[31]

In 1959 Women's Work was renamed Church of the Brethren
Women's Fellowship (CBWF) to reflect its changed emphasis. In
1960 CBWF celebrated the seventy-fifth anniversary of organized
women's activities in the church. Activities at the 1960 Conference
included a presentation of the historical pageant "And She
Ministered Unto Them." A book of poetry *His Pen in Her Hand*,
written by Brethren women, was published. An anniversary thimble,
made of sterling silver and inscribed: CBWF 1885-1960, was produced for the celebration. This project had been suggested by Fern
Mohler, a home economics professor with fond childhood memories
of her mother's involvement in ladies aid.[32] A filmstrip was prepared
by Inez G. Long for use during the anniversary year. "This Radiant
Treasure" called women to find their identity in relation to God and
to determine their place in home, church, community, nation, and
world as a Christian.[33]

These activities attempted to honor the past contributions of
women and to encourage women to commit themselves to support
the total church program. Florence F. Murphy described the tasks ly-
ing ahead in a booklet . . . *Yesterday, Today, Tomorrow*: "We are in
the midst of a transition which should open broader vistas of service
with new meaning and a deeper understanding of discipleship. As
we move forward through the next twenty-five years . . . . may we
conserve the values of the past and exercise our rightful place as
women within the church by helping to form such policies as will lead
us all into a more perfect knowledge of the truth through Jesus Christ
our Lord."[34]

The National Council had been considering since 1954 that the
dissolution of a separate Women's Work organization might be
necessary for women to be integrated into the life of the church. A
decision was made to do so in 1963, after years of discussion among
women and with the Christian Education Commission. Irene Frantz
Bittinger and Anna Warstler led the women through this transition.

Irene was active in Women's Work for several years before being elected to the presidency of CBWF in 1959. She served as director of missions on the National Council from 1945 to 1951 and as
president of the Western Region Women's Work. Born and reared in
a strict Brethren home in eastern Pennsylvania, Irene studied at Eliz-

abethtown College before her marriage to Desmond W. Bittinger in 1927. After two years in the pastorate, the Bittingers went to Nigeria as missionaries from 1930 to 1938. Irene worked in preventive medical care and women's and children's clinics. This work contributed to a marked reduction in infant mortality for the regions the clinics served. Irene also wrote curricula for women's and children's classes and did translating.

Irene influenced many students to go into the ministry and missions during her years at McPherson College. Desmond taught there 1940-44 and was president from 1950 to 1965. Irene taught college French. She was also active in Church Women United and the Parent-Teacher Association, serving both locally and nationally. Irene taught Sunday school, vacation Bible school, and classes at summer camp. She was a devoted mother to her four children, and in 1956 was named "Mother of the Year" for the state of Kansas. She served as a state delegate to the White House Conference on Children and Youth. Irene represented in her own life many of the interests of the Women's Work program.[35]

Anna Warstler (b. 1902) became director of Women's Work and director of Adult Work in 1955. Anna's contribution in envisioning and planning a unified adult program was significant. She joined the Church of the Brethren national staff from the India mission field at the insistence of Norman Baugher, who was the denomination's general secretary. Anna had gone to India in 1931, after study at Goshen and Manchester colleges. She worked for thirteen years as principal and teacher at the Anklesvar Girls' School and then supervised religious instruction in mission schools. Anna also worked in the villages, where she taught women sewing, housekeeping, and child care. In India she came to realize that Christianity was best understood by the quality of one's daily life. This was the beginning of an interest in initiating dialogue with people about their faith, which she later developed as a small group program in the Church of the Brethren, called Mission Twelve. On furlough in 1955, Anna had planned to return to India but instead agreed with Baugher to accept the Women's Work position for a three-year period. Anna discovered that she liked this work and finally agreed to stay indefinitely.

She too saw Women's Work in a period of transition. Within the organization there were differing opinions regarding the focus of Women's Work. Some wanted to retain the program just as it was, some wanted to focus on home and family, and others advocated adult work. Some were afraid to dissolve Women's Work, for fear that women were not fully accepted yet and would not be given a voice in an integrated program. Anna felt that "women were struggling for a rightful place against real odds in the times in which they were." Anna hoped for cooperation between women and men in the church. She wrote: "We need to see ourselves as the whole church —with a deeper concern for all the work. Much of the work formerly done by the two groups should have the attention of every adult. Why settle for dividing it up in groups by sex? In Christ, we are one and should find our ministry together. It is only when we approach a specialized work that we need the fellowship groupings. . . . But both are stronger if they see themselves in a larger context. . . . With this background, the focus for adults is not organization, but mission."[36]

The dissolution of a national women's organization was approved by the 1965 Annual Conference, in response to queries the previous year requesting clarification of the status of Women's and Men's Fellowships. "The direction for lay involvement in the mission of the church . . . was to be through the adult program . . . of the Christian Education Commission in consultation with an Adult Committee made up of women and men." Standing Committee was to see "that the laity is always well represented on the General Brotherhood Board so that they might be vitally involved in the total mission of the church."

District and local women's and men's fellowships were to continue, *if needed*. Their main purpose would be fellowship. The report noted that women's organizations "have made significant contributions to the life of the church through fellowship, worship, family life activities, study, service projects, sewing activities, and projects." Annual reports indicated that 81 percent of the congregations reported women's organization, as did all thirty-nine districts. Yet, "together we are the church. . . . This is true whether we are men or women, trained or untrained, professional or nonprofessional, ordained or unordained. To realize this brings to us a new sense of responsibility and a willing acceptance of and participation in the total mission of the church."[37]

Would this vision of cooperation be realized? Would women be able to "exercise their rightful place"? What was the place of women in the mission and ministry of the church? These questions will be explored in the next chapters.

7

WOMEN AND MISSIONS

The call comes from India today. I am glad the church is not waiting for the morrow to answer it, but is becoming understandably acquainted with her duty toward God in regard to mission work, not only foreign, but home mission work as well. I believe that our love and zeal for home work will grow in proportion to our interest and work in foreign fields. Look into these foreign lands and see the great work to be done, then if you cannot go your desire will grow stronger to do what you can at home. (Bertha Ryan, pioneer missionary to India in an address at the 1900 Annual Meeting.)

An interest in reaching beyond the rural areas they had settled in began to be expressed by Brethren during the 1870s. Their horizons were moving from the unchurched nearby to those in urban areas and overseas. The first foreign mission was established in 1876 when Christian Hope, a Danish immigrant to the United States, was sent to Denmark under the sponsorship of the district of Northern Illinois. Hope had sent Brethren tracts to friends in Denmark. One of these friends requested baptism, and Hope was commissioned to begin work there. The following year Enoch and Anna Eby and Daniel and Julia Ann Fry were sent by the district to join Hope in Denmark in establishing the mission. A Danish congregation was organized during their five-month stay. Hope noted that: "The brethren alone could never have done what they and their wives together did."[1]

Even before organizations were formed to support mission work (see chapter 5), women were contributing funds earned through handwork. A letter published in 1876 indicates such support:

As I am much interested in the Danish Mission, I hold forth the necessity of contributing to it, upon which the following young sisters (mostly sewing girls) resolved to contribute all they could earn by one week's sewing; but while the price of sewing varies so much, the result of their labor (although equally industrious) is also very different. Please credit as follows: Elmira Harley, $4.00; Sara Harley, $1.00; Amanda Cassel, $2.75; Hannah Cassel, $1.00; Rosalinda Cassel, $1.00 Susan Wise, $1.00; total, $10.75.[2]

In 1877 a Brethren's Church Extension Union was organized as an unofficial home mission board. Julia Wood of Virginia supervised the work of women in this endeavor. A March 1878 report of contributions noted that "the sisters generally seem more active than the brethren."[3] Twenty-six sisters, including three groups from congregations, contributed $255.45. The Union was reorganized as the Brethren's Work of Evangelism in 1878, in response to criticism that it conflicted with the work of districts and that its form of organization was worldly. This organization was then taken over by Annual Meeting, and its funds given to the Foreign and Domestic Missionary Board organized by the denomination in 1880.[4] This board funded evangelists in the United States and supported the Danish mission. Outreach through literature was added when the board was reorganized to become the General Missionary and Tract Committee. In 1908 a further reorganization resulted in the General Mission Board.[5] Programs of these boards were to spread the gospel and meet human need, in keeping with the Brethren understanding of doing all "to the glory of God and my neighbor's good."

Women continued to contribute significantly to both domestic and foreign missions. Their contributions included financial support, service as home and foreign workers, and leadership in organizations supporting missions. Some of their stories are told in this chapter.

FOREIGN MISSIONS

Although Brethren missionaries were in Denmark, Sweden (1885), Asia Minor (1895), and France/Switzerland (1899) by the beginning of the twentieth century, the main mission fields for Brethren were in India (1894), China (1908), and Nigeria (1922). Women helped open the India and China fields and joined the work in Nigeria soon after it was opened. Women served in these fields as educators, evangelists, and doctors and nurses. Some were married and hence also responsible for homemaking and childrearing. The contribution of these women is immeasurable.

Bertha Ryan and Mary and Wilbur Stover opened the India mission field for the Brethren in 1894. Bertha had been working in the Chicago mission for about a year before sailing for India with the Stovers. During her six years in India, she organized Sunday schools, cared for those who suffered during the plague and famine which struck India during this period, and helped establish an orphanage for some of the many children orphaned during the plague and famine. Bertha was a tireless worker with a deep commitment to Christian mission. During her furlough in 1900, she did much speaking and writing to increase the support of the Brethren for the Indian mission. Representing the district of India at the 1900 Annual Meeting, she was the first recorded woman delegate. She also spoke to the pre-Conference missionary meeting on "India's Call Upon the Church Today." Her speech focused on the needs of India, including vivid descriptions of the suffering from famine and disease and the condition of women. She concluded with a call to her sisters and brothers in the church in the United States to support both foreign and home missions. (See quotation at beginning of this chapter.) During her furlough, Bertha married Harvey Shirk. They planned on going together to India, but these plans did not work out. Instead they pioneered in Oklahoma. But Bertha's interest in the work in India never waned.[6]

Mary Emmert married Wilbur Stover just a year before their departure for India. Three sons and two daughters were born to them there. Mary's primary responsibility was to be wife and mother. She supervised each of her children's education until he or she went to the States for high school. Mary endured the pain of parting from her children as other missionary mothers would also do—confident that they were in God's care and were being faithful to the command of Christ to go "into all the world." Mary also helped care for orphaned children and worked in evangelism with Indian women. Wilbur and Mary served in India until Mary's ill health prevented their return following their 1920 furlough.[7]

Anna and Frank Crumpacker, Emma Horning, and George and Blanche Hilton opened the China field for the Brethren in 1908. Emma Horning had graduated from McPherson College (1906) shortly before leaving for China, where she was to work as a teacher. After several months of learning the language, Emma began work with women and children in their homes and with classes at the women's Bible school. She also taught toy-making class.[8]

Blanche Cover Hilton, born in Kansas and reared in North

Dakota, helped organize the Chinese Sunday school in Chicago while studying at Bethany in 1907-08. She and her husband were involved in famine relief and orphanage work in China. Because of ill health they were forced to return to the United States in 1913. They did some work in Chinese Sunday schools in Seattle and Los Angeles and served pastorates in the West as well.[9]

Anna Newland also was born in Kansas and studied at McPherson College. Anna married Frank Crumpacker in 1905, while both were students at McPherson. They applied together in 1906 to begin Brethren mission work in China and served there between 1908 and 1941. Frank worked primarily in evangelism while Anna taught Chinese boys, girls, and women in the Brethren schools at the Ping Ting mission station. The Crumpackers sent regular reports to the Brethren at home through the *Missionary Visitor* and the *Gospel Messenger*. Anna worked in the States as an educator after their return.[10]

As congregations were established by these missionaries, Brethren commitment increased. More missionaries were sent, and new stations opened in India and China. Addresses at the bicentennial celebration of the Church of the Brethren in 1908 reflected this commitment and the expectation of a changed world through mission activity. The participation of women in missions was described by Adalaine Hohf Beery in her address on "The Work of Women":

> But 'woman's sphere' is not bounded by home, nor neighborhood, nor city, nor country. The great round world itself is her domain. No matter how 'domestic' her tastes may be, she can make a habitat under an Indian banyan, or in a mining camp of the Cordilleras, or on an Andean slope. And this not for a winter resort, or a summer residence, but to make the 'foreign' land kin to her own. The task is Herculean, but, though her body is fragile, her soul is six feet ten, and in the prime of optimism and working capacity. . . . The Lord of all recognizes her competence, and gives her souls for hire. Maid and matron, mother and wife, alike have received the ambassador's insignia . . . .[11]

Brethren policy was that in preparation for the mission field there was "no discrimination as to the young people, whether they are brethren or whether they are sisters, or both, or whether they are in office." Men were expected to be "in the ministry," but for women "there is nothing of that kind in the way."[12] There were expectations of the wife of a man called to be a missionary: "he must have a companion who is to him a true helpmeet, possessing, so far as may be, similar qualifications, and who is ever ready and willing to help him, in every possible way, to carry forward the Lord's work."[13]

There seemed to be some hesitance to return widowed mothers to the mission field. Ella Miller went to India in 1906 after studying music and Bible at Manchester College and working in urban mission in small midwestern cities. In 1907 she married Charles Brubaker, who had also gone to India in 1906. They worked together in educational work until Charles died of enteric fever in 1910. Ella returned to the States in 1911 because of ill health but then requested to return to India. The General Mission Board wrote her that "It is [our] judgment . . . that since some of your doctrinal views are not altogether in accord with the General Brotherhood as revealed in a letter to the Secretary and that since God has given you two dear little ones to whom you owe a mother duty, and the more so since we secure single sisters who can 'go,' we decided not to use your services in the home field or return you to India."[14]

Single sisters and married women continued to be sent to the mission fields. As the need for health care became more evident, women trained to be both nurses and doctors on the mission field. Laura Murphy Cottrell and her husband, A. Raymond Cottrell, both served as physicians in India, at Bulsar, from 1913 until 1949 with the exception of 1932 when they were on special assignment in China. Laura was a school teacher in Ohio before her marrige to Raymond in 1905. Following their marriage, both Laura and Raymond entered medical school at the University of Chicago from which they graduated in 1912.[15]

Barbara Nickey of Illinois studied medicine at the American Medical Missionary College at the University of Illinos (M.D., 1912). In 1915 she went to India, where she served as a physician and surgeon at the Brethren Mission Hospital at Dahanu for thirty-seven years.[16] Hazel Messer of Iowa earned an R.N. from the Battle Creek Sanitarium after earning a B.S. from Mt. Morris College. She first sailed to India in 1931. After a year of language study she served as the superintendent of nurses at the mission hospital in Dahanu. She also taught the nurses in the training school there. Hazel herself studied midwifery in Bombay so as to better prepare her students to meet the needs of the women with whom they would work. Her contribution through her students was significant toward improving India's health care systems.[17]

Women missionaries also served as educators and evangelists. Minnie Flory Bright of Ohio worked with her husband, J. Homer Bright in China from 1911 to 1940. Minnie had been a home missionary in Ohio and had studied at Manchester College and Bethany Bible School. In China she taught nurses, women, and boys and organized an industrial program of sewing to help Chinese women be self-supporting. She also worked as a doctor's assistant and an interpreter, in addition to rearing her children, two of whom died in China.[18] Minnie's missionary letters were published by her son J. Calvin Bright, who also served as a missionary to China until the field was closed after the 1949 revolution. These letters reflect both her commitment to Christ and her deep concern for the Chinese people. In one of these letters, she describes the women in the industrial sewing program:

> I wish you could see some of the beautiful work they are making. They are very, very poor and hunger is ever stalking at their door but they do the most beautiful work with their needles which requires infinite patience. They really possess wonderful ability in artistic taste. You have bought their work in the past and we are eager for our friends at home to know more about their needle work. . . .
> You and I have never been so near hunger pangs as have they and their children, nor have we known the slightest meaning of what it means to be a widow in this land, and many of these women are widows. This work gives them an honorable living . . . . But it is a crushing grind at the best to be able to feed and clothe themselves and it is mighty little they know of luxury and pleasure.[19]

Nettie Senger worked in China from 1916 to 1939 as an educator and evangelist. During the 1920s and 1930s she worked with others in establishing a program of agricultural extension, mass education, and industrial cooperatives in the Shansi area. Nettie founded a school for Chinese women in which she and Miss Chang taught skills needed for mothering. She wrote textbooks for use in these various programs. Nettie was also a student of Chinese philosophy, and she was working on a doctoral dissertation entitled "A Social Study on the History of Chinese Womanhood" when war broke out in China. After her return to the United States, she worked for two years with the Chinese Sunday school in Detroit. Nettie received a B.D. from Bethany Biblical Seminary in 1923 and was licensed to the ministry in 1947.[20]

Martha Shick (Flory) of Kansas went as an independent missionary to South China in 1916. Martha had been a settlement worker in Chicago and had helped found the Chicago Chinese Sunday School in 1908. Most of the Chinese in this school had migrated from South China and wanted someone to go there to share the gospel. Martha and Soo Ping, the wife of Moy Gwong—one of the Chicago students—founded a primary school in 1918. Moy Gwong returned to China in 1920 and helped in establishing a congregation. This congregation and the primary school became the Brethren South China Mission in 1920. Martha was licensed to preach in 1928. When she returned to the United States in 1931, there were twenty-five members in the congregation.[21]

Chang Shu Mei was a young Chinese woman who served as a village educator and evangelist in China. Shu Mei graduated from the Church of the Brethren's Liao Women's Bible School in the 1930s. Shortly after graduation she went to the village of Feng Hou at the invitation of the village elder. Li Jung Mei was to have gone with Shu Mei but was detained by illness. Shu Mei went alone, trusting that God would be with her in this strange village. The village elder and his wife took Shu Mei into their home and provided a room for the school in which she would teach. They also called in pupils for the school. Sunday services were held in the school room. Shu Mei was adopted by the village elder's wife, who also accepted Shu Mei's God. "Shu Mei is now teaching me to read and when I know more, I too, will witness for Jesus."[22]

Kathryn Kiracofe began thirty-six years of service in India in 1937 after studying at Manchester College and Bethany Biblical Seminary and working as a teacher and social worker in Ohio. She had dreamed of going to India since coming into contact with Ida Shumaker as a child. Her work in India centered in evangelism and education, especially adult education. Kathryn's evangelistic work entailed visits to many villages. Until roads were developed after Indian independence, Kathryn traveled by oxcart and tented in the villages. Later she traveled by jeep, which made it possible to visit each village more often during the year. Kathryn wrote texts for use in literacy work. She remembered one husband being so pleased when his wife learned to read and write that he presented his wife with a Bible of her own to read. Literacy was a means to social and economic development as well as a way to deepen spiritual life.[23]

Kathryn was assisted in her village evangelistic work by Indian women who were known as "Bible women." This was a common practice on the mission field in both China and India among several denominations. Often these women were widows or older women who received a small salary for their work. Their ability to relate to the village women was a significant contribution to the work. Kathryn wrote about Motibai, a Bible woman who worked with her in the early fifties in a mission education program. Motibai was "a village Christian with only a sixth standard education, a love for God, and lots of energy."

Motibai had hoped to go to teacher's training college after finishing boarding school, but her father insisted that she marry. She did so on the promise that she would be able to go to college after her marriage, but that did not happen. Several children were born. Two survived, and Motibai was interested in working as a Bible woman to help support them. Motibai was most helpful in managing emergencies and in "applying the Bible truths" with the village women. She was also a leader in her own village. Women came to her for advice and medicine. During grass-cutting season, Motibai worked as a day laborer. In the evening she conducted evangelistic services. Motibai said, "My greatest desire is to win my people to Christ."[24]

After the Nigerian mission field was opened in 1922 by H. Stover Kulp and Albert Helser, other missionaries joined them in the work there. Ruth Royer Kulp rejoined her husband in 1923 after a year in London studying tropical medicine. She and her infant son died just a year later. Two years later Stover married Christina Masterton, a Scottish missionary to Zambia, whom he met while on furlough in London. Christina returned to Nigeria with Stover and began educational work with women. She was a musician who composed hymns in the Bura and Marghi languages. Two children were born to the Kulps. Christina died in Garkida in 1952.[25]

Clara Harper began her thirty-four years of service in Nigeria in 1926, after study at Ashland College, Manchester College, and Bethany Bible School. Her work in Nigeria was primarily educational and evangelistic, although at times she also did medical work. As a village evangelist, she traveled by foot and bicycle over the hilly terrain of northern Nigeria. In the villages she taught the women how to care for their infants and children, how to sew, how to raise fruits and vegetables, how to read and write, and she interpreted to them the Bible. She worked with any women who were interested, whether

Christian, Muslim, or animistic. "I wanted them to advance and then finally they would see the light and love of Christ and follow him." She then taught in the women's school at Waka. "When they left school they were able to teach Bible classes, sew, plant vegetables and help other women in the villages where they went to live." Clara is still remembered by people in Nigeria for her contribution to the lives of families and villages there.[26]

Mayoksa, a Bura woman, was an evangelist in the leper colony established by the Brethren near Garkida. Mayoksa was one of the the first leper patients at the Garkida General Hospital and was among the first to enter the leper colony after a year of treatment at the hospital. Mayoksa had grown up in Gardemna, where she married and gave birth to three children, two of whom died. Both she and her husband became afflicted with leprosy. Her husband would not go with her for treatment, so she went alone. She was baptized into the Garkida congregation soon after entering the colony. There was no church building in the colony, so Mayoksa held prayer meetings each evening by the door of her hut. At first others in the colony were hesitant to come to her meetings, as many of them were Muslim. But soon the meetings were so crowded that they were divided into several prayer classes. Some of the members of the colony decided to build a church where regular weeknight services could be held. Mayoksa attended these services when she could, as well as continuing her own prayers by her hut. She became known as the mother of the church and was sought out for her counsel and advice by younger church members. Her influence in the church continued after her death.[27]

Marguerite Schrock Burke served as a nurse in Nigeria with her husband Homer, a physician. After working in Nigeria from 1924 to 1938, they served at Castañer Hospital in Puerto Rico from 1946 to 1961. Then in 1962 they returned to Nigeria for another six-year period, after which they worked in Chicago at Bethany Hospital until their retirement to Bremen, Ind. Marguerite was noted for her abilities to "live off the land" and relate to people of many races and cultures.[28]

Without mission boarding schools, it would likely have been impossible for parents of school-age children to serve on the mission field, especially in India and Africa. Thus the missionary teachers assigned to the boarding schools had an important, if largely unheralded, role in the mission work of the church. Though some of these teachers were men, most of them were women.

In this survey, Emma Ziegler will represent these missionary teachers. Over twenty of her thirty years in India were spent on the staff of Woodstock School in the foothills of the Himalaya Mountains of North India. Colleagues, pupils, and parents all held "Miss Ziegler" in high regard. She was known both for her outstanding teaching skills and for the caring way in which she served as a substitute mother to Brethren missionary children at Woodstock while their parents were at work a thousand or more miles away. During all but the first few years there, she also served as elected teacher representative on the board of trustees.

Woodstock's academic excellence and the quality of teacher-pupil relationships drew a student body from mission families of many denominations from all over North India as well as Burma, Thailand, and Nepal. There were also some Indian and Nepalese students.

One of Emma Ziegler's nieces Fran Clemens Nyce reports that on a visit to India twenty years after her aunt's retirement, she found her aunt warmly remembered by North American Mennonite families still in India. The women and men who staffed the mission boarding schools performed a significant ecumenical service.

In addition to the women mentioned above, there were many others who served in similar capacities in India, China, Nigeria and Ecuador. All shared a deep commitment to spreading the gospel and meeting human need. Educational and medical programs were a part of the work in nearly every mission station. As literacy was established and diseases cared for, more specialized educational and preventive health care programs were developed.

The Church of the Brethren committed itself to an indigenization of its mission program in the mid-1950s. Some thought the turning over of mission programs to local and national leadership came too soon; others thought it should have happened sooner. Opinions also differed as to how much Christian mission had imposed Western ways, which were not essential to the Christian faith, onto other cultures. These are questions that must be asked when the history of missions is studied. Yet, the significant contribution of Christian missions to education, health care, and agriculture in developing nations is most evident, in addition to the importance of sharing the gospel with those who had not heard it.

HOME MISSIONS

Brethren were hesitant to develop an organized program of home missions during the nineteenth century. Church extension had come primarily through migration and the development of new congregations from previously established ones. During the 1850s a plan for dividing the denomination into districts received conditional approval by Annual Meeting. One of the purposes of the district was to organize church extension within its sectional boundaries. The plan was opposed by those who thought that the provision calling for districts to pay the expenses of evangelists and missionaries would lead to a salaried ministry, which they saw as unscriptural and out of keeping with Brethren practice. Final approval to district organization was given shortly after the Civil War, and some support was given to home missionaries, particularly those working for church extension to the South and West.

Barbara Kindig Gish (1829-1915) and her husband, James R. Gish, were prominent among these early home missionaries. Shortly after their marriage in 1849, they moved from the Roanoke, Virginia, area to Illinois, where they began farming. Their farming was quite successful financially. In addition to supporting their own home mission work, they made available farms on easy terms to ministers in relatively inaccessible areas. The Gishes traveled through twenty-two states evangelizing and organizing congregations. Barbara was able to travel with James, as they had no children. He preached and she led singing. After James's death in 1896, Barbara donated most of their $60,000 estate to the General Missionary Board and Tract Committee to subsidize printing and distribution of books to Brethren ministers.[29]

The Brethren's Church Extension Union attempted to provide a denominational program of church extension, including preaching in towns and cities where Brethren had moved. This work was later assumed by the General Missionary and Tract Committee (see beginning of this chapter). Until 1896, urban missions were under the direction of this committee or of various districts. Then the 1895 Annual Meeting developed a plan for district and denominational cooperation.[30] There was also a shift from the primary concern of retaining as members Brethren who had moved to urban areas to a reaching out to non-Brethren. Women played key roles in the development of many urban mission programs.

The Chicago city mission began in 1885 when Brethren services

were first held in the city. In 1889 members organized a congregation, called a pastor, and established Sunday school missions in
various parts of the city. Bethany Bible School was started in 1905
across the street from the Hastings Street property of the congregation. Many mission workers came from Bethany, which emphasized
mission study and practical experience in mission work. Some of
these mission workers later entered foreign mission service. An account of these missionaries given in the *Chicago Sunday School Extension* (1904) shows not only a movement from home to foreign
mission but from one home mission project to another:

> First I may speak of Alice J. Boone, whose zeal was without
> measure, and who knew no tiring in her Master's service. She
> began the children's mission work in the fall of 1892. Conscien-
> tiously she endeavored to push the Lord's work into larger and
> wider dimensions, until she went to Brooklyn, N.Y., and began
> the mission work there. Sister Boone is now engaged in mission
> work in Kearney, Nebraska. She remained in the Chicago work
> about five years.
>
> Bertha Ryan came into our work next, and was here about
> one year. Consecrated and truly faithful, but India's hundreds of
> millions claimed her rather than Chicago's millions, and the
> Chicago church gracefully surrendered her; and five years of the
> best of her life were spent in India. She is now married and living
> with her little family in Oklahoma.
>
> Lizzie Howe comes third on the list. Lizzie was one of Chica-
> go's most faithful workers. Her assiduous application to Bible
> study has made her a teacher of exceptional ability. She believed it
> to be wrong to waste time. Brooklyn may well be congratulated
> that she consented to become identified with the work there. Sister
> Howe was also in this work about five years.
>
> Cora M. Cripe numbers fourth on the list, and was the
> youngest of our workers to enter the field, being but eighteen
> years of age when she gave herself to the Master's work in
> Chicago. She has spent eight years constantly at work among
> boys and girls, and also has rendered invaluable service in the
> regular church work. . . . Sister Cripe has had full charge of the
> children's mission for two and a half years.
>
> Next in order comes Susie Forney, one of the purest of the
> pure girls who ever gave their hearts to Jesus. Chicago lost a
> splendid and exceedingly faithful worker when Los Angeles,
> Calif., gained one. The success of the Brethren mission in that city
> shows that some very faithful work has been done by the workers
> there. Sister Susie was in Chicago's work between five and six
> years.
>
> Clara E. Stauffer entered the field as Chicago's sixth mis-

sionary of the Brethren church. She remained here less than a year, when the mission work of Indianapolis, Ind., demanded an experienced worker. . . .

Mary N. Quinter is seventh on the list. And what shall be said of our cultivated, refined Sister Mary? She seemed not as a stranger among us, for in a remarkably short time she had grasped and comprehended the situation, and in a few weeks seemed as much at home in the work as though she had been here from the beginning. And such love and friendship as that which existed between Cora and Mary was very rare among girls, and did one's soul good to realize. It was one of the pitiable sights when Chicago's millions were again called upon to lay upon the altar of sacrifice Mary Quinter for India's hundreds of millions, to see the sorrow-rent hearts of these deeply devoted sisters as they parted after their short year's association. . . .

Gertrude Rowland, eighth and last, finishes our list of missionaries appointed by the board. Gertrude is modest and unassuming. She has been here but a few months, and in that time has won the hearts of many; and she, too, has shown an ability to grasp and comprehend the work in no small degree. . . .

The Chicago church is entitled to some credit for furnishing the opportunity affording these sisters their missionary training, which has helped to make every one of them such an efficient worker.[31]

Often, the organization of a Sunday school was the beginning of urban mission work. This was the case with the Bethany Mission in Philadelphia, established by Julia and Samuel Croft in 1904. The Crofts had moved to Philadelphia from Ohio a year after their marriage in 1883. They were baptized into First Church, Philadelphia, in 1887; Samuel was elected a deacon soon after. In 1898 Julia began working with Geiger Memorial Church, which was built by the philanthropist Mary S. Geiger.[32] Then Julia and Samuel decided to establish the Bethany Mission in Kensington, a working-class neighborhood of Philadelphia with no church.

Samuel and Julia financed the founding of the mission with money Samuel made as a small manufacturer. They purchased a three-story dwelling in the neighborhood for use as a mission. Julia did the pastoral work of the mission. She began by canvassing the neighborhood to invite the children to the mission Sunday school. Sixty-seven children came to the first session on a Sunday afternoon in June. The Crofts hoped to bring a Christian influence into the homes through work with the children. Julia visited the homes of her students, where she "plead for a better life, more wholesome home conditions, and for a family religion."[33] She also conducted funerals, counseled the troubled, and visited the sick. She organized other areas of work, such as midweek prayer meeting for older boys and girls, a mother's meeting, a home department, and a cradle roll for infants. A Loyal Temperance Legion was organized in 1905 to combat drunkenness in the neighborhood.

Regular preaching services were begun in the fall of 1906, and a congregation was organized in 1907. Men from various denominations served as preachers, some of whom were students in the Philadelphia area. A church was built in 1907 on land donated by the Crofts with a loan from a business friend of Samuel's. A pastor was called in 1910. Julia continued to serve as Sunday school superintendent. By 1913 enrollment had grown to over four hundred. A Baptist minister who had preached in the mission in its early days gave this assessment of its contribution to the community: "The planting of the mission seemed to work a mighty change among the people, and a change in every important sense— physically, morally, and spiritually. . . . I have never in all my ministry witnessed such a change wrought in a similar community in so short a time and one of such permanent character. This is to be attributed to the policy of the Mission, and the nature of the ministry fulfilled in the homes of the people by Mrs. Croft."[34]

Some home mission work was directed to specific racial or ethnic groups. Some Brethren were calling for mission work among blacks in the South early in this century. The General Missionary and Tract Committee did begin a mission in Palestine, Arkansas, in 1903 with James and Susan May and Mattie Cunningham Dolby (see next chapter for her story) as staff. The work began well but was discontinued in 1908 after the Mays and then Mattie left the work because of illness.

A black orphanage and a home for the elderly in Denver, Colorado, received some support from Brethren congregations in Kansas and Colorado. But the work was discontinued before 1920 when William Rhodes, the project's founder, was disfellowshipped by the Brethren for personal impropriety. Nellie Morgan (Rainey) had served as matron of the orphanage. Nellie had been taken from an orphanage in Pennsylvania by a Brethren family. She was baptized into the Brethren at an early age. Nellie attended Bethany Bible School from 1906 to 1912, being one of the few black students there. In 1918 she offered to open a mission among black people in the South, but the General Mission Board declined her offer.[35]

It seems that support for home missions did not increase as foreign missions expanded, as Bertha Ryan had suggested. Rather home mission programs were cut as foreign programs expanded.[36] Many denominations, including the Brethren, sent missionaries overseas both to spread the gospel and to bring what they believed to be a better way of life. It was often difficut for them to acknowledge that this "better way of life" had not improved living conditions for many in the United States, as there was much poverty and injustice there also. Not only did home mission programs use funds that could be used in expanding foreign programs, but they also required recognition of need and inadequacies at home.

Some districts and congregations did continue home mission projects. Isolated projects were begun by dedicated individuals, like the Crofts, who supported themselves and later secured institutional support for their projects. Nelie Wampler (1877-1970) of Virginia was a home missionary who supported herself through teaching school. Her story has been told by Nancy Morris.

> She was short, about five feet, with bright blue eyes and red hair. She pulled her hair straight back and tucked it into a small bun on the back of her neck which only accentuated her small face and frame. All this petiteness changed when she spoke. She was quick to tell you what was on her mind.
>
> She was Nelie Florence Wampler, born in 1877 near Weyers Cave, Virginia. Known fondly as "Miss Nelie," she was totally committed to helping the people and especially the children of every community in which she served. She started her lifelong mission work in Staunton, Virginia, where she served for about ten months in 1905. Miss Nelie enrolled in Bridgewater College in 1906 working toward a degree in Sacred Literature. In the summers of 1906 and 1907 she worked at her home church, Pleasant Valley (Va.) while continuing her studying during the school term. In the summer of 1908 Miss Nelie traveled to Greene County, Virginia, to work with people in the Blue Ridge Mountains and particularly Bacon Hollow. After graduation from Bridgewater in 1909 she returned to Greene County to continue the work she had started in the summer of 1908.
>
> "Miss Nelie" began her missionary training and was waiting for a call to the foreign mission fields. While she waited she worked in Greene County, earning her livelihood by teaching school. She became to Greene County folks a Christian symbol, a real "home missionary." Miss Nelie traveled fourteen miles between four churches every Sunday. She was instrumental in the

establishment and operation of the Church of the Brethren Industrial School, a coeducational boarding school from 1922 to
1936.

As a nursemaid, Miss Nelie was frequently summoned in the
middle of the night to administer her home remedies. She was to
some the only way to communicate with the outside world, often
reading the newspaper to listeners gathered around a pot-belly
stove in a general store or someone's parlor. She wrote many wills
and often answered mail for them and helped the ladies with can-
ning and sewing. Miss Nelie reared six motherless children and
was the first director of the hot lunch program in the local schools.

Miss Nelie served Jesus Christ and the people in Greene
County in every way she could. Perhaps her most outstanding
ability was her perception of the mountain folks in Greene County. She recognized quickly these people lacked only opportunity
and she was anxious to help them prepare to use their opportunities which she knew would come along some day soon.[37]

Urban mission projects for particular ethnic groups were established. The Chinese Sunday school begun in Chicago in 1908 continued for many years, as did the ones in Washington, Los Angeles,
and Detroit. The La Verne, California, church sponsored night
school classes in English for Japanese and Mexican immigrants.
After the lessons were finished, the group would be invited to a
member's home for singing, Bible study, and worship. Other classes
were offered in sewing, cooking, music, and arithmetic. Students
from La Verne College organized prayer meetings and play for the
children.

Grace Hileman Miller (1878-1955) was responsible for organizing these activities. She came from her native Pennsylvania to
California in 1902 to be a part of the first class of La Verne College.
She was active in church and community work throughout her years
in California. She was an outstanding teacher, particularly of
children. She taught Sunday school for nearly sixty years, including
twenty years in the Mexican Sunday school. In addition to raising
her own four children, she cared for many other children in camps
and church. Grace was always concerned to bring people from different backgrounds together, whether during a Spanish-American
Christmas program in the local church or in desegregating the local
schools.[38]

Laura Moyer (b. 1899) worked for many years with Italian people through the Brooklyn, (New York) mission established in 1892
by two of the workers from Chicago. A mission Sunday school was

organized among Italian immigrants in 1900 by John Caruso, who had been baptized into the Brooklyn mission. A congregation was organized in 1922, and Giovanni Allegri, a well-educated scholar of Presbyterian background, became pastor in 1923. His wife also was a gifted speaker and teacher.

Laura came to Brooklyn in 1931. Laura had first wanted to be a missionary when she was nine. At that time a missionary had spoken in her church about the need for more volunteers, particularly to Africa. But she went to college and taught elementary school for eight years in Pennsylvania. Then Ida Shumaker came to speak at the Hatfield Sunday school, and Laura again felt the call to be a missionary. She left teaching in 1928 to study for mission work at Pennsylvania Bible Institute and Moody Bible Institute. She was accepted by the General Mission Board in 1931 but was asked to go to Brooklyn rather than overseas as the need in the foreign field was for nurses and doctors, not teachers. Laura agreed to go wherever she was needed.

Adjusting to life in a large city wasn't easy for Laura, but she made the adjustment and stayed for forty-three years. Laura loved the people and her work with them. She visited people in the hospital as well as children who were absent from Sunday school, which she served as a teacher and superintendent. The young people's group met in Laura's apartment on Sunday afternoons. She admitted to having enjoyed playing the matchmaker at times. Laura participated in the street meetings, which were conducted in both English and Italian. She learned to sing in Italian and sang with the Italian choir during the church's Italian language radio broadcasts.

Throughout her years in Brooklyn, Laura worked consistently among the women and children through home visitation and many organized programs. She was honored in 1974 by the Brooklyn congregation for her contributions to the church and community. Among the many letters of tribute was this one:

> When we "look back," there are so many highlights and always there was "Miss Moyer." We were kids in Sunday school, Girl Scouts, going to workshops "downtown" to get ready for D.V.B.S. [Daily Vacation Bible School]. Sunday afternoon with the Gang—and your homemade ice cream, camping, and hiking, trips to Souderton (one with turkey stuffing), visiting in our homes, birthdays, graduation, showers, weddings, children, living at the church . . . and always Miss Moyer.

They were fun times, sad times, busy times, and confusing times . . . but always good times. They helped us grow spiritually, emotionally, mentally, and physically . . . you always "have been" in our lives. We'll take this occasion to say, "Thank you."[39]

Home mission projects also were established by Brethren churches abroad. In the late 1940s, Chinese Brethren sponsored Christian work on a small island near a Bible training school in North China. Both students of the school and its wealthy patrons contributed to the work. Precious Jade, a graduate of this school, was in charge of the mission. Her parents had sent her to a Christian primary school as a child, as they believed in education for girls. During Bible training school, Precious Jade participated in evangelistic work. Her practical experience prepared her to be the logical person to begin work in 1949 on this nearby island with its factory and lime kiln. Within two years a congregation of twenty members had been organized. As in the United States, ordained men were brought in to perform baptisms. But Precious Jade directed the church school, which had an attendance of sixty. She also organized a day nursery for working mothers in 1951. Her work made a difference in the lives of many people on the island.[40]

The home missionaries in the first half of the twentieth century, such as Laura Moyer, Nelie Wampler, and Precious Jade, are a remarkable and commendable story in the pages of Church of the Brethren outreach. Their willingness and ability to be involved with people where they lived opened up possibilities for meaningful contributions to the spiritual and physical well-being of individuals, congregations, and communities.

CONCLUSION

A 1928 report from the Commission on Women's Work indicated that there were more women willing to serve in full-time mission work than there were positions available. The shortage in assignments for women resulted from several causes: lack of funds for their support, inadequate preparation for the tasks, and some "lack of appreciation of their ability to serve in a public way."[41] The commission appealed to congregations to use women as "assistant pastors," either sharing with the pastor visitation and pastoral work or "holding the fort" until a pastor could be called. Women did serve in these ways. But other forms of home mission were developing within the Church of the Brethren at this time. These included youth work, camping, peace education, and relief and service work. There were opportunities within some of these emphases for ministry in either the United States or abroad.[42] Women quickly became involved in these projects.

Naomi Miller and Ivy Miller of Virginia and Melissa McMulin of Iowa were a part of the Peace Caravaners project of 1930. This program was a joint project of the Church of the Brethren and the Society of Friends to promote world peace. Twelve teams were sent out during the summer of 1930. Two of these teams were Brethren: the "Sistern of the Brethren" (Naomi, Ivy, and Melissa) and the "Brethren of the Brethren." The Sistern covered fifty-five hundred miles from June 5 to August 23, traveling from Elgin, Illinois, to Bridgewater, Virginia, in their car, "Modern Priscilla." The Sistern visited towns and cities in the Midwest and Southeast, contacting nearly seven thousand people through various programs. The Sistern kept a journal of their caravan. Among the entries were the following:

> Dr. Ackers, an elderly minister who had made a couple appointments for us, was not able to be present when we filled them, because he had appointments at other places. A few days later he drove several miles to the little town where we were in order to see us before we left. He said, "This is a wonderful work you are doing. Many people hae the idea that the people of the Church of the Brethren aren't well-educated. I think it means much for our church to have three girls who are college graduates to spend several days in this community."
>
> One man said, "When the sisters want to do something, the Brethren ought not to object."[43]

Women were active in relief work as individuals and through their organizations (see also chapter 5). Helena Kruger (1902-78) emigrated from Russia to the United States by way of Germany with her family in 1924. They joined the Church of the Brethren in 1941. Helena was recruited by M. R. Zigler in 1945 for relief work in Belgium, Italy, and Austria. She supervised the conversion of a Nazi labor camp into a tuberculosis sanitarium for refugees. She persuaded the Austrian government to pay nurses and doctors and helped procure the beds, sheets, a truck, and the supplies necessary to operate a 125-patient hospital.[44]

Brethren Volunteer Service (BVS) was established in 1948 at the urging of a group of young adults at the Annual Conference that year. Alma Moyers (Long), a 1948 graduate of Bridgewater College, played a key role in its acceptance. She helped draw up the proposal, spoke with the moderator about its presentation and with two other youth, addressed the Conference in support of BVS. She was subsequently a member of the first BVS unit in September of 1948.[45]

BVS continues to be a highly successful one- or two-year volunteer program for young men and women to meet human need and work for peace. Most assignments are to projects of medical care, community service, overseas relief and refugee projects, and home missions. Many women have served throughout the world in BVS. Edith Merkey served in Europe from 1957 to 1960, working at projects in Germany, Austria, and Greece. Edith was licensed to the ministry after graduation from McPherson College. During study at Bethany she worked in the Chinese mission program. Then for fifteen years she worked among the Navajos at Lybrook, New Mexico, where the Brethren began a mission program in 1953.[46]

In 1974 Yvonne Dilling of Fort Wayne, Indiana, accepted an assignment to work with refugees in Central America for her BVS project. Her experience and service in El Salvador led to her becoming national coordinator of the Witness for Peace project, and ecumenical action program working for a change in United States policy in Central America.

Brethren women also work for peace individually and through non-Brethren groups such as Another Mother for Peace. Jean Warstler Zimmerman, North Manchester, Indiana, home economic professor and mother of two daughters, has focused her work on nuclear disarmament. She has challenged the United States arms escalation in court with other defendents after having engaged in civil disobedience to draw public attention to the issues.

Such work may seem to be quite different from pioneering in mission work in India or Chicago. Yet, all these women have been concerned to bring God's love in word and deed to a world in need of reconciliation.

8

WOMEN AND MINISTRY

God always gave his gifts freely where they [people] were willing
to use them, and I believe in Christ Jesus male and female are
one, just as Jew and Gentile are made one. Every one should do
as much as they can to glorify God with the different gifts of the
Spirit of God (Sarah Righter Major from a letter written in
1835—see Appendix A).

It is a conviction of the Church of the Brethren that all members
are to share in the ministry of the church. All of the original eight in
Schwarzenau "testified publicly to their faith."[1] Yet, the church also
affirms a need for what is called a set-apart ministry for preaching,
administering baptism and communion, and overseeing church
order. These set-apart ministers are elected and installed by the congregation, usually in recognition of their gifts for such a ministry. For
the first two centuries of the denomination, women participated in
these elections but were not eligible themselves for election—having
been "exempted by the gospel" from "the service of the church."[2]

Earlier generations of women have served the church, though,
in many ways. Women as individuals, as ministers' wives, and
through various women's organizations helped establish and maintain congregations in Germany, the United States, India, China,
Nigeria, and Ecuador. They also served the church in local communities and in other areas of their country and the world. Their call
to this service was grounded in the covenant of faithfulness they
made with God and the church through baptism, a call shared by all
members of the church.

The ministry of the Church of the Brethren has found its center
in love of God and love of neighbor. The Brethren at times expressed this ideal by quoting the motto of the Sauer press: "For the

glory of God and my neighbor's good." The New Testament teaches that these ideals are not separable, that love of God is validated through love of neighbor. The Brethren approach to missions exhibited this understanding, as did the work of women's organizations. The love of God has been the focus of Brethren worship, study, and prayer as well.

Brethren worship services are led by the ministers of the congregation. The usual order of service in the nineteenth century included prayer, singing, scripture, and preaching. The congregation knelt for a period of prayer prior to preaching. Two or three ministers would pray aloud, and then the congregation would pray the Lord's Prayer. In some congregations two or three ministers might preach upon a text.[3]

One sister fondly remembered such services from her childhood. She wrote in 1914:

> With much pleasure we remember the joy we experienced in going to meeting, with the whole family, on the big springwagon. This usually meant that there we would see our grandmother, with all the other grandmothers and aunties who assembled on one side of the large church, while the brethren occupied the other side. Because of their uniform appearance, as they were assembled for worship, they reminded us of soldiers, ready for marching orders . . . . Behind the long table sat a row of devout, reverent elders and ministers, facing the congregation. In front of them, on the opposite side of the table, sat a long line of deacons, one of whom usually read the chapter which contained the text for the sermon. Sometimes the whole chapter was the "basis of the remarks" by the minister, whose turn it was to preach.[4]

Both the leadership of deacons, ministers, and elders and the presence of loved ones among the gathered congregation contributed to a meaningful meeting.

The elected deacons and ministers of the congregation were also the leadership for the Brethren love feast. They read the scriptures and gave the meditations during the service. The presiding elder administered communion. But the service would not have been possible without the work of women—usually the wives of deacons—beforehand. Sisters baked the unleavened bread that was used for communion. Sometimes the grape juice which was used had been prepared and canned by some sisters when grapes were in season. They also prepared the food for the fellowship meal, with the assistance of the deacons in some congregations. Many sisters felt it was a privilege to be able to serve the church in this way.

Prayer meetings, which were also called social meetings, were organized by some congregations in the nineteenth century. This was an addition to the usual Sunday services of a Brethren congregation. Some members opposed these meetings, as they seemed to imply that regular worship services were inadequate in meeting members' need for spiritual nurture. Supporters pointed out that Brethren preaching services were infrequent in frontier areas. Annual Meeting approved these services in 1859.[5] These meetings were led by the laity. A query came to Annual Meeting in 1861 asking if their approval of such meetings meant that "liberty be given to any brother or sister, or if time admit, for all to rise to their feet, and exhort" and, if not, what should the order of such meetings be. The answer was that "the order should be according to . . . 1 Cor. 14:27-40."[6] A later query (1891) asked if this scripture was to be understood as prohibiting sisters "leading or rising to speak" at these meetings. Annual Meeting answered that it was not to be so understood.[7]

On into the twentieth century, women continued to be involved in the leadership of similar meetings. A report of the first time Nigerian Brethren women led a prayer meeting was published in the *Gospel Messenger* (1935).

> The first cautious step in leading the Bura women to take part in the church service was when Mrs. Bittinger taught them a new song and asked them to sing it in church. Oh, such consternation as showed on their . . . faces! "Why, no, truly, such things just weren't done. What would the men say?" They insisted the men would laugh at them right in meeting. But finally their fears were partially dispelled, and the women all sat on the front mud benches at church that morning . . . . Then they sang, and their first public performance was history. Several other appearances in song followed. . . .
> Then came the invitation to the women to take full charge of the prayer meeting. Their verdict was eagerly awaited. Their answer was to be made entirely by themselves. Then came the word: "Yes, we will do it. We have a program all arranged."
> When Friday night came, the church was quite well filled. No one wanted to miss this program. The women filled the first six or seven benches. Many of them had little curly headed babes fastened on their backs or held in their arms. It was plain to be seen that they were nervous. But each one did her part, and did it well. They were quite shy as they stood on the pulpit to tell a Bible story or to sing a song.[8]

Many women in the United States certainly shared these feelings of shyness and nervousness when they first began participating in church services. They also must have shared the joy their Nigerian sisters felt in glorifying God publicly.

Some congregations who believed religious instruction to be part of their ministry began organizing Sunday schools in the mid-nineteenth century. These, too, were questioned by some members of the church who feared they would relieve parents of their responsibility for religious instruction and who found no scriptural command for such schools. The Annual Meeting of 1838 considered it "most advisable to take no part in such things" (Article 10).

A Sunday school was organized in the White Oak congregation (Pennsylvania) in 1845 by Jonas Gibble and his wife. Classes were given in both German and English. The Philadelphia congregation permitted a Sunday school to be organized at the insistence of Henry Geiger, who agreed to accept their call to the ministry on condition that he could establish one. The German Baptist Sabbath School Association was organized in 1856 and contributed significantly to the growth of the congregation. Its influence spread, and in 1857 the Annual Meeting declared that "we know of no scripture which condemns Sabbath-schools, if conducted in gospel order . . . ." (Article 11).

Although Sunday schools continued to be a subject of controversy until late in the nineteenth century, many were organized throughout the denomination.[9] Often mission programs began with the organization of a Sunday school (see chapter 7), and then a congregation was formed. Established congregations also organized Sunday schools. Dedicated women were usually involved in organizing and continuing such schools. Many teachers were women; at times the superintendent of the Sunday school was also a woman from the congregation.

Martha Zug Eckert was the founder of the Sunday school in Lebanon, Pennsylvania. She wanted her sons to have the same kind of instruction she had received as a child in a rural Brethren congregation. As there was no Brethren church in Lebanon, she asked the Midway congregation to open a Sunday school in Lebanon. Permission was granted, and a Sunday school was started in 1899. The classes were held in the home of Martha's father. Her sister Mary Zug Francis was its first superintendent. Mary had attended Lebanon Valley and Mt. Morris colleges, as she felt education would be helpful in furthering the growth of the church. She and her sister remained active in the work of the church. Martha was especially concerned with the welfare of the children and adults, and she regularly visited the sick and needy within the congregation. Mary was a quiet source of moderation and reconciliation during a period of transition in the church. She also was active in the community as a pioneer in organizing children's playgrounds and parent-teacher associations.[10] The Battle Creek (Michigan) Church of the Brethren also began with the organization of a Sunday school in 1916 by two sisters. Goldie Mullenix Early and Maurine Mullenix Kilpatrick were assisted in their work by some women working as nurses at the Battle Creek Sanitarium.[11]

Eva Kindell of southern Ohio was the superintendent of the Pleasant Hill Sunday school for over twenty years. She was first elected to that office in 1900 and was re-elected yearly.[12] Before her marriage in 1889, she had attended Mt. Morris College. Clara Alstadt was installed as district Sunday school superintendent of the District of North Dakota, Eastern Montana, and Western Canada in 1897.

Elizabeth Myer was one of the organizers of the Sunday school of the Elizabethtown Church of the Brethren in 1903. She was appointed to an advisory committee with a deacon and a "lay brother." Both the primary and home departments of the Sunday school were organized through her efforts. Her contributions in education extended beyond the Sunday school movement. Elizabeth was a respected public school teacher as well, although it seemed for a while that she might not be able to teach as there was opposition to anyone in "plain dress" teaching in Pennsylvania public schools. Elizabeth had joined the church in 1886, during her senior year at Millersville State Normal School. She thought that she would not be able to return to school, as she had adopted the plain dress required of Brethren at that time. But the principal of the school insisted that she return, telling her: "Your scholarly attainments at this school have won the esteem of all of us. I shall, therefore, recommend to the faculty that you be allowed to continue your work at this place. . ."[13] Elizabeth did return and graduated that same year. She was salutatorian of her class, and gave her address in a simple gray dress and with a prayer covering over her hair.

Elizabeth was invited to teach in the Lancaster County schools. She taught in various schools over a period of fourteen years and was well respected as a teacher "second to none." At one point she accepted the challenge of teaching in a school where several teachers had been "thrown out of their jobs" by some older, unruly boys. Miss Myer met them on the steps her first day with a pleasant "Good morning." But they soon discovered they now had a teacher who combined firm discipline with sincere interest in each of them. She successfully completed her assignment.

Then in 1900 she devoted herself to the task of establishing a Brethren college in Elizabethtown, Pennsylvania. She began by soliciting funds for the college and then became an instructor in mathematics, elocution, and English when the college opened in 1901. She was also a preceptress (dean) of the college. In addition to teaching, she sponsored many student activities, edited the faculty paper, and organized literary societies, a museum, and the library. Her service to the college extended until her death in 1924. A campus hall was later named in her honor.

Elizabeth Myer's contributions in education were recognized by the larger church family when she was asked to present a paper at the bicentennial celebration of the founding of the Church of the Brethren in 1908. In its report on this conference, the *Gospel Messenger* noted that "Sister Myer read a spendidly prepared essay on 'The Growth of the Sunday School Movement.' She put much work on the essay and read it well."[14]

A General Sunday School Board (GSSB) was established by Annual Meeting in 1911 in response to queries asking for denominational development of Sunday schools. The five appointees to the board were men. A query came to that same meeting requesting that "sisters be used more frequently" on committees "inasmuch as the sisters do so much teaching in Sunday school, prayer meeting, and other church work."[15] A motion to return the paper, claiming that sisters were used in such positions, passed. The GSSB continued to consist of male members until its merger in 1923 with the Christian Workers' Board (CWB). This board had been established in 1919 to supervise Christian Workers' organizations, which united the concerns for youth work and evangelism. CWB consisted of three members, one of whom was Eva Lichty Whisler. She continued on this board until its merger in 1923 with the GSSB and then was a member of that board until 1925.

A Board of Religious Education was established in 1928 from a merger of the GSSB and the General Welfare Board. It consisted of seven members including Eva Trostle from 1928 until 1933. Eva had served on denominational committees since her appointment to the Dress Reform Committee in 1914. Among her appointments were committees to study the loss of Brethren children to the church (1915), the use of music in the church (1916), and the revision of the credential blanks used at Annual Meeting (1918). Her tenure on the Committee on Dress Reform (1914-24) was longer than that of any other member.

Eva was born in 1878 near Mt. Morris, Illinois. She studied at Mt. Morris Academy (1899-1904) and College (B.A., 1928) and Bethany Bible School (1907-1915; B.D., 1929) and several Bible institutes. Eva was a mission worker in Illinos, 1904-07. While at Bethany, she supervised the practical work (1907-12) and taught Bible and music as well as serving as dean of women (1911-23). She later taught Bible and was chaplain at Bethany Brethren Hospital and Nurses' Training School.[16]

Cora Miller Stahly was appointed to the General Music Committee established by Annual Conference in 1919. Her service on the committee continued until 1928, including several years in which she chaired the committee. Cora was born in Ohio in 1877. When she was only ten she led congregational singing, using the metrical tunes without notes common among the Brethren at that time. She studied music at several schools, among them Manchester College. She headed the music departments at Manchester (1911-20), and Bethany Bible School (1920-22). She and her husband traveled in the western states (1925-26) to promote the new Brethren hymnal which she had helped compile.[17]

Women participated in the governing boards of some districts during this period. Their presence seemed to be strongest in areas which had been frontier areas, such as the Great Plains, and areas where the Brethren were not as concentrated, such as Michigan. In 1920 women were serving as district Sunday school secretaries in twelve of the fifty-one districts of the church. However, the district Sunday school boards were all male. Three districts had women serving as district missionary secretaries. Six of the 138 temperance officers at the district level were women. The members of the ministerial and mission boards of the fifty-one districts were all men.

In 1930 women were serving on the home mission boards of three districts. Of the 143 members of the district boards of religious education (successor to the SSB), 21 were women. Some districts still had district welfare boards. Of the 73 members of these boards, 26 were women. In two districts, women chaired boards which included men.

As the various denominational boards carried out their tasks, it became necessary to employ a full-time staff to administer the program. The General Mission Board was the first to engage several staff members, and it was instrumental in the expansion of denominational staff. The Brethren Publishing House (BPH) came under the control of this board in 1897. Women were employed as assistant editors by BPH. Maud Newcomer was named to the editorial staff in 1910 after teaching public school for five years. She continued in this position until 1937, editing several Sunday school papers for children and youth. Maud also wrote the teacher's page in the *Bible Study Monthly*. Teaching in the primary department of the Highland Avenue church in Elgin, Illinois, kept her in touch with the needs and characteristics of children.[18] Other women have served quite ably as editors of Brethren Sunday school papers. Among them are Edith Barnes and Hazel Kennedy. Edith was on the staff for thirty-eight years (1921-59), then volunteered her skills to the Brethren Historical Library and Archives (also at Elgin, Illinois) for more than twenty-five years. Hazel edited curriculum from 1949 until 1974.

The General Sunday School Board was the first to hire a woman as field staff. Ruth Shriver was appointed director of Children's Work in 1927, a position she held for nineteen years (see chapter 5). She was exceptional in her ability to recruit, train, and work with a network of regional, district, and local volunteers in a shared ministry.

Writing was a form of ministry for many Brethren women. During the nineteenth century when their speaking publicly was limited, women expressed their views and feelings through letters, poetry, meditations, and columns for the various Brethren periodicals. Twentieth century Brethren women have also written inspirational and historical books.

Myra Brooks Welch (1877-1959) spent her childhood in Illinois, Nebraska, and Oregon. During her adult years, she lived in California. She and her husband were the parents of three children. Myra published three books of poetry. Her poem "The Touch of the Master's Hand" has been quoted extensively and has received worldwide acclaim.[19]

Myrtle Crist Porter was born in Kansas in 1901. Following

elementary school, she attended La Verne Academy and Bethany Bible School. She married and with her husband reared two sons. Although she struggled with ill health, Myrtle wrote poems and stories for both children and adults. Several appeared in Brethren periodicals and Sunday school papers. She also wrote historical pageants, including "And She Ministered Unto Them" for the seventy-fifth anniversary of Church of the Brethren women's organizations (1960). The Kansas churches honored her in 1961 with a citation "In recognition of her contribution to the spiritual inspiration and the literature of the Brethren people." As is true of many Brethren women, her life of faithful love of family, church, and friends was "a continued message to all who knew her."[20]

Women married to pastors often have had a unique ministry within the congregation. In addition to supporting their husbands and caring for their children and home, these women have provided support and counsel for many women in the congregation. Sometimes they were involved in the leadership of women's programs or musical or educational programs. The stories of Ruth K. Lehman and Santosh are illustrative of women who have shared the ministry of the parsonage family.

Ruth Kurtz Lehman was born in Ohio. After graduation from McPherson College, Ruth taught high school home economics and English. Then in 1928 she married Harvey Lehman, a minister and teacher. Ruth and Harvey were in pastoral work for nearly thirty-seven years in Ohio, Kansas, and Nebraska. During this time they reared two sons and two daughters and also welcomed a German exchange student into their home for a year. Ruth has these memories of her work as a pastor's wife:

> As a full-time pastor's wife, I soon became interested in the Women's Fellowship programs that were being promoted through the Elgin [denominational] Office. Gradually, I was able to enlarge on the Aid Society which most of the churches had—the change was slow and not always accepted too readily. But eventually a good many of the women became interested in a variety of creative programs, study groups, playlets, service projects and so forth. Soon, the women were going through their closets, bringing good clothing for relief, mending and remodeling, cutting out and making layettes and various sizes of chilren's dresses, suits, sleeping garments, etc. Some of the churches served dinners for groups who needed this service and the money often went for some area of relief work. We made soap, packing it and sending it along with

the clothing on the Church World Service trucks whenever they arrived in our area[21]

Ruth served as district and regional CBWF president. She and her husband look back with gratitude for these "rich experiences" of service.

Santosh was the wife of the pastor of the Jamoli congregation in India. She was a leader of women in her congregation and the surrounding area. She reared a family of six girls and four boys. After they were grown she was able to give even more time to her work with the church. As the president of her local women's group, she attended to the spiritual welfare of the women of the church. She also coordinated a monthly devotional meeting of women and girls as well as a midweek meeting which included devotions, fellowship and handwork.

Home visitation was another part of Santosh's ministry. At times she made these visits alone and at other times with a woman missionary. Usually she read the Bible, led in prayer, and read articles to those she was visiting. She also visited during times of illness and grief. A third aspect of her ministry was serving as a group leader during the evangelistic week sponsored by all the Christian denominations in India. Santosh and her group of women would go each morning to a different village to share the Good News with the women and children of the village. Santosh also took evangelistic groups to the villages during other times of the year. Her ministry played a critical role in unifying the women of the church [22]

Some women find the role of pastor's wife a difficult one at times. Inez G. Long, wife of John Long, has written about these feelings, as well as about the rewards of being a companion in the pastorate:

> I chafed under the complexities of public-private life when I was younger, especially when our children were small. Now I can see the benefits which came to us as a family in the public life we all shared. . . . Perhaps I was chafing not so much against my husband's public life and our need for more private life as I was chafing against the second-rate role I had as pastor's wife. I was sort of an appendage to his position, and I resented this. Not because I was neglected or frowned upon, but because, very simply, I wanted to have a career of my own. I had a good career before I was married, as editor of Youth Publications at Elgin. I had had teaching experience while John was at Yale Divinity School. I was

accustomed to an identity apart from John's. So when I returned to teaching—and I had a wonderful teaching career for twenty years at McCaskey High School in Lancaster as an English teacher—I felt a lot of problems resolved. . . . A pastor's family, whether the pastor is man or woman, can put their family life into church life with wonderful benefits. The church is family, and offers many family-centered activities in which all ages can participate.[23]

Women married to Brethren college professors and presidents also have had opportunity to provide support and counsel to many other women. Elva Burr Bowman (Mrs. Joseph L.) was born in Indiana and studied art in Chicago. After her marriage she moved to McPherson, Kansas, where her husband taught math and physics at McPherson College. Elva often spoke to young women about making a career in homemaking, and she continued to address high school girls on this topic into her eighties. Her commitment to the importance of education was evidenced in that in 1984 she was listed among the top one hundred contributors to McPherson College.[24]

Rowena Stoner Peters was a college president's wife. Rowena was born in 1889 in Indiana. She and her seven sisters and brothers all graduated from Manchester College. Her mother, Lina Norris Stoner, had been a schoolteacher in Maryland before her marriage. When Rowena began college, she enrolled for a math course but was told that the course was only for men. She protested to president Winger, who contacted her father. Rowena took the course. She taught school in Indiana for four years, before graduating from Manchester in 1915.

Rowena married Woodward W. ("W. W.") Peters in 1917. Two children were born to this marriage. Rowena and her family lived in Ohio and North Manchester, Indiana, before moving to Mt. Morris, Illinois, where W. W. was president of the college for three years. During their years at Mt. Morris, Rowena worked with the women's group of both the church and the faculty. She worked with a "mission" church in Champaign, Illinois, from 1927 to 1936 while the family lived there. W. W. was named president of McPherson College, Kansas, in 1941, which turned out to be a nine-year stay for the Peters family. He also served as moderator of Annual Conference in 1943. After retirement, Rowena and W. W. spent three years in Austria while W. W. was director of Brethren relief work. Rowena worked with the women, helping sell their handwork. She also helped distribute clothing contributed by American church women.[25]

Women also have had opportunity to serve on the faculty of Brethren colleges. Gladdys Muir is remembered by many Brethren women and men as the most influential professor of their college years. Her students remember her as one who was "soft-spoken and hospitable." She welcomed them into her home, where she lived with her mother. "She created an atmosphere and setting where growth could occur, but didn't dominate."

Gladdys Esther Muir (1895-1967) was born in McPherson, Kansas. She received her B.A. from McPherson College in 1915, then engaged in graduate study at several universities in the United States and Europe. She taught for over forty-five years at La Verne College (California) and Manchester College (Indiana). In 1947 she proposed that the Brethren colleges establish programs for the study of international conflict. Muir founded and directed the Peace Studies Institute at Manchester College, the first program in which students could receive a degree in peace studies. This institute became a model for others. Gladys was a historian and wrote a history of *The Brethren on the Pacific Slope*.[26]

Among other women who especially are remembered for their college teaching are Sadie Stutsman Wampler (1886-1963), who taught drama and music for many years at Manchester College, and Rebeccah Schaeffer, a popular professor of English literature and drama at Elizabethtown College (Pennsylvania).

The ministry of many women in congregations and districts often has been a multi-faceted one. Their commitments embrace children, youth, and women near and far. Their concern extends from their own families to the church family and beyond. In their ministry they create or participate in programs which they hope will help meet the physical, spiritual, and emotional needs of those for whom they care. Accounts of the ministries of several women representative of this significant discipleship were given by congregations and family members for inclusion in this volume.

Bertha Eikenberry Glein (1890-1947) directed children's work and served as chorister and Sunday school superintendent in the Froid (Montana) congregation. She had come as a single teacher to Montana in the 1920s. She and the homesteader she married worked in evangelistic efforts, such as tent meetings. Bertha organized Bible camps in her yard for youth, as there were no other camps in the territory. She was remembered by children as a wonderful story-teller.[27]

Ethel Henderson Masters (1899-1960) was a district and local organizer of educational ministries in the Carolinas. Most of her adult years were spent in the Mill Creek church (North Carolina). Her ministry in the congregation included teaching primary Sunday school classes, serving as Sunday school superintendent, and as church organist. She organized the congregation's cradle roll, mother and dauther banquet, and women's work. She was a generous contributor to the church and to those in need in the community, whether black or white. Ethel was a leader in the regional and district camping movement, beginning with the first camp in 1934. The administration building of Camp Carmel is a memorial to her. Her district involvements also included serving as a member of the district board, as writing clerk of several district conferences, and as district field worker.[28]

Florence Baker Gibble (1878-1971) is still remembered by many women who knew her as a Bible teacher or camp counselor. She taught Bible and counseled at both Camp Harmony and Camp Conewago, a predecessor of Camp Swatara. Florence corresponded with many of her campers, as well as with many missionaries. She was also a Sunday school teacher in the Lititz (Pennsylvania) congregation, of which she was a charter member. From 1923 to 1943 she served as either president or secretary of Women's Work of Eastern Pennsylvania District. She also served on the board of trustees for Juniata College (1927-56).[29]

Ada Miller Brandt Burd (1904-78) was born in Pennsylvania to the family of a Brethren minister. She gave a lifetime of service to the Mt. Olivet (Pennsylvania) congregation. Her ministry included teaching Sunday school, serving in various offices in Women's Fellowship, conference delegate, wife of a deacon, *Messenger* representative, and filling various church offices. Her granddaughter noted that "she was a friend of all—"enemy" was not in her vocabulary. Her smile would light up an entire room. Her beautiful alto voice would ring above all others when singing the songs she loved best—any old-time hymn. Her faith in God and courage to face whatever was in store for her never ceased. . . . she strived to do everything to the glory and honor of the Lord."[30]

Elizabeth Owens Roller (b. 1902) was born in Minnesota and reared in North Dakota, where her father was a farmer. She was christened in the Old Welsh Church. Elizabeth rebelled against and to assist the local doctor. When she was a teenager, she went to a revival meeting to hear a Brethren minister from Canada. She then joined the Church of the Brethren and served it faithfully for many years.

Elizabeth went to Chicago to study at Bethany in 1922. She hoped to be a missionary nurse. In 1927 she graduated (R.N.) from Wesley Memorial Hospital. She married Mark Roller in 1930, and they moved to Virginia, where Mark was a school principal. Elizabeth was the "bumps and bruises doctor" in Tom's Brook. She organized the first county clinics for inoculation against children's diseases. In addition to caring for her own two children, she taught Sunday school and organized a local WCTU chapter. She was active in district children's work and women's work. The Roller home was a depot for Church World Service relief clothing for about forty years. Elizabeth washed and mended the clothes that were donated. She helped cook and can for Civilian Public Service (CPS) camps during the war and then sponsored refugee families after the war. She served as president and secretary-treasurer of the Shenandoah Council of Churches and as president of her local CBWF from 1965 to 1980. After the death of her husband, she joined a "Post"-30 BVS unit and worked at Cross Keys Home in southern Pennsylvania. Elizabeth trusted God's guidance throughout her life: "If a door slams in your face, others will open" was her testimony.[30]

Eva Meiser (b. 1904) was committed to keeping open the doors of the Zion Church of the Brethren in Prescott, Michigan, during the fourteen years it was without a pastor. Eva was rearing her eight children during this period. Yet she found time to serve as Sunday school superintendent and chair of both the ministerial board and the church board. She continued to be active in the aid work of the congregation even in her seventies. Those who have followed Eva in making Zion Church their church home have been grateful for her early labors to help the congregation survive.

Mary Elizabeth Petty (b.1936) was baptized into the Broadwater, Missouri, congregation in 1945. She graduated from McPherson College in 1956, shortly thereafter married Charles Petty, and began teaching public school in 1957. Her teaching career has spanned her entire married life with the exception of three years when she gave primary care to her two small children. She also has been active in mental health work and much involved in many church programs: Sunday school teacher, district camp leader, youth group sponsor, choir director, and church treasurer. She and her husband together work with church and community youth. The Broadwater congregation also has had periods without a pastor. They credit her with carrying on much of the work of the church.[33]

The contributions of women to the ministry of the local church were noted by an Annual Conference paper on "The Role of Women in the Church," adopted in 1952.[34]

> We believe that the division of labor which assigns to women a special function in home and family life is Scriptural, and that normally this offers the greatest opportunity open to women for the service of mankind and the kingdom of God. It is also true that experience proves that women can make outstanding contributions in other areas. We believe this also is Scriptural and in harmony with the spirit and teaching of the Bible.
>
> Regarding the role of women in the church, on the basis of a questionnaire answered by four hundred twenty-three congregations, we find some women serving on almost every board and committee of the local church. One-third of the congregations reporting have at least one woman on the board of administration, trustee board, finance board, and ministerial board. Two-thirds report at least one woman member on each board of Christian education, music committee, and Brethren service committee. Eighty-two percent reported a woman on the missionary committee. The following percentages of church-school teachers are women: adult division, 42%; youth division, 64% children's division, 92%.[34]

The paper concluded that although women do hold "a significant place" in the life and work of the church, "women do not have representation equal to their numerical strength on the boards and committees of the church." Therefore, it was recommended that there be "a more extensive use of their wisdom and ability. . . . Especially do we urge that women be more widely represented on boards and committees on the local, district, and brotherhood level."

Many Brethren women have made a career of home and family. For many, this has been personally rewarding. Their contribution continues through their families. Brethren women have been encouraged to "give their sons to the ministry of the church" as recently as 1960 in Church of the Brethren Women's Fellowship (CBWF) materials. Some Brethren women did encourage their sons to be ministers or missionaries. Some encouraged their daughters, also. Many of these women also found time to be involved in the work of the church themselves, such as Mary Etta Fike Bittinger Sanger and

Vinna Helstern.

Mary Etta raised her family in the mountains of West Virginia. Two of her children became ministers, and two became missionaries. Her son Desmond, a minister and missionary, remembers her as giving herself to service: "midwife, doctor with herbal medicines, donor of food and clothings, quilts to the deprived, sponsor of missions." She also taught Sunday school and spoke at district conferences.[35]

Vinna Helstern reared her daughters in Ohio. Her husband, Russell, was a minister and educator. Vinna was quite active in Women's Work locally and in the district, region, and denomination. Between 1945 and 1951 she was the district director of Brethren Service and Aid. She was well aware of the need for such work, but she also felt that women needed to improve their minds. She thus established "The Fellowship of the Informed," first in the district, and then nationally. This was to encourage reading and discussing good books. Her involvement in the life and work of the church was a significant influence on her daughters. Joy Helstern Dull served on the district board and was the first woman moderator of the District of Southern Ohio. She also served in a national field staff position concerned with rural issues. Mary Sue Helstern Rosenberger became a pastor's wife, nurse, and a member of the Church of the Brethren General Board. Before her marriage, Mary Sue worked in Vietnam with Mennonite Service. Both Joy and Mary Sue are writers, and Mary Sue is the author of one book.[36]

The involvement of four women will represent many other women who assumed leadership in the congregation, district and denomination.

Estelle Baile Mohler (1916-78) was born in Missouri and was active in the district program there as an adult. Estelle graduated from McPherson College. She married Harold I. Mohler in 1939 and with him reared three children. Estelle was minister of music of the Warrensburg congregation for thirty-two years. She served as president of the local and district CBWF, and the local Church Women United organization. Estelle was district clerk, Standing Committee delegate, and its first woman moderator.[37]

Darlene Bucher is an educator and minister's wife. Her husband, Gordon, has been the district executive of the Northern Ohio District for several years. Darlene has been quite active in the local church. She chaired the Christian education commission of the church board and was a member of the church building committee.

Her dramatic abilities have been quite helpful in directing plays with the youth of the church. Several of the plays have been given at district conference. Darlene was a delegate to Annual Conference Standing Committee from the Northern Ohio District, and chaired its nominating committee. She has been a representative of the Alumni Association on the Manchester College Board of Trustees. The recipient of a Jennings Foundation Award for outstanding achievement in educational administration, Darlene has been an elementary school principal since 1970.[38]

Patricia Kennedy Helman is a minister, writer, spiritual life consultant for the Church of the Brethren, and college president's wife. She has been involved in local, district, and denominational leadership. Pat was born in Iowa in 1925. She and her brother and sisters were proud of the fact that their mother was a registered nurse.

After graduation from McPherson College in 1947, Pat married A. Blair Helman. They moved to Ottawa, Kansas, where Blair was a pastor and professor at Ottawa University. Pat taught junior high school during these years, interrupted only by the two brief periods when their two daughters were born. She kept teaching because of financial necessity, but she also loved her work.

In 1956 she and Blair moved to North Manchester, Indiana, where Blair became president of Manchester College. Pat assumed the role of president's wife quite graciously, although she sometimes missed teaching. She was often asked to speak to women's groups and developed a speech using hats to illustrate the various roles and identities of modern women. She would conclude with a Brethren bonnet, which symbolized her heritage and faith. Pat gave her first public access after finishing college. During the 1970s she twice addressed Annual Conference.

Pat was influenced by her mother's artistic gifts and mystical bent. She developed a ministry in spiritual direction and has written meditations for *Disciplines* (from the Upper Room publishers) as well as a regular column ("Pilgrim's Pen") for *Messenger,* and several books. Her book *Free to Be a Woman* focused on the spiritual identity of women. It has been her conviction that a gift women bring to ministry is "a sense of the wholeness of life." Her second book, *In League with the Stones,* traced her own spiritual journey. *At Home in the World* developed Pat's perception of that wholeness and integration. She has also led spiritual life retreats for several different denominations. She has sensed her mission is that of helping people experience personally the reality of God's presence. In response to world hunger concerns and the sensitivity of artists to those concerns she founded "Art for Hunger." Over $50,000 has been contributed through 1984 to this project for hunger relief.

Pat was elected by Standing Committee to the Brethren delegation to the National Council of Churches of Christ (NCCC) in 1978 and has served for two triennial sessions. She is a member of the NCCC committee dealing with farm worker labor relations and the Campbell Soup Company. Pat has twice been nominated for moderator of Annual Conference.

Pat felt a call to the set-apart ministry during the 1977 Conference after making her first public speech from the conference floor. In supporting adoption of a structured ballot which would insure more equal representation of gender and ethnic groups on the boards and in the offices of the denomination she noted that women had used their gifts on behalf of someone else's calling, but the time had come to use their gifts for their own calling. The support of the church was needed in doing this. She was subsequently licensed and then ordained in March, 1981 and has served as a visiting chaplain at Timbercrest Home in North Manchester for three years. In May of 1984 she gave the commencement address at McPherson College, her alma mater. She was then honored with the degree, Doctor of Letters (Litt.D.).[39]

Nganu Gamece was born in a small village in northeastern Nigeria. As was the custom, she was engaged as a baby to a boy by his parents Gamece, who lived in the same village. Nganu grew up helping her mother. Gamece went away to school. When Nganu was in her mid-teens, she and Gamece were married during one of his school vacations. Gamece left her with his parents when he returned to school. But within a week he was back with a missionary who wanted Nganu to come with Gamece. She gathered together a cloth to wear, some cooking pots, and a blanket, and went with Gamece.

Nganu studied in the women's school, where she learned to read and speak the Bura language. During the years Gamece continued his education, Nganu worked as a matron in the girl's dormitory at Waka. Gamece had begun teaching her English. During his absence she took English classes. Five children were born to them. Nganu took a secretarial course and then worked as a secretary in a hospital when Gamece was working on his bachelor's degree. Upon completion of his degree, he became the first Nigerian principal of the Waka Secondary School. Nganu entertained staff wives and many other guests in their home.

Recently Nganu was elected denominational president of "Zumuntar Matan Ekklesiya" (ZME), the "Fellowship of Women of the Church." Each of the more than 100 congregations of Ekklesiyar 'Yanuwa a Nigeria (EYN—The Church of the Brethren in Nigeria) has a ZME. These groups usually meet weekly or biweekly. The women worship, share concerns and pray, clean the church, and make visits. Small monthly dues are paid, which are used to aid needy women and to hold retreats and a yearly ZME conference. Several ZME groups combined to form a choir to provide music for Sunday morning worship services.

In June of 1983 Nganu and seventeen other ZME choir members arrived in the United States for a four-week tour of Brethren congregations. Nganu came both as a choir member and as president of ZME. She shared information about the faith, work, and goals of the women of EYN with United States sisters and brothers. Nganu often told the churches, "We are here to share our joy and peace as Christian women."[40]

While working full time as homemakers, teachers, or nurses, women, such as these above, have given service and leadership in the church wherever it was needed. Their contributions were not made so that they might receive recognition. Rather, they ministered to express their love of God and neighbor. But their contributions have been recognized and remembered by those to whom and with whom they have ministered. The contributions of women in shared ministry have opened the way for women to enter the set-apart ministry of the church.

Patricia Kennedy Helman (1925-), teacher, author, minister, retreat leader

Laura Moyer (1899-), worker in Brooklyn, N.Y.

(personal photo)

Nigerian women's choir, ZME, 1983

WOMEN AND SET-APART MINISTRY

I conceive it would be very inconsistent in an apostle, who had laid his hands on men and women, and pray'd over them, that they might receive the Holy Ghost, to quench the gift of the Spirit of God, because it was given to a woman—in answer to prayer—when at that time it may not be given in such measure to more experienced Christians. God always gave his gifts freely where they were willing to use them, and I believe in Christ Jesus male and female are one, just as Jew and Gentile are made one. Every one should do as much as they can to glorify God with the different gifts of the Spirit of God (Sarah Righter Major from a letter written in 1835—see Appendix A).

Although the Brethren believed that all who were baptized were to be ministers, they also set apart some members of the congregation by election to minister as deacons and ministers (see chapter 2). The Brethren attempted in ordering these offices to follow the teachings of the New Testament.

The qualifications for deacons were those given in 1 Timothy 3:8-15. Responsibilities of the deacons included: visit made by teams of deacons to members of the congregation before the love feast to give spiritual counsel and to reconcile differences, supervising preparation of love feast, and serving the tables during the meal at love feast. The deacons were also overseers of the poor. They were to distribute food and money to the congregation's ill and needy. In worship the deacons assisted by reading scripture and leading prayers and congregational singing. In the absence of a minister, they could preach and schedule meetings.[1]

Three degrees in the office of minister were recognized by the Brethren by mid-nineteenth century. The first degree minister was a speaker who could preach with permission of the advanced degree ministers or conduct an entire worship service in their absence. A second degree minister could preach, schedule meetings for worship, administer baptism, perform marriages, and officiate at the love feast at the request of an elder. The third degree of ministry was that of the elder, sometimes also called the bishop. The elder presided at congregational council meetings, installed deacons and ministers, anointed the sick, and officiated at love feasts. The elder was also responsible for congregational discipline and well-being. Ministers of the first two degrees, as well as deacons, were installed into office by the elder, who extended the right hand of fellowship and gave the kiss of peace. The elder was ordained into office by at least two other elders by the laying on of hands.[2]

In the nineteenth century it is clear that the position of the Brethren excluded women from election to the offices of deacon and minister on scriptural and traditional grounds. There is, however, some evidence that women were not excluded from these offices by the early Brethren (see chapter 1). Alexander Mack, Jr., names three women as elders in his list of deaths.[3] The first was Sister Schneider, whom he called "the first women elder [Ältestin in German] at Schwarzenau." One of the others was Margaret Bayer, whose election as a deaconess was recorded in the Germantown Poor Book.

There are no existing records that indicate what the responsibilites were of these early set-apart women leaders. Could they have been the same as those of elders in the ninteenth century? In a German Bible which may have been used by Alexander Mack, the word Ältestin is used in those passages which in English speak of elders or bishops (Acts 24:23, 20:17-35; 1 Timothy 5:17; Titus 1:5; 1 Peter 5; James 5:14); not in the passages which speak of deacons, such 1 Tim. 3:10-11. But the record of Margaret Bayer's election refers to 1 Tim. 5:9 as scriptural authority. This verse is about the enrolling of elderly widows in the congregation. There is a printed note with this verse in this Bible which refers to Romans 16:1, in which Phoebe is named as a deaconess (Diener in German, feminine form Deinerin). This would seem to indicate that these women were deaconesses, and not elders. But why would Mack, Jr., refer to them as elders? An adjective form of Ältestin is used in 1 Tim. 5:2 in speaking of older women—in German, "die älten weiber." So perhaps he was referring to them as older women who were elected deaconesses.

Thus it is not certain that women were elders in the early church. It does seem clear that some were deaconesses. It is not evident, however, why the Brethren changed this practice so that the only women who became deaconesses were those whose husbands had been elected deacons.

Although the early Brethren generally were opposed to women preaching, some congregations permitted Harriet Livermore (1788-1868) to speak in their churches. Harriet was an evangelist, non-Brethren, who was known in both the United States and Europe. Daughter of a United States Congressman, she addressed Congress four times.[4] Sarah Righter (1808-84) of the Philadelphia congregation was converted under Harriet's preaching in 1826 at age 18. Soon after she experienced a calling to preach, which she was hesitant to act upon as she knew of the opposition of Brethren to women preachers. She shared her call with her father, John Righter, when he asked her why she was so melancholy. He was sympathetic and suggested they confer with Peter Keyser, elder of the Philadelphia congregation. Keyser encouraged Sarah to preach, as did Israel Poulson of the Amwell (New Jersey) congregation. Sarah preached in both these churches, beginning in 1828.

Her preaching met opposition. A query came to the 1834 Annual Meeting "concerning a sister's preaching." Annual Meeting stated disapproval of women preaching, adding that "such sister being in danger, not only exposing her own state of grace to temptation, but also causing temptations, discord, and disputes among other members." A committee of elders was sent to counsel with Sarah. They decided not to enforce the Annual Meeting decision, although they did not give her official permission to preach. A committee member later explained that "I could not give my vote to silence someone who could outpreach me."

The next year Sarah wrote a letter to Jacob Sala, a Brethren printer in Ohio, giving the biblical basis for her preaching. The letter was published that year in a pamphlet with another letter from a Swiss Pietist on millenialism. In regard to those who cited Paul to forbid women to preach, Sarah wrote: "I conceive it would be very inconsistent in an apostle who laid his hands on men and women and prayed over them that they might receive the Holy Ghost, to quench the gift of the Spirit of God because it was given to a woman . . . ."[5]

So Sarah continued to preach.

In 1842 she married Thomas Major, who had been elected a minister in the Philadelphia congregation the previous year. They moved to Highland County, Ohio, where they remained except for a brief period in Philadelphia (ca. 1857). Five children were born to them; three survived infancy. The Majors helped establish the Fall Creek church (Ohio); Thomas was elected elder in 1847. Sarah and Thomas also helped establish the Frankfort (Ohio) congregation in 1865. This congregation began with the baptism of a black couple converted by Samuel Weir, a black Brethren minister.

Sarah and Thomas Major also held preaching missions in Ohio and Indiana. They preached in homes, churches, infirmaries, and prisons. Thomas would usually open the service, and then invite Sarah to speak. If the congregation had asked that she not preach, she would often lead in prayer. One brother who heard her preach left this account:

> When she entered the churchhouse . . . she took her seat down in front of the stand while Elders Shively and Major went up on the stand and, after some little talk among themselves, Brother Major invited her up, and she took her seat on his right side. In dress she was neat and plain—a very plain bonnet which she soon laid aside, and a little shawl around her neck and over her shoulders. . . . After the opening exercises she was invited by Brother Major to preach. She arose, and slowly announced her text, an old, plain, simple one. I was disappointed. I expected something new . . . I was disappointed in a text, but was interested in the preacher, and I gave attention. It did not take long to discover that out of the common came forth the sublime. I could see a wonderful unfolding of the text. I think I am safe in saying that I have never heard a text so expounded, illustrated, and so transformed into newness of life as was done in that discourse.[6]

Other Brethren women were also beginning to preach. A letter came to the *Monthly Gospel-Visiter* in 1852 asking for counsel about "a very interesting sister, and some of our brethren think she ought to preach, which she can do and get her at it sometimes, while some think she ought not to preach, and seem displeased at those who had her to exhort in their houses. (The sister is a Virgin.)" The case was brought to the congregation for counsel, but was not resolved as there was no copy of Annual Meeting minutes available and members had different recollections of what the minutes actually said.

The *Gospel-Visiter* editor, Henry Kurtz, had been clerk of Annual Meeting since 1837 but had taken personal notes on Annual Meeting decisions prior to that date. However, for an unexplained reason, he was reluctant to share those notes and asked his readers if there were extant minutes which included the query on sisters preaching. He also sought the counsel of brothers and sisters near him in Ohio. They suggested that the issue needed to be more fully discussed in Annual Meeting and that in the meantime the congregation should neither forbid nor encourage such meetings. He concluded his reponse with a word from the sisters in Ohio:

> Our sisters have desired to ask those brethren, who want our dear young sister to preach, the following questions, viz. What they would think of a shepherd sending forth one of the most tender lambs of the flock "into the midst of wolves," this being the mission of preachers according to the express words of our great Shepherd? See Matt. x. 16. And if that lamb should be destroyed by those wolves, who would be responsible?
>
> To their beloved young sister . . . our sisters here would send in love for her most serious consideration in the closet, accompanied by fasting and prayer, the words recorded Luke ii.19. "But Mary kept (mark! kept) all these things and pondered them in her heart." Your sisters in Ohio think that this Mary was a wise Virgin.[7]

Six years later the August issue of the *Gospel Visitor* received other questions on "the duty and liberty of women in the church." The editor, still Henry Kurtz, responded with a discussion of various New Testament passages on the subject and then reached the following conclusion: "It appears proper and lawful for pious and devoted women to labor for the promotion of the cause of Christianity; to exhort, to prophesy, and to pray, especially in social meetings. But they should not speak with the authority of bishops or overseers in the church; in this respect they should be 'under obedience' and 'learn in silence.'"[8]

A query came to the 1859 Annual Meeting asking if "the gospel admit of female preaching." In answering this time, a distinction was made between teaching, ministering, and prophesying. Annual Meeting decided that a sister could prophesy, but not preach or teach: "As Paul recognizes a distinction, in Rom. 12:6,7, between teaching, ministering, and prophesying, and as he evidently approves of females prophesying (1 Cor. 11:5), we think that a female cannot teach or preach, according to 1 Cor. 14:34, 1 Tim. 2:12, in the ordinary acceptation of those terms, yet we cannot, under all, forbid them to prophesy" (Article 7).

The question continued to be debated in church periodicals, with writings on both sides of the question. But Sarah Righter Major continued preaching, including a sermon during the 1878 Annual Meeting. This assessment of her ministry was given by James Quinter, editor of the *Gospel Messenger*: "A remarkable woman with a good and discerning mind. Although she had considerable prejudice to contend with in our Brotherhood, such was her modesty, her humility, her discretion and her exemplary life, that as she was known she was loved. Generally wherever she went once to preach, she was invited to repeat her visit."[9]

Mattie A. Lear (1838-1903) began preaching in Illinois in the 1870s and continued until her death in 1903. Mattie was an educator who taught at Mt. Morris College and led in organizing the first Sunday school there. She also was a regular contributor to the *Brethren At Work* and the *Gospel Messenger*. In addition to regularly filling the pulpit in her home congregation, she also addressed Sunday school and ministerial meetings. Her obituary in the *Gospel Messenger* claimed that "as a scripturist she had few equals, and possessed a most graceful and fluent way of giving expression to her views.[10]

Bertha Miller Neher (1873-1948) began teaching when she was sixteen. Shortly after her marriage in 1894, she and her husband went to Alabama to teach in Brethren schools there. During this period she wrote a popular children's book *Among the Giants*. She also wrote for Brethren periodicals, including a column in the *Brethren Teachers' Monthly* for twenty years. The Nehers returned to Indiana where they helped build the Bethel church. Five children were born to them there. Bertha was authorized to preach and did evangelistic work. She also served a year as interim pastor of the Winona Lake church. Bertha was a leader in the dress reform work of the denomination (1915-27).[11]

Mattie Cunningham Dolby (1878-1956) was the first woman to appear in the ministerial list of the Church of the Brethren. Born in Indiana, Mattie was baptized when she was sixteen into the church of her parents. She and her brother Joe were the first black students to enroll in Manchester College. They were forced to cook their own meals off campus the first year. The next year a group of students worked to create a more welcome environment for Mattie. After college (1903) Mattie went to Arkansas to establish a Sunday school in the Brethren mission at Palestine. She felt deep concern for her people: "The history of the Negro is the history of a downtrodden and neglected race. America boasts of her freedom and Christianity, but we, as American Negroes, have known little but to be abused and misled." Mattie believed that educational opportunities needed to be improved as "it has long been proven that we can be somebody if we only have an opportunity." Mattie wrote to Brethren asking for support of the struggling mission: "We appeal to you who are comfortably situated in good homes and whose tables are spread with an abundance of good things, we appeal to you, dear brethren and sisters, to divide your luxury money with God to be used for his poor, benighted, neglected dark-skinned children in this place." Mattie was forced by ill health to leave Arkansas in 1906. The mission was closed by the Brethren the next year.

Mattie moved to southern Ohio and soon married Newton Dolby, son of a Baptist minister, who later joined the Brethren. Mattie and Newton became active in the Frankfort church (which the Majors had helped establish) and were elected deacons in 1907. Mattie was installed into the ministry by this church on December 30, 1911. Elders Horning and Bookwalter performed the "laying on of hands ceremony." Mattie's installation was reported in the *Gospel Messenger*, and she subsequently was placed in the denomination's list of ministers.

Six children were born to the Dolbys during their years in Ohio and Illinois. They were asked in 1924 by "a new administration" to leave the Brethren congregation they had attended in Ohio for seven years because of racial prejudice. Mattie then ministered nine years in a Methodist congregation and twenty in a Church of God congregation.[12] She rose above the prejudice against her, as had Sarah Righter Major.

Now queries began coming to Annual Meeting questioning by what authority some districts were giving women permission to preach. In response, a ministerial statement brought to the 1922 Annual Meeting included a provision for "licensing sisters to preach." This recommendation caused considerable controversy. The leading spokesman for those who felt that women preaching was contrary both to scripture and to the tradition of the church was B. F. Kessler, who later withdrew from the Church of the Brethren.

Others supported the recommendation. Otho Winger, president of Manchester College, cited references the Apostle Paul made to women who worked with him and pointed to the preaching of Sarah Righter Major. Wilbur B. Stover, a pioneer missionary to India, spoke highly of the work of women on the mission field, including their preaching. Naomi Shaw, one of the first women to speak during Annual Meeting debate, called for "man to follow the example of his head (Christ) and woo instead of rule" so that "woman could fill her mission" given by God. The recommendation for licensing sisters to preach passed by a vote of 389 to 149. Congregations now had permission to authorize women to preach. For men, licensing was the first step toward ordination to the full ministry. For women it was possible to be "permanently licensed to preach," but not to be ordained.[13]

After this decision, the number of "licensed sisters" in the ministerial list of the church grew year by year. Their ministries were varied. Some preached regularly—on a circuit like Wilma Waybright of West Virginia; or in evangelistic meetings, like Mary I. Cook of Michigan. Wilma Bittinger Waybright and her husband, Noah, were dairy farmers. Noah cared for their five children while Wilma preached. Her preaching ministry as a free minister spanned fifty years.[14] Mary Cook, who remained single, also pastored several churches in Ohio and Indiana.[15]

Some women served in team ministry with their husbands. Alice D. Lehman Sell of California was licensed to preach in 1924 by her husband's congregation in Pennsylvania.[16] Martha Hilary Keller of Iowa was also licensed in 1924. She had assisted her husband, David, in congregations in Iowa, Ohio, Michigan, and Minnesota from the time of their marriage in 1897.[17] Cora Kohr Keller was licensed in 1925. She assisted her husband, Walter, in Maryland, Pennsylvania, and Ohio. Cora was in demand for special services, such as funerals for children and speeches for the WCTU.[18]

Some women served in home and foreign missions, like Alice Eisenbise of Nebraska and Ida Shumaker in India. Grace Deal Showalter of Michigan was a minister of music. Nancy Blain Underhill of Colorado wrote for many Brethren periodicals. Her correspondence with Brethren who appreciated her writing on Christian living led her to unite with the Church of the Brethren, although the nearest Brethren congregaton was two hundred miles from her home.[19]

Elizabeth Jennings Broughman pastored several churches in Virginia during a preaching ministry that spanned nearly sixty years. One of the circles of the Hollins Road Women's Fellowship chose as its name the "Elizabeth B" Circle in her honor.[20] Bertha Cline, a graduate of the National College of Education and Bethany Biblical Seminary worked in missions in Chicago for fifteen years before being licensed to the ministry in 1937. She then pastored churches in Oklahoma and Colorado.[21]

Since women were serving in the ministry of the congregation, some thought they should be able to serve as deaconesses. The Central church of Roanoke, Virginia, brought a query to the 1931 Annual Conference which included the request that local churches be given the privilege of electing sisters to the office of deaconess, independently of the deacons. A committee appointed to study this and other aspects of "the deacon question" brought reports in both 1933 and 1934 which included such a recommendaton. The report which Conference finally accepted in 1935 omitted this recommendation; wives were to continue to serve when their husbands were elected deacons, but women could not be elected in their own right.[22]

Women serving as pastors also faced limitations in their ministry. Licensed sisters were not permitted officially to perform all ministerial functions, such as weddings, baptisms, and administering communion. The 1922 decision had stated clearly that the licensing of sisters was only for preaching. Recognizing the difficulty this caused, the McClave church in Colorado petitioned Annual Conference in 1949 "to allow women equal rights with men in the ministry." At this time, Bertha Cline was their interim pastor.

Annual Conference referred the petition to the General Brotherhood Board, which requested the following Conference to appoint a committee to study this question as part of a larger study of the role of women in the life of the church.

The five-member committee (T. F. Henry, Eva Bowman, E. R. Fisher, DeWitt Miller, and Ruth Shriver) brought a report to the 1951 Conference which included a recommendation that "a woman who is the pastor of a church be granted the privileges of the ordained minister to function in the congregation of which she is pastor." This report "was recommitted for further study." The report brought to the 1952 Conference broadened the previous recommendation to one that "women be allowed equal opportunity with men in the ministry." In supporting this recommendation, the committee claimed that "there can be neither male nor female in Christ Jesus."[23]

A heated debate ensued. Edward K. Ziegler, alternate moderator of the 1952 Conference, remembered it well: "At that time, some old elders made impassioned pleas to defeat it, professing their concern that sisters be spared the pain and burden of the kind of counseling which pastors have. Also, they were concerned about the propriety and the difficulty that a woman minister would have in baptizing big adults by immersion."[24]

J. L. Miller and S. S. Blough were among these elders. J. L. Wine opposed the recommendation, saying that there were no biblical references supporting the ordination of women and neither was there an apostolic precedent.

Calvert Ellis, president of Juniata College, raised other objections. He claimed that ordaining women would not be progress. Charging that the feminist movement of the past half-century had contributed to the breakdown of the home, he cited studies that claimed that this movement had spent itself. Women's central place was to be a mother.

Supporters of the recommendation gave equally impassioned speeches. The first was from Florence Fogelsanger Murphy, who had been installed into the ministry in 1935 by her home congregation in recognition of her ministry in Women's Work. She claimed that there is "no sex in Christ." Equal opportunity in the ministry was dependent on the leading of the Spirit. "It is the Spirit we are to follow, not biblical literalism," she said.

In response to Ellis, DeWitt Miller pointed out that the feminist movement had been a needed "corrective in a masculine dominated society." He granted that it may have gone too far but pleaded that the church not go too far in the other direction. "Women need to be able to answer the call of the Spirit."

Cora Fisher, president of the National Women's Work Council and a pastor's wife, questioned the claims of protecting women. Pastors' wives already bore many of the burdens of pastors, she said, including counseling. She also pointed out that men did not rush to protect women from the hard work of packing relief boxes. "Had the work of women's hands loomed so large that it had been forgotten that women also had minds and hearts?"

After several hours of debate and the loss of an amendment that would have granted women the privileges of the ordained ministry but not ordination, Paul Robinson declared that a compromise was needed. Citing the shortage of pastors and the number of women who were currently serving as pastors, he moved that "a woman who is the pastor of a church be granted the privileges of the ordained minister to function in the congregation in which she is pastor."

One supporter of the original motion argued, "If women have the gift of the Spirit, how can men forbid them to minister?" Robinson's substitute motion passed and replaced the committee's recommendation in the report on the role of women in the church, which subsequently was adopted.

The question of women serving as deaconesses in their own right was not addressed in this report on the role of women in the church. A study of the office of deacon, including the question of deaconesses, was initiated by the 1955 Conference. The report brought by the study committee included a section on "Women in the Deaconship," which recommended that:

> 1. A deacon's wife shall be considered a deaconess and her term of service shall coincide with that of her husband, provided she is a member of the church in a position to serve. If a deacon has been elected for a life term, his wife may continue to serve as a deaconess in her own right, provided the church asks her to continue in the office.
> 2. Qualified women may be called to the office of deaconess in their own right.
> 3. The functions of a deaconess shall be the same as those of deacons.[25]

The report was adopted by the 1956 Conference, thus permitting women to "serve in their own right."

In 1958 a query came to Conference requesting ordination for women in their own right. Edward K. Ziegler had been disappointed with the 1952 decision that granted the privileges of ordination only to women functioning as pastors. While pastor of the Williamson Road church in Roanoke, Virginia, he wrote a query requesting the 1958 Annual Conference "to grant to women full and unrestricted rights in the ministry."

Standing Committee recommended favorable action on the query. "There is no female or male in Christ," said L. John Weaver, speaking for Standing Committee. He also referred the delegates to the 1952 report the "Role of Women in the Life of the Church" and asked that its original section on women in the ministry now be accepted.[26]

A very brief debate followed. One brother opposed the motion as not being acceptable in a New Testament church. Reuel B. Pritchett repeated the concern he had shared during the 1952 debate. "Scripture supports women praying and prophesying, but they are not to be put in positions of authority." He asked the delegates to look carefully before making a change, "so as to be scriptural."

Then, the author of the query made an impassioned plea for its acceptance. He pointed to the ability of women and the greatly increased needs in pastoral ministry, as well as to action in favor of the ordination of women in sister denominations. He concluded that "the time is here in the anniversary year [1958 was the 250th anniversary of the eight original Brethren baptisms in the River Eder] . . . to recognize that the gift of God may be bestowed equally on sisters of the church."

After one more supporting speech made by the husband of a "licensed sister," a hand vote showed "a strong vote for passage." A local newspaper reported less then fifteen dissenting votes.[27] Women finally had been granted "full and unrestricted rights in the ministry."

Within the next few years, a number of women were ordained. Among them were three who had been licensed to preach in 1922 —Elizabeth Jennings Broughman, Mary Cook, and Madolin Taylor. Others included Anna Beahm Mow, former missionary to India and professor at Bethany Seminary; Nettie Sanger, former missionary to China and pastor in Michigan; Harriet Bright, in team ministry with her husband; and Opal Pence, a pastor in the Midwest. The stories of these two women, Anna Mow and Opal Pence, illustrate the unique ministry women have had.

Anna represents those women whose ministry has been one of preaching, speaking, mission, and writing rather than pastoring a congregation. She is well known among the Brethren, as her "flock" seems to embrace the entire denomination. Anna was born in Virginia in 1893 to Mary Bucher and I. N. H. Beahm, a prominent Brethren educator and evangelist. She had decided by age eighteen that she would be a missionary to India. She prepared herself through study at Manchester College (B.A., 1918) and Bethany Bible School (B.D., 1921). She married Baxter Mow in 1921. After teaching two years, the Mows were sent to India as missionaries. Their work in India, mainly with the Muslims, lasted seventeen years. Three children were born to them there.

Anna taught education, missions, biblical studies and devotional life at Bethany Biblical Seminary from 1940 to 1958. During her early years there, she completed both a Master of Religious Education (M.R.E., 1941) and Master of Theology (M.Th., 1943) degrees. She was ordained in 1960 in Roanoke, Virginia, with Edward K.

Ziegler officiating.

Anna served as a Brethren representative on the Evangelism Committee of the Federal Council of Churches. She also served three terms as a member of the General Board of the Church of the Brethren and as a member of the Review and Evaluation Committee. Anna has written more than a dozen books for both adults and teenagers. At age ninety she was still traveling cross-country speaking and preaching. Sister Anna often has been the first ordained woman many Brethren have known.[28]

Opal Pence was one of the few women serving as full-time pastors in 1958. She had been given the privileges of ordination in 1955 and with this decision was able to receive full ordination. Opal felt an inner call to be a minister or missionary while still a high school sophomore. She shared her call with the moderator of her congregation (Pleasant View, Indiana), in which she had been baptized a few years earlier. He encouraged her to finish high school and prepare for the ministry. After high school graduation in 1943, she attended Fort Wayne Bible College for three years. In September of 1945 she was licensed to the ministry by her home congregation; the following year she received a permanent license.

Opal's first summer pastorate was with a woman pastor in a Christian church in Iowa, an assignment she received through the American Association of Women Ministers. This woman was an outstanding leader, and working with her was a good experience. Opal's next two summer pastorates were in Brethren congregations in southern Illinois (Hurricane Creek and Pleasant Grove).

About 1948 Opal went with her parents to the Elgin offices of the Church of the Brethren to make herself available for service as a missionary with the General Mission Board. But the one who interviewed her felt that as an only child it would be difficult for her family for her to go to the mission field. Within six months after that, she had decided to go into the pastoral ministry. Opal then studied religion at Manchester College from 1946 until 1950.

After college she worked as the part-time pastor of the Auburn church (Indiana), a position she was helped to find by her regional executive. Opal worked a forty-hour week in a card and calendar company and then made pastoral calls in the evenings and weekends. She enjoyed calling and also preaching. Her experience in this pastorate from 1950 to 1954 confirmed her call to the ministry, and she decided to request a full-time pastorate.

She accepted the pastorate of the Blissville (Indiana) congregation in 1954. As a full-time pastor, she received special ordination in 1955 so that she could marry, baptize, and officiate at communion. Those occasions were moving ones for Opal. Calling continued to be her primary emphasis. "Sitting at the kitchen table, eating apples under the tree, finishing chores" were ways of getting close to people. Her eight years in this congregation were good ones.

After a two-year period as director of Christian education in South Bend, Indiana, Opal went to Elizabethtown College (Pennsylvania) in 1964 as director of student activities. She also married John Nees, an accountant she met in South Bend. During her years at Elizabethtown, she provided pulpit supply in nearby congregations. Women preachers were not common in Brethren congregations in this area at that time. She sometimes felt that some parents were afraid that if their daughters heard her they might want to become pastors. Opal would have been happy to open up this possibility for other girls and women.

In 1976 Opal left Elizabethtown to return to the parish. Her husband had died in 1974 of cancer. At that time his surgeon had encouraged Opal to consider pastoring again, as she had now been "on the other side." She returned to Indiana, accepting a full-time pastorate in the Liberty Mills congregation. Again calling and preaching were her priorities. Her ministry among this congregation for more than eight years has been welcomed, especially by the women who are glad to have a pastor "who is one of them".[29]

For the Church of the Brethren, the 1958 decision opened up the possibility of many more women entering its ministry, and the number of women doing so has steadily increased. These women have ministered quite ably as pastors and associate pastors, as seminary professors, as campus ministers and hospital chaplains, as retreat and spiritual growth leaders, as denominational staff members, and as district executives.

Some who in the past opposed ordination of women now accept women as pastors. Calvert Ellis spoke against ordination for women during the 1952 Conference debate as being inappropriate for women. Although he still believes that the first responsibility for both women and men is to their families, he sees that this can be done cooperatively. "The whole conception of men and women has changed since the fifties," he noted in 1982. "Women are taking responsible positions in all areas of life, there is no reason they should not be ordained."[30] Yet, there is still resistance to women serving as pastors. Most district executives report difficulty in placing women in congregations.

But there are also congregations that are supportive of women in ordained ministry. Such support has helped some women accept a call to set-apart ministry. Eleanor Painter is one such woman. For her a change of career was involved in accepting her call. Eleanor's ministry has included service in the congregation, district, and denomination.

Eleanor Painter grew up in a small church in northern Ohio where she was given many opportunities for service and for developing leadership abilities. After graduation from Manchester College, she taught high school near her home for fifteen years. She was a science instructor until some students began entering the field to learn how to build better armaments. She then switched to guidance counseling, earning a master's degree in that area. During this time she was asked by her congregation to teach Sunday school and to serve as a youth advisor, church board member, and delegate to Annual Conference in 1953.

That experience was a turning point for her. During her Annual Conference report to the congregation, she included inspirational highlights as well as business decisions. After her report, her uncle told her that she would one day be a preacher. At first Eleanor laughed at the thought. But the pastor of her congregation did not; he urged Eleanor to preach and gave her theology books to read. Eventually she did agree to preach. The congregation affirmed her preaching, and she received other requests to preach.

Eleanor was hesitant to preach without district approval, so the congregation's ministry commission recommended she be licensed. She struggled in making that decision. She knew that early church teaching disapproved of women in the ministry, and she could not identify with the only woman preacher she knew. But after much thought and prayer, she agreed to be licensed. After her licensing in February 1956, she continued in her guidance counseling position while preaching occasionally and serving as district children's work director.

During this period, Eleanor received three calls to full-time ministry. Then in 1962, after much struggle, she accepted the call to serve as associate pastor in the Elkhart City (Indiana) congregation. After ten years of service in the Elkhart congregation, Eleanor directed a community day care center sponsored by seven churches.

Then in 1974 she accepted a call to serve as pastor of special ministries of the Palmyra (Pennsylvania) congregation. At their request, she was ordained. In her ministry there she has performed marriages and baptisms, baptizing five teenaged boys. She also performed her niece's and nephew's weddings. Her family have been long-time supporters of her ministry.

Eleanor also has served the larger church family in various leadership positions. She chaired the Northern Indiana District Board in 1973 and was moderator of the Atlantic Northeast District in 1980. She was the second woman to serve on the Annual Conference Central Committee (1972-75), first organized in 1960.

Throughout her years of service to the church, Eleanor has been encouraged to participate more fully in the ministry and leadership of the church. She has encountered some who oppose women as pastors. But Eleanor "continues to follow God's leading as I experience it." One elder who opposed women as pastors responded to her story of entering the ministry by saying, "You couldn't stay out any more than I could, could you?"[31]

Congregational support was also significant for Connie Burkholder, a 1983 Bethany graduate, in responding to her own growing sense of call to the parish ministry. She was licensed by her home congregation in Chambersburg (Pennsylvania) with the encouragement of the Polo (Illinois) church—site of a successful field experience. A research paper on Sarah Righter Major for a seminary course further strengthened her call. She was then ordained in 1983 after accepting the call to be pastor of the Wooster (Ohio) church.[32]

The preaching and pastoral ministry of women within the Church of the Brethren spans 155 years—from the first sermon of Sarah Righter Major to the ministries of the nearly 150 licensed and ordained women in the denomination in the mid-1980s. Their ministries join with those of their lay sisters to enrich the total church family in service to God and neighbor.

10

TOWARD FULL PARTICIPATION

In times past the church has often closed her doors to the services of women. This situation has no doubt been prompted by the cultures in which the church has lived and served. Today amazing doors of opportunity stand open awaiting the response of women who are willing to serve. Now it is up to women to accept their new challenge by offering themselves for service in the church where they are needed and able to minister. (Local CBWF booklet, 1960)

As the Church of the Brethren entered the 1960s, there were amazing opportunities for women in her service. The contribution of women in mission and lay ministry had been recognized by Conference in 1952 when it "urged that women be more widely represented on boards and committees."[1] With the decision to open the ordained ministry to women in 1958, there were no longer any official policies limiting the participation of women in the church. Women's Work and later CBWF had worked to create places for women within church policy-making bodies. Thus when CBWF dissolved themselves as a national organization in 1963, they firmly expected the integration of women in the life of the church to continue.

New opportunities for the participation of women, as well as laymen, had been created with the denominational reorganization in 1947. A Committee of Fifteen—all male—had been appointed by the 1945 Conference to study the structure and polity of the church. They proposed that a twenty-five-member General Brotherhood Board (GBB) replace the various denominational boards in existence.[2] This board would be elected by Annual Conference. The GBB would consist of three representatives from each of the five regions and ten at-large members. Any qualified "elder, minister or member of the laity" could be elected to the board. Previously some boards, such as the General Ministerial Board, had been opened only to elders.

Districts were also to organize one district board, consisting of a minimum of five members. Each district was to continue its elders' body, which was composed of all the ordained elders of the district. This body was to serve as an advisory board in handling district problems, as well as "passing upon the ordination of ministers and elders." As women could not be ordained at this time, this body would continue to be all-male.

Two plans for local church organization were suggested. One plan was that a board of administration be elected by the church council. "In this selection men, women, and youth should be considered in order that all interests of the church might be represented." The second plan was that the church board be made up of representatives of the functional groups of the church, including women's work, men's work, et cetera. At this time the moderatorship of the local church was opened to the laity. However, only ordained elders were eligible to serve as district and Annual Conference moderators. Laity became eligible to serve as district moderator in 1959 and Annual Conference moderator in 1960.

Membership on the Standing Committee (SC) of Annual Conference was opened to the laity during the 1947 reorganization. This committee was to suggest answers to the queries which came from districts to Conference, to review the reports of the GBB, and to serve as a nominating committee for Conference officers and committees and the GBB. Standing Committee members were elected by the districts they represented. Representation was proportional to the size of the district, with smaller districts having one representative and larger districts two or three.

The first women to represent their districts on Standing Committee were elected in 1949, two years after the committee was opened to laity.[3] As with the election of women as congregational delegates, the churches in India and China were the first to elect women to represent them on Standing Committee. Mary Royer represented India; Anna Crumpacker, China. There were no women on SC in 1950. Then in 1951 there were four: Gladys Royer, Nigeria; Lillian Grisso, India; Leta Wilson, Oklahoma, Texas, and New Mexico; and Ada Scrogum, the Second District of West Virginia. Modena

Studebaker, representing Nigeria, was the only woman delegate to SC in 1952. Three women were district delegates in 1953: Mrs. Harold Hoff, Northern Illinois and Wisconsin; Mrs. E. E. Butson, Texas and Louisiana; and Mrs. J. T. Glick, Second Virginia. Goldie Swartz, who represented India, was the only woman SC delegate in 1954. Lucille West from Northern Indiana and Etta Bowman from Northern Virginia were the women delegates in 1955. During this period, the membership of Standing Committee varied between eighty-six and eighty-nine yearly. So although the inclusion of women was significant, their numbers were far from proportional. By 1960 six women were members of Standing Committee. Six of seventy-eight members were women in 1965, and six of forty-five in 1970.

The number of women on the General Brotherhood Board (GBB) fluctuated from one to three of the twenty-five elected members during this period. Sarah Halladay and Charlotte Weaver were members of the first board in 1947 and continued until 1950. Sarah was active in Women's Work and the Women's Christian Temperance Union. Charlotte was active in the Brethren young people's organization. Sarah was the only woman between 1950 and 1952 to serve on the GBB. In 1952 she was joined by Modena Studebaker (1952-56), former missionary to Africa, and Anna Beahm Mow (1952-57, 1967-68), professor at Bethany Biblical Seminary. Eva Bowman, former president of the NCWW, replaced Sarah in 1953 and served until 1959. Dessie Miller Myers, who had been a member of the denominational staff, served from 1958 until her resignation in 1961. Naomi Will, a member of the NCWW, served from 1959 to 1964. Inez Goughnour Long, an educator who also had been on the denominational staff, was elected to the board in 1964 and served until 1968. Anna Mow rejoined the board in 1967.

The General Brotherhood Board was reorganized in 1968. The number of commissions was reduced and the name changed to the General Board (GB). Anna Mow and Inez Long continued their terms from the GBB. Phyllis Carter, a pastor, was elected in 1968. Two more women were elected in 1970—Anna Mary Forney Dubble and Gladys C. Weaver. There were thus four women serving on the GB in 1970.

During this period women were seldom appointed to Annual Conference study committees. They did serve on some other Conference committees. Women began serving on the Committee on Credentials in 1945, with Naomi Will being the first. Gladdys Muir, college professor and church historian, served periodically on the Committee on Resolutions, beginning in 1947. It was not until 1969, with the election of Mary Workman, that a woman served on Annual Conference Central Committee. This committee was formed in 1960 to make the arrangements for Conference. Its function was later broadened to include strengthening "the leadership of Annual Conference for a more effective exercise of its policy-making function."[4]

The number of women in the Brethren delegation to the Federal Council of Churches, later the National Council of Churches, decreased during this period. The first Brethren delegation was sent in 1948. Cora Fisher, president of NCWW, was the first woman to join the delegation (1951). In 1952 two women were in the delegation—Lucille West and Eleanor Curry. Lucille continued until 1956, at which time Cleda Zunkel was appointed the one woman in the delegation. Cleda served through 1958. From 1959 to 1970, there were long stretches with no woman in the delegation. Glee Yoder served in 1960, Inez Long in 1965 and 1966.

During this period (mid-1960s) Inez was the only woman both in this delegation and on the GBB. The number of women on Standing Committee stood at about 25 percent. Some were questioning whether women were achieving their "rightful place" or "proportional representation."[5]

Carole Ziegler and Nancy Peters (now Nancy Lamia), educators and ministers' wives, were concerned about the position of women in both church and society. They brought this concern to the 1970 Conference and were instrumental in the adoption of a "Resolution on Equality for Women" by the Conference. This resolution called the church to "support action to bring women into full participation in the mainstream of American society exercising all the privileges and responsibilities thereof in truly equal partnership with men." This call was grounded in the "worldwide concern for human rights for all persons" and the commitment of the church as the body of Christ "to persons affirming their full worth and humanity." The General Board was directed by the resolution to:

> appoint a committee composed of at least 50 percent women to write a major paper stating the church's position on women in our church and society . . . ; consider the possibility of creating vehicles to educate and sensitize persons, institutions and

organizations to their dehumanizing attitudes toward women; investigate the feasibility of creating and funding specialized ministries which will increase the options from which women can choose, enabling them to create more equitable life styles . . . ; support the Equal Rights Amendment . . . ; and report annually to the Annual Conference on progress toward achieving these goals.[6]

Donna G. Forbes, Ruth S. Hogan, Eldon Morehouse (replaced by Paul Keller in July 1971), Nancy J. Peters, and Duane Ramsey were appointed by the GB to prepare a position paper. Reports were brought by the committee to the Board in June and November of 1971 and again in March of 1972. At that time the Board endorsed the November report and asked the Goals and Budget Committee to consider the report's recommendations.[7] The paper as adopted affirmed that "the very essence of the Christian message, which finds its roots in the Hebrew faith lies in the equal dignity and rights of all human beings as persons, for . . there is neither male nor female; you are all one in Christ Jesus." It further urged "that all policies and practices of the church at national and local levels which create or permit a subordinate status for women be changed, and we recommend that new ways be developed to promote the full participation of women in both church and society with equal opportunities and responsibilities."

Particular concerns expressed in the report raised awareness of the issue of discrimination against women within the church, women's participation in leadership within the church, exploitation of women by the media, and discrimination under the law. The recommendations of the report were to address these concerns. Although the Board did not endorse the specific recommendations of the report, it did take some action over the next few years to address the concerns raised by the report. Several events to raise awareness and encourage wider participation of women were sponsored by the Board, beginning in 1972. The Board adopted an inclusive language policy in church publications, prepared by a committee it appointed in 1973. The denomination's support of the Equal Rights Amendment to the United States Constitution was expressed through publications and lobbying efforts.

A women's caucus developed from the work of Carole and Nancy at the 1970 Annual Conference. The following year an all-day meeting of women was held during Conference.[8] Nelle Morton, feminist theologian and professor at Drew University, was the resource person for the meeting. Women caucused informally and asked Nancy Peters to coordinate their activities. Their primary concern that first year was to nominate women for positions to be filled at Conference. Although some of the women felt timid about speaking in front of the delegate body, they did make several nominations. Among them was that of Virginia Showalter Fisher, the first woman ever to be nominated for Annual Conference moderator. Virginia had a long history of service and leadership in the church and was thus well qualified for the position.

Virginia was born in Virginia in 1908. She studied at Blue Ridge College, George Washington University (B.A., 1932) and Lancaster Theological Seminary (M.R.E., 1956). In 1934 she married Nevin Fisher, a professor of music and a church musician. Virginia taught public school in Virginia and Kansas and also taught at Elizabethtown College and Lancaster Theological Seminary.

Her lay involvement in the church began with the encouragement of Ruth Shriver. In 1937 Ruth asked Virginia to take charge of children's programs at Annual Conference. That same year she also was appointed Western Region Director of Children's Work. Thus she was a part of a grass-roots program just being organized by Ruth.

Virginia was then employed as regional or district administrator first in Kansas, then in Virginia, and finally in Pennsylvania. She was one of the first women to hold such a position. In the 1940s letters from the denominational offices came to "Dear Regional Men and Mrs. Fisher." In the fifties Virginia helped originate national youth conferences. In the sixties she worked full time for the Pennsylvania tri-district. Her job included relating to thirty-two different organizations, including Women's Fellowship, although she had never had time to be active in women's work herself.

Virginia wrote *The Story of the Brethren*, a book for junior highs, for the 250th anniversary of the Church of the Brethren. She also wrote Christian education curricula for all ages. Virginia never wanted to be a minister and rebuffed the suggestion that she become one of the first ordained women in the Church of the Brethren. She found fulfillment in her lay ministry.

Virginia became a supporter of the Equal Rights Amendment when she was told by a prominent church leader, "We only pay heads of families on scale." As is true of many other women, Virginia gave generously of herself to the church.[9]

In spite of efforts of the women's caucus at the 1971 Conference, Virginia Fisher was not elected moderator. However, the interest shown in the goals of the caucus prompted an informal continuation of the group. Publication of a caucus newsletter, *Femailings*, was begun, with Yvonne ("Von") Schroeder James giving significant editorial leadership. Mary Cline Detrick and Mary Blocher Smeltzer became coordinators of the caucus in 1972. The caucus continued its efforts to nominate women for the Conference ballot and to meet together during Conference. They requested that Central Committee include women as speakers during the evening services of the Conference. In 1972, one or two women began appearing as speakers on the Conference program. Often these women were General Board members or pastors. In 1973, the caucus began holding insight sessions on issues of concern to women. In June of 1973 about fifty women voted to formally establish the "Womaen's Caucus," for each woman and for all women. A steering committee would carry on the work of the caucus. During its first meeting in August of 1973, the steering committee decided to continue as an independent organization within the church. Financial support of their program was requested from the Parish Ministries Commission. A grant of $2,500 yearly was approved at the November 1973 General Board meeting.

Mary Blocher Smeltzer was the primary inspiration behind the movement of women through the caucus. A feisty spirit herself, she encouraged other women not just to have ideas but "to do it." Mary met with women across the country to raise awareness and to organize. She was an effective and articulate advocate for women's concerns during General Board meetings and at Annual Conference.

Mary had a long history of involvement in social justice work. Trained as an educator (La Verne, B.A., 1937; Claremont Graduate School, M.A., 1938), Mary taught school for several years. During World War II she and her husband, Ralph, worked together resettling Japanese Americans from internment camps. After the war, they worked for a few years in Austria with refugees. Ralph then joined the denominational staff to work with peace and social justice issues. During this period, Mary taught school, raised their three children, and was active in peace groups, interracial ministries, and local politics.

The Smeltzers moved to Washington, D. C., in 1971, where Ralph became the director of the Church of the Brethren Washington office. Mary taught school and was active also in the National Organization of Women and the Women's Equity Action League. Ralph was supportive of Mary's work in the women's movement. Mary used well the political advice of her husband, who had been active in the civil rights movement.

Mary was the first woman moderator of Mid-Atlantic District and the first woman to chair the board of the Washington City church. After Ralph's death, she spent two years with the Peace Corps in Botswana and a year in Japan at the Hiroshima Friendship Center. In 1978 the caucus established the Mary Blocher Smeltzer Leadership Development Scholarship in recognition of the leadership Mary had given the church through the years. In 1983 Mary was one of the two Church of the Brethren delegates to the Sixth Assembly of the World Council of Churches in Vancouver, B.C.[10]

Not all women welcomed the Womaen's Caucus. Some were afraid that it would jeopardize the gains that women had already made within the church. Some thought that it was breaking with what Eva Bowman had claimed as the pattern of Brethren women— to not ask for more power.[11] But the caucus did not understand power as something which was sought for selfish purposes to be used against others. Rather, power was a creative force necessary to work toward realization of the Christian vision of mutuality within community. This understanding was expressed in the caucus's statement of purpose: "We, the Womaen's Caucus, are impelled by Jesus' example to affirm personhood by working to eliminate sexual discrimination and empowering the oppressed so all may participate more fully in life."[12]

The work of the caucus on behalf of full participation of all was welcomed by many of those who had long been concerned that women be more fully included in the policy-making structures of the church. Naomi Schrock Hartzler, the first woman to serve as Standing Committee delegate from Michigan, was one such person.

Naomi was born in 1907 into the family of a Brethren elder in Indiana. Her mother, who was paralyzed from the hips down by polio, raised a family of thirteen children. Naomi had these memories of the church from her childhood:

> I was quick at memorizing and liked to sing and because these activities were more a part of our required education then, they were happy opportunities to be a part of the church program. Those first memories are clear: woman's place within the church was

meagerly defined. She could sew prayer coverings, make communion bread and grape juice, clean the church and wash dishes. They taught children's Sunday school classes, could be choristers, but were not elected to positions within the church.[13]

Naomi married Russell Hartzler in 1928, and they began their married life in Wisconsin. During the thirties Naomi and Russell moved to rural Michigan. Four children were born to them there. They attended the Grand Rapids church, where Naomi taught Sunday school. She soon was elected to the Christian education commission. Naomi was visited by the deacons and then the elder for not covering her head while teaching the junior high girls. She was able to persuade them that her prayers and teaching were valid without her head being covered.

Naomi served as chair of her local building committee, president of the district Women's Work, and chairperson of the district camp board. She and Russell opened their home to displaced persons and exchange students. She also served three months as cook and housemother for a Brethren Service unit work camp in Germany in 1955. Then in 1956 she was elected to represent Michigan on the Annual Conference Standing Committee.

Naomi and Russell moved to Lansing in 1960 and became active in the church there. Naomi chaired the CROP committee and Church Women United. In 1966 the Hartzlers opened their home to women who were ready to reenter society from mental institutions. Their lives were richly blessed with the friendship of the many people they had befriended.

Yet, Naomi did not forget the discrimination she felt women faced in the Church of the Brethren. She participated in many of the activities of the Womaen's Caucus in the early seventies. She still felt that men had acted unfairly in insisting on controlling funds which women had collected during projects, a view she first expressed publicly during a district conference keynote address in 1948. Naomi was also concerned about the position of women in society. She marched in support of the Equal Rights Amendment. Naomi believes that women still face discrimination within the church today, but "attitudes are changing, to the benefit of all. I believe Womaen's Caucus has been an important element in this change."

The General Board adopted an affirmative action plan in 1975. This plan was a commitment to increasing the percentage of women and minority persons among the Board's employees over a five-year period. The Board also began electing women as commission chairs. In this capacity, they served as members of the Board's executive committee. Ina Ruth Addington, a businesswoman, was elected chair of the General Services Commission in 1972. Phyllis Carter, an ordained pastor, became the chair of the World Ministries Commission in 1974.

Wanda Will Button from Iowa became the first woman to serve as a member of the Brethren delegation to the World Council of Churches. The WCC had requested its members to include women, racial-ethnic minorities, and youth in their delegations. The Womaen's Caucus asked the 1975 Conference to honor this request. Wanda, a General Board member, was then selected by Standing Committee to represent the Brethren along with Robert Neff, executive secretary of the denomination.

Wanda grew up knowing diversity. Her school years were spent in Chicago, where her father, Harper Will, was pastor of First Church of the Brethren. Wanda attended neighborhood schools with Jewish and Italian children. Then came study at Manchester College, where she majored in philosophy and religion. After graduation, Wanda spent 1953-55 in Germany with Brethren Volunteer Service working with the student exchange program. While in Europe, Wanda met Glendon Button, who was a BVSer working with the Heifer Project. Wanda and Glendon married in June of 1956. Their life together has been full. Wanda taught while Glendon began medical school, but was forced to quit when she became pregnant in 1958. To make ends meet, Wanda provided child care for working mothers in the Buttons' small apartment. Upon receiving his medical degree, Glendon established his practice in Conrad, Iowa. The Buttons have reared five children, including two Korean children adopted by them. In addition to her busy life as a mother, Wanda assumed major leadership in the Ivester Church of the Brethren.

Wanda's election to the General Board in 1974 continued a family tradition. Her father had served on the Board from its organization in 1947 until 1953. Then her mother, Naomi Royer Will, served from 1958 until 1964. Naomi had received a B.D. degree from Bethany Biblical Seminary and served as an associate pastor in Oregon before her marriage in 1928. After her marriage she saw her ministry as being a helpmate to her husband. She served on the National Council of Women's Work and wrote some articles on family life for *Messenger* in that capacity.

Wanda's work on the Board was with the World Ministries Commission, which she chaired for four years. She was hesitant to accept her nomination to the WCC delegation but did so with the encouragement of her husband.

Wanda has been deeply committed to the ecumenical movement. She has been involved for several years in the Iowa Council of Churches and helped organize the Consortium on International Peace and Reconciliation in 1976. She believes that the Brethren have three gifts to give the world: our historic peace witness, servanthood, and our commitment to the simple life. "This witness needs to be ecumenical."

Wanda considered her role a bridge between women. She has felt called to accept the leadership positions which have been offered to her, as "she values the visibility of more women in church structures."[14]

The Womaen's Caucus initiated a petition in 1975 which led to the formation of the person awareness program of the Parish Ministries Commission of the Board in 1976. Beth Glick-Rieman was employed as part-time field staff for this program. Beth, who was born and raised in Virginia, is an ordained Church of the Brethren minister with a doctor of ministry degree from United Theological Seminary in Dayton, Ohio. A musician and teacher, Beth and her husband, Glenn, raised four children. Beth put her full energies into the person awareness program. One of her early tasks was the organization of district person awareness task forces. Several were formed within a year.[15]

A query came to the 1976 Conference from the Northern Plains District asking that a committee of "three women and two men" be elected to study, update, and implement the 1972 General Board paper on "Equality for Women." Conference approved this study and elected Louise Baugher Black, Wayne Buckle, Violet Cox, Barbara Enberg, and David Markey to the committee.

Their report was adopted by the 1977 Conference, after deleting three recommendations for nominating and balloting procedures to achieve a more equitable representation of women and men on conference-elected boards and committees. The report as adopted began with a section on the biblical basis for equality of women and men. It affirmed that the intention of creation (Genesis) was a partnership and equality between male and female. But when brokenness entered creation, a fallen order of patriarchal subordination came to prevail. However, a new order is anticipated, beginning in the Old Testament and more fully with Jesus as he breaks with relations of subordination of women. Paul, too, envisions "full equality and full partnership of women and men."

The second section of the paper presented an historical overview of women in the Church of the Brethren. The primary focus was on the contribution women have made to the church, with some mention of the restrictions upon women that had been changed. The section included this assessment:

> Currently the unexamined restrictions on the role of women are under intense scrutiny by many persons in the Church, partly because of the total focus of the Womaen's Caucus on women's place in the Church, partly because of the 1972 General Board paper on Equality for Women, but mostly because of the social milieu in which such examination is occurring throughout all structures of society.[16]

A review of current activity found that "some progress has been made" in developing an awareness of equality of women and men, but that "more remains to be done." Exhibits were included with the paper to support this claim.

Exhibit B reported on various positions in church-related colleges and Bethany Seminary. In 1970 Bethany had no women at any faculty level; by 1975 one woman was a part-time instructor. One woman served with thirteen men on the board of electors of the seminary. The number of women in the student body had grown from a ratio of 5 in 74 in 1970 to 18 in 73 in 1975. Although all of the Brethren colleges except McPherson had as many, if not more, women students as in the past, none had a significant number of women as faculty or trustees. Exhibit C indicated that the ratio of women to men on the General Board staff at Elgin had remained approximately one to four from 1970 to 1977.

Exhibit D reported on the number of women and men serving in various positions at local, district, and denominational levels. In 1970, 3 out of 879 pastors were women; in 1976, 10 out of 894. Local church moderators in 1970 were 18 out of 809; in 1976, 48 out of 918. The number of district moderators had grown from 0 in 27 to 4 out of 19. There were no women district executives during this period. The number of women on the General Board had peaked at 10 out of 15 in 1975 and dropped to 8 of 17 in 1976. In 1970, 5 in 38 was the ratio of women to men on Standing Committee; in 1976, 14 out of 30. The participation of women had increased, although it was still not proportional to their strength in the church.

The report concluded with a section of recommendations. To clarify priorities and practices, Conference affirmed:

— a commitment to the achievement of equality for all its members, male and female, and

— a commitment of staff to provide leadership in the Church to assist all persons in becoming aware of their worth in God's total creation, to enable women to experience greater fulfillment in leadership roles in the Church, and to develop denominational strategy and program for witness to society in eliminating sex discrimination; and

— that, while the Church will support all its members in their choices of professional and vocational pursuits, it stands firm in its belief in the importance of the family. The nurture and training of children is a responsibility of primary importance belonging to both men and women . . . .

Specific recommendations included making available opportunities for women "to assume leadership and service responsibilities in full-time ministries"; forming talent banks of women locally, and at district and national levels; review of hiring policies; development of "awareness and recognition of the worth of parenthood experience"; encouraging positive images of women; and support of legislation promoting equality of women and men.

The paper, as adopted, concluded with the conviction that these actions are justifiable "for a people long concerned about the commonality of *all* Christians and the priesthood of *all* believers."

The 1977 Conference elected Phyllis Ann Kingery (Ruff) to a five-year term as Annual Conference Secretary. Phyllis thus became the first woman ever to serve as a conference officer. In addition to being responsible for the official minutes of Conference, the secretary is a member of the Central Committee and serves as secretary of Standing Committee and its nominating committee. Phyllis had been a kindergarten teacher in Omaha, Nebraska, before moving to Iowa after her marriage to Clifford Ruff. She also had served as a district moderator.[17]

Two national conferences for Church of the Brethren women were held in 1977 and 1978, under the sponsorship of the Parish Ministries Commission.[18] Beth Glick-Rieman designed these conferences, working with committees representing a broad range of women from across the United States. Two hundred and fifty women from twenty-four districts gathered at Elizabethtown College in 1977 for a conference on the role and status of Church of the Brethren women. The conference program included plenary sessions led by Shireen Subramanya, a native of India from the staff of Church Women United; Barbara Thain McNeel, professor at Hartford (Connecticut) Seminary; and a panel of Brethren women who had served the church throughout the world. Thirty-four workshops were centered on themes of women as persons, women in the church, and church women in the world. A mini-Annual Conference provided experience in parliamentary procedures as well as a discussion of some of the business coming before the 1977 Annual Conference.

Three hundred women from twenty-two districts came together in July of 1978 at North Manchester, Indiana, for a Gathering of Church of the Brethren Women. Theology, drama, music, and an address by Ruth Ann Knechel Johansen, author of *Coming Together: Male and Female in a Renamed Garden*, were topics of plenary sessions. Forty different workshops were held, as well as daily meetings of small dialogue groups. During the business sessions, resolutions were brought from groups to be acted upon by the women present. A report from the conference indicated that ten resolutions were passed, including: a directive to the General Board to explore ways to develop and receive leadership abilities of CB women; a pledge of support (in response to the request of lesbian sisters present) of a resolution to go to the Human Sexuality Committee and the 1979 Annual Conference, urging acceptance of gay church members as Christ accepts all, encouraging dialogue to promote understanding, asking for programs of education on human sexuality, and desiring that the church support civil rights for gay persons; the formation of a Global Women's Project; and a recommendation that the person awareness position become a full-time position for a five-year period.

The resolution in relation to the person awareness position arose from concern that the program might be ended. The Board had terminated Beth Glick-Rieman's employment as staff for the program. The future of the program seemed questionable. In additon to this resolution from the gathering, the Womaen's Caucus again circulated petitions in support of the program. The Board did decide to continue the program. Mary Cline and Ralph Dietrick, denominational staff members responsible for life cycle ministries, were given the person awareness portfolio.

The Global Women's Project was a response of the conference participants to Ruth Ann's moving address. "The feminist call to liberation," she claimed, "must be set within a wider context which recognizes that a global apartheid of rich and poor, developed and developing, exists." She called women to prepare the way for the birthing of a new world through a conversion to oneness with the oppressed. The GWP was created by the women at the gathering, who urged the GB to implement it as a denominational program. The Board agreed and appointed a steering committee of three conference participants and three staff members.

The project was a challenge to affluent Christians "to increase the awareness of our own overconsumption and misuse of resources"; to change that lifestyle; and "to contribute funds saved through relinquishment or taxing of luxuries" to projects "engaged in the fulfillment and empowerment of our global sisters."

The first project of the GWP was a water supply system for the Miriu Health Center in Kenya. The center was constructed by the local women themselves. The primary focus of the center is obstetrical care. The GWP contributed $15,000 to the project. World Ministries Commission made a matching grant. More recent projects have included underwriting publication of Julia Esquival's book of poetry, *Threatened by Resurrection*. Julia is living in exile from Guatemala. Her poems speak powerfully of the suffering and faith of the people of Central America. The current project is helping to support women's groups in Costa Rica who are organizing sewing cooperatives among rural women. In addition to funds, treadle sewing machines are being contributed by Brethren women.[19]

Ruby Rhoades became the executive of the World Ministries Commission of the Church of the Brethren in 1980. Ruby was well qualified for this position. She and her husband, Benton, had opened the Brethren mission in Ecuador in 1946 and remained in Ecuador for twelve years. Ruby taught during most of this period, as well as helped care for their four children. Then came twelve years of working for a New Jersey publisher, after which Ruby became director for *Messenger* promotion. She moved from that position to being the Brethren Washington representative in 1976.

Her appointment to the World Ministries executive position was featured in *Messenger*, as she became the first women to serve as an associate executive secretary of the General Board and thus the first woman to serve on the Board's Administrative Council. Ruby shared her vision of the work of World Ministries as she began her assignment:

> My vision is as old as that of the early church. Its followers had seen and experienced something meaningful to them and they went out to share it. That is our task for the '80s. . . . [The Great Commisson and the Great Commandment—to love one another] together define well the World Ministries task. I see mutuality in mission as a continuing guideline in developing program. We are at the threshold of discovering some exciting, new ways to work in partnership.[20]

In response to a question about her concerns for leadership opportunities for women in the church, Ruby noted:

> In filling leadership positions, women come up on the short end, unless it is mandated as it was in my case. And it is not because we are incapable but simply because we're women. The report of the Annual Conference study committee on elections showed that to be true. I see capable women serving as local church or district moderators and as board chairwomen. They are dedicated and do their jobs well. We recognize that not everybody can be moderator of Annual Conference nor general secretary; all we're asking is that women be considered and judged for our leadership skills and capabilities, and not our sex.[21]

Thus, the concern to participate fully in the church's worldwide ministry and mission continues to move Brethren women as it has throughout the years—from Sarah Righter Major to the Sisters' Mission Band to Ruby Rhoades, Wanda Will Button, Mary Blocher Smeltzer, and many others.

Some doors are still opening to women. Harriet Ziegler was the first woman to serve as managing editor of *Messenger*. Phyllis Carter was the first woman to serve as a district executive. Elaine Sollenberger became the first woman chair of the General Board in June of 1984.

A few doors, however, still remain unopened to women. One is that of Annual Conference moderator. When two women were nominated by Standing Committee for this office in 1978, protests were raised that the ballot had been structured. Four men were nominated from the floor, and one was elected. Yet, no charges of a structured ballot were raised the next year when two men were nominated by Standing Committee. Only men were on the ballot in 1981 and 1983. Women were defeated by men again in 1982 and 1984.

A statement on "Annual Conference Elections" was adopted in 1979. The church was challenged to face the issue of "representative leadership." Among the goals adopted by that Conference were "to provide for fair and equitable participation by all of our people— men, women, various ages, racial and ethnic minorities, rural and urban segments of our church and to develop an effective plan that will be in practice in 1982."

A Parish Ministries report in March 1983 noted that these goals were not being met. The ratio of women to men on the General Board had remained eight women to seventeen men since 1976. An analysis of Conference elections of 1980 through 1983 indicated two trends: "1. With only two exceptions in 22 elections, women are on- ly elected . . . when women run against other women. 2. With only one exception in five elections, racial/ethnic men are only elected when they run against women. Racial/ethnic women aren't elected."[23]

Some women and men are discouraged with the slowness in implementing this goal. The National Council of Women's Work recommended to Standing Committee in 1958 that as women par- ticipate more fully in the life of the church, they should be more fully represented on its boards and committees. A few women have left the church because of its resistance to fully welcoming the leadership gifts of women. Others stay, hoping that the day will come when their "call to serve Christ and the Church . . . in ways that have tradi- tionally been available only to men" wil be affirmed.[24] Still others are satisfied with the opportunities available to them for leadership and service in the church. They all strive to be faithful to their calls, as did their sisters who went before them.

Virginia Fisher (1908-), teacher, church administrator, and author

Ruby Rhoades (1923-1985), first woman to serve as an associate general secretary for the Church of the Brethren

One Hundredth Anniversary Steering Committee, 1984
Left to right: Mary Cline Detrick, Martha Dubble, Pam Brubaker, Shirley Kirkwood, Mary Eikenberry, Fran Clemens Nyce

EPILOGUE

For as many of you as were baptized into Christ have put on
Christ. There is neither Jew nor Greek, there is neither slave nor
free, there is neither male nor female; for you are all one in Christ
Jesus . . . . For freedom Christ has set us free; stand fast therefore,
and do not submit again to a yoke of slavery . . . . For you were
called to freedom, brethren; only do not use your freedom as an
opportunity for the flesh, but through love be servants of one
another. For the whole law is fulfilled in one word, "You shall love
your neighbor as yourself" (Galatians 3:27-28; 5:1,13-14).

This call to freedom has rung out down through the ages—at
times in muted tones but at other times with amazing clarity. Many
women and men within the Church of the Brethren have heard the
call and have attempted to live out this freedom. The early Brethren
in Europe and America seemed to have organized their common life
so that women were not as confined to a subordinate role as was the
usual custom for that period. Although there was not a "perfect
equality" with men, women did speak publicly and held some church
offices.

This freedom was soon curtailed. Perhaps because of the disturbances experienced by Brethren who had once been part of the
Ephrata Cloisters, a woman's place within the church came to be
seen as clearly subordinate. She was not to preach, hold church office, break the bread of communion with her sisters, or form
women's organizations within the church.

Yet some women did feel a call to participate in church life in
these ways. At their baptism they had vowed to be faithful to Jesus
Christ. Scripture recorded his command to break bread in remembrance of him, to love and serve both God and neighbor, to go into
all the world preaching and teaching. How could they be disobedient
to these commands? For some, faithfulness to their call meant chal-

lenging the place assigned to them in church life.

Throughout the nineteenth and twentieth centuries some women and men struggled together within the church to open again the doors to the freedom and equality brought by Jesus Christ. Many of their early efforts were not successful. At the end of the nineteenth century, a system still existed in which women were clearly subordinate. During the 1891 Annual Meeting several policies were adopted which reiterated this: women were denied again the privilege of breaking bread with each other or representing their congregations at Annual Meeting; and they were told explicitly that they were not installed into church office in their own right, but only as "helpmeets" to their husbands. But a system in which women were more equal participants began to emerge with the dawning of the twentieth century. There was a woman among the delegates to the 1900 Annual Meeting. In 1910, the year in which a denominational Sisters' Aid Society was organized, women finally received the privilege of breaking bread with each other. Then in 1922 women were given the right to preach.

Many women used their increasing freedom of participation to serve others—within their congregations and communities and beyond to the far reaches of the world. Through their own organizations and through congregational and denominational programs, women cared for the ill and elderly, the hungry and homeless; taught literacy, nutrition, and the word of God; supported colleges, orphanages, congregations, and home and foreign missions.

The particular structures for carrying out this service were shaped by the current thinking of church and secular leaders. Often the structures were paternalistic; women who were serving were to be directed by men, and those who were served were to be passive recipients of the service being given. These structures maintained a relationship of power in which one group of people is seen as dominant to another group, which is kept in a subordinate position. Often the dominant group is considered more naturally suited to leadership, which is exercised for the well-being of all.

Such a form of "love paternalism" is expressed in Christian teachings about headship and submission (1 Corinthians 11 and Ephesians 5). It may be appropriate in rearing young children, but it has been questioned as an appropriate form of relationship for men and women, whites and blacks, and members of local and global communities. The dominant group often benefits economically or psychologically at the expense of the subordinate group. The subordinate group is kept in a dependent, childlike position and not given opportunities to develop the skills for self-direction or leadership, as the position of the dominant group is not to be challenged. Without the chance to develop such skills, mutual forms of relationship will be difficult to live out.

Within the dominant-subordinate form of relationship, mission and service can become distorted. Along with the desire to genuinely meet the needs of others, there can be insistence that the language and customs of the dominant group are the best ways to meet those needs. The church has often mistakenly identified Christianity with "Western civilization." In doing so, we have closed ourselves to the presence of God in the experience of those from other cultures and removed our own culture from needed judgment.

Women often have been forced into a subordinate position within many cultures, including "Western civilization." Yet the liberating love of Jesus has enabled many women to break with traditions of subordination. Padma Gallup, an Asian theologian, describes it this way:

> Jesus sought to affirm women, as he did Mary and Martha and the Samaritan woman. He demonstrated the equality inherent in God's creation when, in refusing to condemn the woman taken in adultery, he indicated that the guilt from the act falls equally on the man involved. Tradition and society would have happily dismissed the woman as *the* temptress and sinner. Jesus broke with a tradition that would diminish one half of humanity. Centering on Jesus gives women the courage to break with tradition. . . .[1]

Brethren women also witnessed to the experience of this liberating love of Jesus Christ. They identified it as the source of their service to others. A 1929 Sisters' Aid report expressed it in this way:

> What lies back of all this giving of time, energy, money and self-denial? Of all these deeds of mercy and good-will and love? Is it not, an outward expression of the gratitude in women's hearts for the liberty and equality brought to them by the Lord Jesus? Since the dawn of Christianity women have thus expressed themselves. Mary and Martha ministered to Christ himself; Lydia welcomed the gospel to Europe; Dorcas made garments for the poor and so on until our time. Now since this precious heritage has come to us, we the women of the Church of the Brethren rejoice in the privilege of serving others in the name of Christ.[2]

Recogniton of this liberty and equality contributed to the transition within the church from a subordinate place for women to one in which there is the possibility of more equal partnership with men. The organization of a secular women's movement certainly was also a force in this transition. But this vision of equality and fuller participation predated the 1848 Seneca Falls Women's Rights Convention. Sarah Righter Major's 1835 letter (see Appendix A) gives eloquent testimony to this.

Recognition of this liberty and equality also contributed to the development of more mutual forms of service. Structures and programs have been created which seek to empower *all* to be full participants in a common life. Decisions as to what needs are to be met and how best to meet them are made by all. There are no passive recipients of service, but a community to which each contributes and from which each receives.

As a denomination, the Church of the Brethren has made significant strides in becoming a church in which all members are full participants. We continue to be nourished by a heritage and a vision of liberty and equality which moves us to love our neighbor in word and deed. Women continue to joyously serve others in many ways. From the congregation and local community to the far reaches of the globe, women respond to the needs of others through ladies' aid societies, women's fellowship groups, and the Global Women's Project. They serve with men in congregational ministries such as Sunday school teachers, choristers, deacons, secretaries, board members, and pastors. Women also serve in district and denominational programs as board and staff members, as volunteers in district homes for the elderly, and through programs such as MICAH Mission and Brethren Service.

Although we have come far as a church in which all members are full participants in its life and work, there are still areas of concern which are expressed by some members. Although there are no longer official policies which limit the full participation of women, the participation of women in policy-making bodies and the ordained ministry is not nearly proprotional to their membership. At least three means of addressing this situation have been suggested.

One proposal is the formation of a denominational women's organization. Previously, denominational women's organizations such as Sisters' Aid Society and Women's Work were resources for leadership development of women within the church. Although there were other resources for leadership development after the dissolution of denominational organizations, a lack still seems to exist in this regard. Many local and district women's organizations have expressed the need for program resources and facilitation like that provided by the denominational organizations. It seems that there is again a need for denominational organization of women. This organization could include the currently existing groups, as the National Council of Women's Work did when it was organized in 1929. Thus, local and district CBWFs, Womaen's Caucus, ladies' aid, the Global Women's Project, and person awareness task teams could be represented in a denominational women's organization which would enable women to coordinate their programs with each other and with other denominational programs.

Perhaps also there are practices within the church which discourage full participation of women. The language we use powerfully shapes our view of the world. Although some women insist that they are included in male language, other women and men find such language contributing to the past invisibility of women in leadership positions. If women have not been specifically named in our language, will they be fully included in the structures of the church and society? The expectations of children especially are shaped by the presence or absence of women both in the language they hear spoken and in the leadership they see. The General Board has adopted an inclusive language policy for church publications. Annual Conference Central Committee has also encouraged the use of inclusive language during Conference worship services. Some ask, though, if it is possible that the name of our denomination—the Church of the Brethren—may render women invisible? We have changed our name before to represent more fully who we are. Perhaps it is again time to consider such a change.

As the church grew and spread around the globe, practices were developed to insure representation of members from each geographic area. The ballot for General Board members has been structured since the board's organization in 1947 so that each region of the denomination is adequately represented. As a concern for fuller participation of the laity was expressed, ballots were often structured so that both clergy and laity would be elected. As a denomination we also need the full participation of women and racial/ethnic minorities in leadership and policy-making positions. Ballots could also be structured to insure proportional representation of racial/ethnic members and women.

At this time the church is not of one mind in regard to the use of inclusive language or the adoption of structured ballots. Discussion of these issues is often emotionally charged. There is a need for continued dialogue and openness to the positions of others. But we must not let fear of differences or conflict keep us from facing the question of how we encourage the full participation of all within the life and work of the church. Within our faith community, we must nurture and call out the gifts of *each* member. This is particularly urgent as the gifts and contributions of all are needed to adequately respond to the tasks facing women and men today.

We live in a world deeply divided by race, religion, culture, and ideology. The gap between rich and poor continues to grow, both within the United States and between the so-called first and third worlds. The continued escalation of the arms race endangers us all.

The need for global community has never been greater—a community in which all participate and benefit equitably. Such a community cannot be built without doing the work of justice. The inequities and injustices which contribute to poverty and oppression must be overcome. We are called not only to comfort but also to confront. Our service needs to include not only relief to the victims of poverty and oppression but also creation of systems in which there are no victims.

The challenge is immense, the task difficult. We may not see this vision of global community realized in our lifetime. But we have the heritage of a living faith which frees us to love and serve each other as we work to live out our vision of a community free from the barriers of race, sex, and status. May this heritage call each of us to renewed commitment to love our neighbors throughout the world by making peace with justice.

A LETTER FROM SARAH RIGHTER MAJOR

April 1, 1835

May Grace, Mercy and Peace be with thee and all those who love our Lord Jesus Christ—to whom be praise now and forever, Amen. . . .

Through a number of your friends, you have heard of me as sustaining an extraordinary character, feeling it my duty to make known even publicly, the unsearchable riches of Christ. You remind me of the Savior's parable of the woman having ten pieces of silver, and losing one piece, doth light the candle, and sweep the house, and seek diligently till she find it, and when she hath found it, she calleth her friends and neighbors saying, "Rejoice with me, for I have found the piece which I had lost." So they rejoice in heaven over one sinner that repenteth, and so you have heard of me, that as a repenting woman I call on my dying friends, to see "the pearl of price" I have found, "the unsearchable riches of Jesus Christ my Lord." Well, well, my dear brother, may our dear Redeemer give me grace to be faithful, that you may never hear any worse report of me than this.

You once thought this liberty I use an assumption not belonging to the female character, because the Head of the Church, in sending out into the world, chose his first heralds from your sex. My dear brother, I shall ever acknowledge the head of the woman to be the man, and the head of every man is Christ. He did not send many men, and gave them no authority to forbid any that should do works in his name and kingdom. You recollect when the apostles return'd they said, they saw one casting out devils in his name, and forbid him, because he followeth not with us. But he said, "Forbid him not, no man can do a miracle in my name, and speak lightly (or in the least) of me." They forbid him, because he went not with them when he might have as strict command to go home, and shew the people, how great things the Lord had done for him, as they had to go shew the kingdom of God to the cities of Israel.

I believe man to have been first in creation, but I also believe woman was made to be an help meet for or equal to him, having a soul and body, capable of helping him, in his natural, and spiritual, world, the companion of his joys and sorrows, in heaven and on earth, who looks up to him as for her power and protection, and on whom he is bound to look with feelings of care and love, so as to secure that confidence to himself which belongs to his high station. I am happy to say, that at this dark age of the world, I have met with men, who are always the same faithful friends in temporal and spiritual things, but believe me these are the fewest, who are brethren indeed, in every time of need, especially when the truth is suffering, and many are asham'd to defend it.

I believe my character is not so uncommon as that of "Anna the prophetess" of great age, the widow of 84 years, which took the liberty of staying in the temple to serve God, with fastings and prayers night and day. Simeon was singing his dying song with the infant in his arms, in the presence of many who came daily to the temple, and no doubt knew the time was then when the Child (wise men came from far to worship), must be offer'd to the Lord. They came looking for redemption in Israel, she coming in that instant, as he did, so she gave thanks, and spake of Him to all who look'd for redemption in Israel.

Let me say, Christ has not only honored your sex, but he has comforted mine. When he was to come into the world, he sent his angel, not to Joseph, but to Mary, face to face, to tell her she was "bless'd among women" and by the Holy Ghost gave her words to magnify God with Elizabeth in a loud voice, in the very city of the priests, where Zachariah dwelt. When he came first in the temple, his spirit moved the lips of Simeon and Anna, and some historians whose sects oppose a woman's testimony, call her the first herald of the gospel, and say she went from house to house, and to the Towns of Israel, proclaiming to them that Christ the Messiah had come. And when he burst the bars of death, his few disciples are in fears and tears—at home, but Mary seeks him—living or dead, and finds him alive and receives his dear command to go and tell his disciples and Peter too, that he is risen from the dead, and the resurrection of our Savior, believe me, I rejoice to tell you saints and sinners, for this living fact hold up the kingdom of the living God, the kingdom of heaven.

Happy woman! methinks, many often sat silent to hear her tell, what she saw and heard that joyful morning, when beside his tomb her Master stood and as he call'd her Mary, dri'd her tears away, and put such tidings in her lips, as heavenly angels wonder'd with joy. But when the day of Pentecost was fully come, you know they were all together with one accord in one place, the number of the disciples was 120 (men and women) in prayer and supplication they waited for the promise to endue them with power from on high, and cloven tongues like as of fire sat on each of them, and they were all filled with the Holy Ghost, and spake with other tongues as the spirit gave them utterance, even so that none of their many enemies could dispute Peter's testimony when he said to them, This is that which was spoken by the prophet Joel, "And it shall come to pass in the last days I will pour out my spirit on all flesh and your sons and your daughters shall prophesy." And that this gift continued in the church, just as they receiv'd the Holy Ghost, I am well convinced, and was the gift of the Holy Ghost, to some women at Corinth, to whom Paul wrote, to prophets male and female, how they should dress, when either of them pray'd or prophesied. Let Paul explain prophesy. "He that prophesieth, speaketh to edification, exhortation and comfort," and the gift of speaking to edify, to exhort and to comfort is not given at the schools, nor at any time we please, nor by the power of man. Therefore, I conceive it would be very inconsistent in an apostle, who had laid his hands on men and women, and pray'd over them, that they might receive the Holy Ghost, to quench the gift of the Spirit of God, because it was given to a woman—in answer to prayer—when at that time it may not be given in such measure to more experienced Christians. God always gave his gifts freely where they were willing to use them, and I believe in Christ Jesus male and female are one, just as Jew and Gentile are made one. Every one should do as much as they can to glorify God with the different gifts of the Spirit of God.

You once thought in reference to the church the apostle said "Let the women be silent." Now in two places in the scripture they tell me, Paul says so—but there is much in the Old Testament about holy women, in the old and new church of Moses and of Christ. Now if all the rest of the scriptures prove that Paul in these two passages forbids all women to speak by the spirit of God, to edify, exhort and comfort the church of believers, and convince the unbelieving men and women of the truth, then it might be so believed. But if the rest of the testimony proves the contrary, then Paul in these two letters is not understood. I believe he very honorably would not suffer any woman to come in and teach doctrines she never received from Jesus or his apostles, as many believing women do oppose their wise men, and do as they please in word and deed. Again he will not suffer them, to talk in meeting, nor ask questions, who have not wisdom enough to know when to ask their husbands, they who know not the time to speak, know not what to speak.

My Love to all who love the Lord . . . Sarah.

Sarah Righter Major
(1808-1884)
First woman preacher of the
Church of the Brethren

WRITINGS ON THE ROLES OF MOTHER AND WIFE IN THE NINETEENTH CENTURY

TO MOTHERS

Monthly Gospel-Visitor—February 1854

Dear mothers! Have you ever considered the influence that you have over your children, to bring them up in the fear of the Lord? If you have not, let me tell you, that there is a great responsibility resting upon you. For it is in your power to instill those sentiments in the hearts of your children, that will give you great joy in the after life.

While your children are small, their mind is like soft clay; you can make any impression thereon you please. If then you take your child upon your knee, and tell it of heaven and of heavenly things, it will listen with great interest. It will cause its innocent mind to bring forth many questions, which if properly answered, will cause it to desire this place of happiness very much. And often will their little tongues prattle to you about that good Being, that took little children in his arms and blessed them.

Then it is your duty to tell them to pray often to their Father, that is in heaven; to teach them the Lord's prayer, learn them to say it morning and evening, and teach them to shun all kinds of wickedness and bad company. . . . Yes teach them to frequent the house of prayer, and all will be well; for God will bless thy labors. . . .

And dear mothers, do you not want your children all to be good citizens of this country? Do you not want them to be respected by all those that are honest people? And I know you often wish that they may get to that land, where joy and peace abound. Then teach them the ways of the Lord. If you are unconverted, oh renounce your sins, for fear your children may be like you, and be banished from the presence of the Lord! Devote more time to training them in the path of truth, and less time to making useless and frivolous articles about their dress! . . .

Then, dear mother, let thy conduct be that of a true believer on the crucified Redeemer, and instruct thy children in the way of truth and soberness, and then will you see pleasure in your travail, and you will be blessed by him, who committed their tender charge into thy care.

Thy poor brother feels thankful unto God, that he was blessed with a pious mother, who often took occasion to point me home to God, and to guide my erring footsteps in the path of peace. . . .

CEPHAS

SOME OBSERVATIONS AT CHURCH

One Saturday Night

by J. H. Moore

While seated in the pulpit, one Sunday morning, I observed a care-worn woman entering, carrying one child and leading another. Three other children followed. She gathered them around her as a hen would her little chicks. Presently the husband entered, a strong man, looking as though he enjoyed life as well as the table. He picked out a good, comfortable seat at one end of the bench, and fixed himself to take things easy. So far as I could discover he had no concern about the mother and her five children. He came to meeting to enjoy it, and meant to get all the good possible out of the service.

I looked at the woman. She seemed tired and yet she did her best to appear cheerful. Hers were good children, accustomed to attending services, and yet they required her constant attention. She was a hard-working woman in her home, for the family was poor. Instead of having to care for the entire little flock she should have been relieved in some manner. I wondered why that strong husband of hers could not have taken at least two of the children to the seat with him. That would have been a relief to the overworked mother. Then it would have looked manly for him to have assumed at least a part of the family burden. It would have given the mother a better opportunity to enjoy the service and get some of the rest she needed. I certainly pitied the woman, and felt very much like preaching a sermon on the text, "Husbands, love your wives."

Presently, a man entered, carrying a child, which he took care of during the meeting. His wife looked real cheerful and happy. She occupied another seat with some of the larger children. To me that looked sensible, and I felt like commending the man for his fatherly and sensible conduct. His good wife got the full benefit of the service and went away from the meeting a stronger woman, spiritually. To her the service was restful as well as instructive.

A WIFE'S REMORSE

Gospel Visitor—August 1860

"Sick—sick again!" said the heedless wife with petulance. "I'm so tired of seeing a pale face from morning till night, of hearing groans, and of mixing doses. . . ."

"Mary—Mary," cried a quivering voice.

"Coming, coming,"replied the woman. "Oh, dear! how I have to run. He's so impatient, and I must always be there. Men never ought to be sick; they make so much trouble."

There was but little tenderness in the voice that answered the faint queries of the sick man, and yet Mrs. Nash was not a hard-hearted or an unfeeling woman. Her character leaned somewhat to the side of selfishness, and being in robust health, she had no knowledge of the heart-wearing that continued pullbacks cause to men of the strongest wills.

"Oh, dear!" sighed the man, half childish. "It seems as if my head never did ache as it does now."

"I've heard you say that a hundred times," said Mrs. Nash, not in the softest manner.

"But I'm sure it is worse. If you will only pull the curtain down— the least light strikes through my eyes, even when they are shut." . . .

"I'm a great deal of trouble," said the sick man, seeing the cloud on his wife's brow.

"Oh, no!"—her face cleared up—"you are notional, of course—all men are. Men don't know what sickness is, and they're so frightened at the least pain."

"But this is terrible!" cried the invalid, pressing his closed eyelids together. . . .

Mrs. Nash had been down stairs preparing the supper. She had just laughingly said, in reply to a neighbor's question concerning her husband: "Oh, going to die, as you men all are, if you happen to cut your finger."

Little she thought how true was the prophesy she so unthinkingly uttered! In another moment her oldest son came into the room. . . .

"He didn't know me, because I kept calling pa, and he would look at me so strangely and keep asking me if I had that will all made out."

Her cheek paling a little, Mrs. Nash hurried up to the chamber. Her husband was talking wildly to himself, and his appearance had changed frightfully. Now, seriously alarmed, she sent for the physician. . . .

"The man must have shown symptoms of more than ordinary distress this morning," he said . . . .

The wife was forced to confess that the symptoms had been unusually severe, but he was so liable to attacks that she didn't think much of it. Her heart, however, condemned her. . . . Now she was ready to make amends. With tears and loving thoughts she hovered over that sick bed, accusing herself, as every wild cry for her rang out, and still there was no consciousness.

Tears and wild prayers to heaven, sweet and fervent words of love availed nothing. The death hour came, and with it consciousness. Arrows could not have pierced that sad heart as did the last words of that dying man: "Dearest, you have been a good wife to me."

"If I had been tender to him that day," she often sobbed out as she accused herself, "I would give worlds!" But the sorrow, dreadful as it was, has not been without its salutary influence. Now the widowed woman is the welcome visitor by the bedside of the sick. . . . And if she is ever tempted to think an impatient thought. . . there comes up before her the vision of a pale face! that but for her neglect might be smiling on her *now*.

THE HUSBAND'S REMORSE

Gospel Visitor—May 1861

Brethren:—Reviewing some of the past numbers of our valuable *Visitor*, I observe several articles designed expressly in their character for the admonition of the sisters. . . Thinking all well enough in their places, though not liking part of the reproof being entirely intended for the sisters, I think it may not be amiss merely to ask the brethren if they are altogether exempt from the feelings of regret which so surely follow the errors we are all liable to commit?

Woman's life is one of continued toil, anxiety, and suffering, to which man's is not worthy to be compared. And too often, indeed is many a pang and heart sorrow added thereto by the unkind treatment of those who should fondly cherish and protect them. Methinks many is the bitter cup of remorse that has been drunk, and will be drunk to its very dregs by those unthinking "lords of creation," who deem it no part of manliness to treat with tender regard the helpless ones who cling to them next to God, be they mother, sister, wife. Those who can truly appreciate the faith of trusting, confiding woman will never be the subjects of this remorse. And oh! if woman should sometimes fail to discharge her whole duty amid her unceasing labor, is it a wonder. Brother, first remove the beam from thine own eye, then canst thou see clearly the mote in thy sister's. . . .
C. C.

ON THE DEATH OF A HUSBAND

Monthly Gospel-Visiter—February 1855

[For Henry Ebersole by his Widow]

Hark! A mournful voice of sadness, born upon the passing gale,
Sorrow takes the place of gladness, grief's sad echo fills the vale.
All around kind friends were weeping, for a blessed husband dead,
For a father, brother sleeping, in the grave's cold lonely bed.
Long had sickness traced with sorrow every feature once so gay,
And to him the hopeful morrow brought no bright or gladsome ray.

When the summer leaves were dying obeying nature's high behest,
When the autumn winds were sighing, they laid my husband down
to rest.
Sweetly sleep, departed husband, in the quiet grave so low,
Sweeter far than this another life immortal thou shalt know.
Long thy memory we will cherish, as a sacred holy thing,
They last farewell shall not perish but will sad remembrance bring.

ON THE DEATH OF A WIFE

A Letter of the Gospel Visitor—October 1858

I, some twenty months ago, married a very interesting young
woman at Nittany Hall. . . Pennsylvania, some sixty miles from
where I now live and also where I was raised. This last spring I
bought a farm and built a barn, and at the very time that our struggle
in our building and removing was pretty well over, and my heart had
been made glad by being the first time a father, and fortune seemed
to have especially contributed in our behalf, as far as this world's
comforts are concerned, but alas! affliction approached, (and) fever
prevailed. One Tuesday evening, I was compelled to witness the
awful change—awful indeed inasmuch as the one thing needful has
to a great extent been neglected. (Neither husband or wife had yet
joined the church at that time.)

And now we return to the hour of death when the breath was
visibly growing shorter, and the eyes were glazed never to brighten,
the tongue which uttered fervent prayers to Almighty God for par-
don and mercy could utter no more, and the clammy sweat was rolling in streams. . . I, unconscious of myself, uttered a few despairing
groans, which she seemed to understand very well, and could only
answer them by bursting out in tears. . . and she was gone—a
traveler to return no more. . .

I would occasionally awaken and find myself in a fervent prayer
to the God of the universe to guide me in the event, and to give me
only such a companion as she turned out to be. And the only promise I extracted of her after a very serious and somewhat lengthy conversation on the subject of religion was that she would take the
unadulterated word of God for the man of her council, let it lead her

wherever it would. This she cheerfully and frankly assented to, and I verily believe that she was trying to fill every letter of her resolution. (She would often put in my hand. . . the word of God and ask me to read to her whilst her busy hands would pursue what seemed to be her duty.) But the time was short for such a transposition to take place. . . . When I reflect on these things as above, it give me a lively hope that she still found redemption in the blood of Jesus. But since it has been the will of God to remove from me my little babe (their infant daughter), now I am left with no companion or family than the church of God, in which I find delight and consolation.

Rufus R. Gish (1826-1896) and Barbara Kindig Gish (1829-1915). Home missionaries. Barbara gave most of their estate to the work of the General Missionary Board.

*Martha Cunningham
Dolby (1878-1956)
First Black sister to
be called to the ministry*

*Portrait to illustrate style of plain dress for sisters, Mt. Morris, IL,
1891*
*Left to right: (back row) Ella Amick, Mary Royer, Lilly Royer; (center row)
Mary Lair, Hattie Meany, Anna Royer; (front row) Josephine Royer, Minnie
Windel, Minnie Buck, Ida Royer*

APPENDIX C

DESCRIPTIONS OF
EARLY ORGANIZATIONS

OUR AID SOCIETY MEETING YESTERDAY

by Ida M. Helm

Gospel Messenger—June 9, 1917

It was such a good meeting that I feel I must tell the *Messenger* readers about it. It was a *real* Aid Society—practical, spiritual, and social. When Lydia Foss and I arrived, about a dozen of the sisters were busy quilting. Elsie Lee and Marguerite White were making sun-bonnets. . . . Some of the girls were making door pockets, clothes-pin pokes, and laundry bags.

I looked at the clock. It was half past nine. I was wishing we had gotten there earlier, but I thought, "That's pretty good for a rural Aid Society. These women had their morning work to do, dinner to prepare for the menfolk, and some of them have children they had to see started to school before they chould start to Aid."

Some of them had three miles to drive. But they believe in giving a full day to the Lord. There was Aunt Sarah and Mary Anne Dulabaum. They came four miles. Aunt Sarah isn't so young anymore, either. She will be seventy-three her next birthday. . . . Her fingers are crippled with rheumatism, and she can't sew, but she is a great help to us. She has a book entitled "Children of Other Lands." She is reading it to members of the Society. Yesterday, while we worked, we listened to the sad story of little girls dedicated for life to . . . Indian temple service . . . or little Turkish girls imprisoned in harems, and of little boys taught and trained to consider their sisters far beneath themselves and to believe that girls have no soul and are very little better than beasts. We heard how heathen girls are taught to make long pilgrimages to some heathen shrine and . . . utter numberless vain prayer repetitions to some . . . man-made god. Our hearts were filled with pity . . . . "We must show our sympathy," said Sister Patterson, "by being more diligent and more self-denying, so that we may send more missionaries into the field. Then the people may be taught to know and worship the true God. Then the children will be set free from these heathen deceptions and practices."

"One good way for us to help the mission cause," said Grandma Wright, "is for us to help bear the expense of educating the young brethren and sisters who have volunteered for the mission field, but must work and earn money before they can finish their preparation for the field." Each of the sisters decided to have a missionary educational vegetable bed this summer, the proceeds to be used for that fund.

The time seemed short until Sister Gordon announced: "Dinner." . . . Each member brings a basket containing nourishing, appetizing eatables, but we never encourage extremes or extravagance. Yesterday we enjoyed Sister Holben's beef loaf, Sister Rowe's good bread and butter and applebutter, and Sister Root's floating island. Sister Ritter knows we all enjoy her cherry pie and she brought some. Sister Roonick brought sponge cake. There were canned peaches and pickles . . . Sister Wilkes asked the blessing in so impressive a way that we could not help but appreciate the Source from which every good gift comes, and we thoroughly enjoyed our dinner, as God intended we should.

While we were eating, Etta Darrow said: "I received a letter from Grace Leiter yesterday and she told me she has volunteered for the foreign mission field. She says she has passed the medical test, and the Chairman of the General Mission Board has visited her and she feels sure she will be approved by the Conference." How we all rejoiced at the good news! Grace used to live in our congregation, and we all love her. We always rejoice when one of our number makes a success of any good undertaking. . . .

After dinner the food that was left was gathered into a basket, to be carried to a poor family in the community. Then we went back to our work and we listened while Aunt Sarah read some more. . . . By and by the quilt was out of the frame and the sewing was finished.

Then our worthy president stood up and read a chapter from the Bible, and we all knelt while Sister Alsdorf led us in prayer.

The reading of the minutes of the previous meeting told that we had pledged $100 for the Mary Quinter Memorial Fund. The sisters are all enthusiastic in working for it. Sister Good has a baking powder recipe that she used for years. . . . She offered to manufacture the powder and the sisters are going to buy their baking powder of her, [as are] some of the women of the community who are not members of the Society. We decided to invest $20. Then we can clear $22. That will be used to help pay the expenses of educating one missionary. We donated some clothes to the Farris children. Now they are going to come to Sunday-school. The offering was lifted and we counted it and found . . . $5.20. There were twenty women present. . . . Some one had put in a whole dollar but we do not know who it was. Not one of the members ever sounds a trumpet when doing a good deed. . . . Our Aid Society hopes to accomplish much by working earnestly, unostentatiously, and prayerfully.

LAY LEADERSHIP—THE WORK OF THE WOMEN OF THE CHURCH

by Florence Fogelsanger Murphy

Gospel Messenger—June 13, 1931

"And he touched her hand, and the fever left her; and she arose, and ministered unto them."

Lay leadership as it applies to women, places the emphasis upon individual Christian responsibility. Women's Work is the work of the church—that is, the Christian program of the church. And through the larger Women's Work we are endeavoring to determine the scope and activity of that program, and to shoulder our responsibility in carrying it forward.

The women have always been vitally interested in the evangelistic and missionary activities of the church. So much so that when these enterprises seemed to lag, the women earnestly besought themselves as to how funds might be raised to meet the emergency. The fact that during the past twenty years $1,500,000 has been contributed by and through the women toward carrying forward the program of the church is itself a service worthy of the fine spirit of consecration that prompted it. Yet the sum total of the dollars is not half the story of service. In most cases the "mite" had already been given before the dollars were earned, the latter expressing a consecration of time and energy over and above the "tithe." All of this was an expression of a very earnest prayer seeking guidance and direction from the Master himself. It was an expression of love as was the breaking of the alabaster box of precious ointment. And the story of it, as well as the sweet scent of its odor, shall be as a memorial to those who have gone on.

But now, even though the dollars seem to be needed more than ever, we are stressing what may be a more difficult task. This task lies more especially in the field of Christian education—Christian education in the home, community, nation and throughout the world.

Our five-fold program means just this: first, that we shall continue to be vitally concerned about the necessary funds to carry forward the church's program; second, that we shall assume the responsibility of making not only our own homes beacons of Christian light but of casting that light into other homes as well; third, that we shall exercise to establish in our children and young people the fundamentals of Christian character and refinement; fourth, that we shall strive toward a fuller realization of the brotherhood of man and the fatherhood of God by concretely and practically interpreting the teaching of Jesus concerning social barriers, race prejudice, and false nationalism; and fifth, that we may do all this because of our love for Jesus Christ and the impelling power of his spirit as an active force in our daily lives.

This, then, is the work of the women of the Church of the Brethren, and may I venture to say that it ought to be a work peculiar to them. During the past we have taken considerable pride in applying the term "peculiar" to ourselves. But the world in this twentieth century A.D. is not attracted toward external or temperamental peculiarities. There is one and only one peculiarity in the realm of Christian experience that attracts. It is the vital, living spirit of Jesus Christ expressing itself in and through the lives of his followers. The much criticized youth of today stands on tip toe earnestly peering into our very souls to find out if this Jesus is a Force to be counted on in the every day experiences of life.

The beautiful and holy symbolism of immersion, feet-washing, the love feast and what we term the simple life, means little today unless it becomes incarnate in daily living. Therefore, if we would be a peculiar people attracting folk toward Christ, we must live day by day as though we were buried to sin and had arisen a new creature—as though we actually experienced the dignity and beauty of humble unselfish service as it relates to others regardless of race or creed—as though we actually were willing to sit around the common table and break the bread of life with our fellows—and as though we really respected our bodies and our intellects as the medium of expression of the spirit of God to the extent that we are unwilling to subject them to physical degradation and personal vanity.

Although we would not exclude the men from such a program, yet perhaps because of our experience in relation to our church, we, as women, have been driven to the feet of the Master, and the love of him has so crept into our souls that we are much more interested in the breaking of the alabaster box in loving service than in the discussion of theological issues.

Anna Warstler (1902-), missionary and church administrator

Women's Work Cabinet, 1947

Seated left to right: Eva Bowman, Ruth Shriver, Leah Francis Bowman, Lucille West, Florence Schwalm; standing, left to right: Kathren Holsopple, Etta Bittinger, Zola Detweiler, Naomi Will, Alma Metzger, Ellen Forney

Women's Fellowship Cabinet, 1956

Seated left to right: Ruth Miller, Mildred Baker, Anna Warstler, Sarah Halladay, Esther Crouse, Harriet Bright; standing, left to right: Pearl Murray, Cleda Zunkel, office secretary (not identified), Mary Blickenstaff, Thelma Replogle

APPENDIX D

WHY GIRLS SHOULD BE EDUCATED

by Bhuri Gamya, Age 16, of India
A Student at the Anklesvar Girls' School

Brethren Sisters Around the World—1952

What is meant by education? To strengthen our mind, spirit, and health so that we may overcome difficulties.

Need of girls' education: The girls are even more in need of education than boys. The progress of any country depends much on its women. If the women are educated, they can lead their country in good progress. Though they cannot preach in public, they can teach their own children as no one else can. In order to make the future generation helpful to the country, there is a great need of female education. From education we know how to conduct ourselves in this world. For instance, some women pass their leisure time in speaking ill of others and thus more than waste their time. On the other hand if girls are educated, they may pass their extra time in knitting, sewing, and embroidery. Thus they may earn and save money. Educated mothers teach their children how to keep clean, how to study, how to be orderly and obedient, and how to help other needy people.

Education makes women more courageous. The girls of the future should know how to look after their own homes. This requires proper education. To carry on their affairs, men often need advice and help from women. It is therefore necessary that women should be educated as well as men. Educated women can easily carry on their own household affairs with economy, bring up children in the right path, know the value of time, and assist their menfolk. Some people think female education is unnecessary because women cannot work like men. This is a great error. Girls should be educated in order that they may be useful in the future.

Some people believe that education makes girls proud and that they want to become independent of men. Sometimes this does happen. But if girls are given proper education and helped to realize their responsibility, this will never happen. Therefore the girls who are studying should behave themselves in such a manner as to give no opportunity for others to think them haughty.

Benefits of education: In countries such as England and America, progress is rapid because their girls are educated. Educated women can work as efficiently as men. They may even have inventive power. At present it is women who are carrying on temperance work. Also it is women who can better help the poor and nurse the sick. God has bestowed upon women such qualities as mercy and love. One educated woman can create good impressions upon illiterate women of a whole village and can set a good example for them. Truly educated women are seldom idle. They are happy, diligent, and kind. Educated women always desire to see their country and people on a high level and try their best to help raise the standards of life. . . .

Conclusion: It therefore appears that female education is very essential. In order that girls may be a blessing to themselves and to others, girls should not neglect the good opportunities to receive education.

Mildred Grimley (1919-), teaching in Nigeria, 1947

Eleanor Painter (1926-), pastor of special ministries, Palmyra Church of the Brethren

"Sistern" in the Brethren Peace Caravan, 1930, changing a flat

Yvonne Dilling (1955-), social justice advocate (Manchester College photo)

Anna Mow (1893-), missionary, author, minister, retreat leader

Laura Wine (1899-1969), victim of Lassa fever, at work in Garkida Hospital.

Winnie (Winifred) Cripe (1884-1934), opening of China missionary girls school, at Liao Chow, ca. 1915

Sewing Club at Garkida, ca. 1951

NOTES

Chapter 1. Brethren Beginnings

1. Donald F. Durnbaugh, *European Origins of the Brethren*, p. 121. This collection of source materials supplied most of my information in the first section of this chapter, including the chapter title.
2. William Willoughby, *Counting the Cost: The Life of Alexander Mack*, p. 57. This book is another important source for this chapter.
3. Durnbaugh, *European Origins*, p. 119.
4. Willoughby, *Counting the Cost*, p. 59. I will refer to this group as the Brethren, which is the name by which they later came to be known.
5. Durnbaugh, *European Origins*, p. 202.
6. Durnbaugh, *European Origins*, p. 171. A letter from the deputy administrator of Dudelsheim, November 5, 1712, to the city councilors indicates that a husband sought the deputy's help to prevent his wife from being baptized by the Schwarzenau Pietists.
7. Willoughby, *Counting the Cost*, pp. 67-69.
8. Durnbaugh, *European Origins*, pp. 365-76. This discussion on avoidance is taken from *Rights and Ordinances* by Alexander Mack, Sr.
9. This is a paraphrase by Willoughby, *Counting the Cost*, p. 81. An English translation of the original is in Durnbaugh, *European Origins*, pp. 141-42.
10. Durnbaugh, *European Origins*, p. 151.
11. Donald Durnbaugh, *The Brethren in Colonial America*, p. 597.
12. Durnbaugh, *European Origins*, pp. 144-45.
13. Durnbaugh, *European Origins*, p. 283.
14. Willoughby, *Counting the Cost*, p. 107. Also see the sketch by Inez Long, *Faces Among the Faithful*, pp. 11-18.
15. Durnbaugh, *The Brethren in Colonial America*, pp. 61-62.
16. Durnbaugh, *European Origins*, p. 389.
17. Information on Beissel and Ephrata may be found in *The Brethren Encyclopedia* (1984); *Chronicon Ephratense: A History of the Community of Seventh Day Baptists at Ephrata* by "Lamech and Agrippa"; Durnbaugh, *The Brethren in Colonial America*, and Walter Klein, *Johann Conrad Beissel: Mystic and Martinet*.
18. *Chronicon Ephratense*, p. 91.

19. *Chronicon Ephratense*, p. 91. The Moravians, with whom Beissel was acquainted, had a similar practice. At times feetwashing services for women were held, with a woman presiding, see Ruether and Keller, eds., *Women and Religion in America*, p. 225.
20. *Chronicon Ephratense*, p. 158.
21. *Chronicon Ephratense*, pp. 158-59.
22. Martin Grove Brumbaugh, *A History of the German Baptist Brethren*, p. 177.
23. Durnbaugh, *The Brethren in Colonial America*, p. 601.
24. *The Brethren Encyclopedia*, p. 1344.
25. Henry Kurtz, *The Brethren's Encyclopedia*, pp. 10-11.
26. Durnbaugh, *The Brethren in Colonial America*, p. 209.
27. Durnbaugh, *The Brethren in Colonial America*, p. 261-62.
28. Durnbuagh, *The Brethren in Colonial America*, pp. 265-66.
29. Durnbaugh, *The Brethren in Colonial America*, pp. 263-64.
30. *The Brethren Encyclopedia*, p. 175.

Chapter 2. The Order of the Brethren

1. Durnbaugh, *European Origins*, p. 347. The entire manuscript of *Rights and Ordinances* is reprinted in this volume, pp. 344-404. For a brief summary of its contents, see Willoughby, *Counting the Cost*, pp. 95-98.
2. Durnbaugh, *The Brethren in Colonial America*, p. 464.
3. Durnbaugh, *The Brethren in Colonial America*, p. 469.
4. Various writers have claimed that among the Anabaptists and Pietists women enjoyed equality with men. In an 1895 article on "The Anabaptists," W. E. Griffis said that one of their fundamental doctrines was "education of women and the equalization of the sexes, especially in religious life and privilege" (*The New World*, December 1895). George Williams would later make a similar claim: "Akin to the prominence of the laymen in the Radical Reformation and the functional extension of the priesthood of all believers in the direction of personal witness to Christ in missions and martyrdom . . . was the corresponding elevation of women to a status of almost complete equality with men in the central task of the fellowship of the reborn" (*The Radical Reformation*, p. xxx). More recently, Elise Boulding claimed that Anabaptists "practiced complete equality of women and men in every respect, including preaching" (*The Underside of History: A View of Women Though Time*, p. 548). Joyce Irwin does an excellent critical analysis of these claims in her source book, *Womenhood in Radical Protestantism: 1525-1675*. She concludes that "inspite of democratic tendencies, the [Anabaptist] women remain entirely subordinate to the men, both in the home and the church (p. xxi).
5. Durnbaugh, *European Origins*, p. 379.
6. *Chronicon Ephratense*, p. 36.
7. *Chronicon Ephratense*, pp. 59-60.
8. *Chronicon Ephratense*, p. 55.

9. Durnbaugh, *The Brethren in Colonial America*, p. 476.

10. Brethren had developed by the mid-nineteenth century three degrees of ministry, in addition to the deaconate. All these were elected by the membership of the congregation. Ministers of the first degree were permitted to preach, ministers of the second degree could administer baptism and communion. The third degree minister was the elder who was overseer of the congregation. Kurtz, *The Brethren's Encyclopedia*, p. 44; *The Brethren Encyclopedia*, pp. 844-45. Ministers were non-salaried until the twentieth century, although some congregations still maintain the "free" ministry.

11. Sources for this discussion of church polity are *The Brethren Encyclopedia*, pp. 1041-45; Floyd Mallott, *Studies in Brethren History*, pp. 164-85; and *Minutes of the Annual Meetings of the Brethren (1909)*.

12. Kurtz, *The Brethren's Encyclopedia*, p. 60.

13. *Proceedings of the Annual Meeting of the Brethren*, 1881, p. 67.

14. *Proceedings of the Annual Meeting of the Brethren*, 1881, p. 71.

15. *Proceedings of the Annual Meeting of the Brethren*, 1882, pp. 4-5.

16. *Proceedings of the Annual Meeting of the Brethren*, 1882, pp. 4-5.

17. *Proceedings of the Annual Meeting of the Brethren*, 1883, p. 10.

18. A three-way schism occurred among the Brethren in the early 1880s. Some four to five thousand traditionalists withdrew to become the Old German Baptist Brethren. They were opposed to innovations which were being made in the church. In 1882, Annual Meeting upheld the disfellowshiping of a progressive elder, Henry Holsinger. He and supporters organized the Brethren Church in 1882-23, with about five thousand members. A large middle group of some sixty thousand continued as the German Baptist Brethren, the official name the Brethren adopted in 1871. This group, which changed its name to Church of the Brethren in 1908, included many tending towards both conservatism and progressivism. See *The Brethren Encyclopedia*. pp. 178-79.

19. The New Testament instructs Christians to greet each other with a kiss of charity (love), also called the holy kiss. This has been the practice of the Brethren, with sisters kissing sisters and brothers kissing brothers. The kiss is also given after the feetwashing and sometimes during the fellowship meal of the love feast. *The Brethren Encyclopedia*, pp. 698-99.

20. Kurtz, *Brethren's Encyclopedia*, p. 27.

21. Durnbaugh, *The Brethren in Colonial America*, pp. 238-39.

22. *Minutes of the Annual Meetings*, (1909) 1843, Article 5.

23. Durnbaugh, *European Origins*, p. 392.

24. *Proceedings of the Annual Meeting of the Brethren*, 1915, p. 166.

25. *The Brethren Encyclopedia*, pp. 399-404; E. F. Rupel, "An Investigation of the Origin, Significance, and Demise of the Prescribed Dress Worn by Members of the Church of the Brethren" (Ph.D. Dissertation, University of Minnesota, 1971), p. 133.

26. *Minutes of the Annual Conference of the Church of the Brethren, 1923-44*, p. 35.

27. Quoted in Rupel, "Dress," pp. 135-36.
28. Some women wore prayer caps during waking hours, others for prayer in the home and for church services. A few Brethren women still wear the covering all through the day. Some Brethren women wear the covering only for worship or love feast. Very few Church of the Brethren women still wear what was once the prescribed order of dress.
29. Mallott attributes the change in policy on carpets to the lowering of their price with increasing industrialization. They were thus no longer considered an expensive luxury item. Mallott, *Studies*, pp. 155-56.

Chapter 3. Women in Home and Congregation

1. Freeman Ankrum, *Sidelights in Brethren History*, p. 70.
2. Earl Kaylor, Jr., *Out of the Wilderness: the Brethren and Two Centuries of Life in Central Pennsylvania*, p. 54.
3. *History of the Church of the Brethren of the District of Southern Ohio*, p. 594.
4. *History of the Church of the Brethren of the District of Southern Ohio*, p.487.
5. Sappington, *The Brethren in the New Nation*, p. 34; *The Brethren Encyclopedia*, p. 631.
6. Sources for the Wolfe family include Roger Sappington, *The Brethren in the New Nation*, pp. 54-56; *The Brethren Encyclopedia*, pp. 1356-57; and Inez Long, *Faces Among the Faithful*, pp. 32-38.
7. Sappington, *The Brethren in the New Nation*, pp. 97-98.
8. Sappington, *The Brethren in the New Nation*, pp. 89-99.
9. Sappington, *The Brethren in the New Nation*, pp. 93-94. I have edited the letter so that it is in standard English.
10. *Monthly Gospel-Visiter*, July 1856, p. 176.
11. *The Brethren Encyclopedia*, p. 1358; Sappington, *The Brethren in the New Nation*, pp. 101-2.
12. Sappington, *The Brethren Along the Snake River*, pp. 18-19.
13. *Gospel Messenger*, May 19, 1914, p. 290.
14. *Gospel Visitor*, March 1872. This article was contributed by Olive V. Roop, great-great-great-granddaughter of Mary Herring.
15. Ankrum, *Sidelights in Brethren History*, pp. 123-27; *The Brethren Encyclopedia*, p. 1126.
16. *The Brethren Encyclopedia*, p. 704.
17. This biography was contributed by Evalena's daughter Mary Blocher Smeltzer, to the "She Will Be Remembered For This" project of the One Hundredth Anniversary Celebration of Women's Organizations in the Church of the Brethren, 1984.
18. *History of the Church of the Brethren in Indiana*, pp. 302-3.
19. *Minutes of Annual Meeting*, 1919, pp. 8-12.
20. Sappington, *The Brethren in the Carolinas*, pp. 58-60.
21. *History of the Church of the Brethren of the District of Southern Ohio*, p. 426.

22. A letter from Isaac Hoke in *The Monthly Gospel-Visiter*, May 1854, pp. 281-82.

23. *History of the Church of the Brethren of the District of Southern Ohio*, p. 379.

24. *Gospel Messenger*, January 23, 1904, p. 52. Also see the chapter on Anna Kline in Long, *Faces Among the Faithful*, pp. 39-45.

25. *History of the Church of the Brethren of the District of Southern Ohio*, p. 393. A more detailed description of the Arab capture is given in *The Brethren Encyclopedia*, p. 1344.

26. Mrs. C. O. Beery, "Two Mothers," the *District Echo*, May 1936, pp. 1-2.

27. From a letter of Beverly Cayford to the author, May 12, 1983.

28. Howard Miller, "Tea Table Tattle," *Progressive Christian*, February 21, 1879, p. 1.

Chapter 4. Sisters and Communion

1. *Monthly Gospel-Visiter*, June 1851, p. 64. Writers in this periodical often were not identified, or else identified only by initials or geographical location.

2. *Monthly Gospel-Visiter*, November 1851, pp. 118-19.

3. *Monthly Gospel-Visiter*, September 1851, pp. 91-92. Some of the claims in this letter are questionable, as the writer states not only that this account is from older Brethren but also that it is the way he has seen communion celebrated at Annual Meetings. There are other accounts from the same period that would differ from this one.

4. *Monthly Gospel-Visiter*, January 1852, pp. 164-66.

5. *Monthly Gospel-Visiter*, March 1852, pp. 192-93

6. *Monthly Gospel-Visiter*, March 1852, pp. 192-93.

7. *Monthly Gospel-Visiter*, March 1852, p. 194.

8. Kurtz, *The Brethren's Encyclopedia*, p. 180.

9. *Christian Family Companion*, February 25, 1868.

10. *The Brethren's Family Almanac* of 1890 published a "History of the Far Western Brethren," by W[H]. W. Strickler. This was a greatly abridged version of a manuscript by Elder John Clingingsmith, "Short Historical Sketch of the Far Western Brethren of the Dunkard Church . . . to the year 1885"; an unpublished typescript is located in the Brethren Historical Library and Archives, Elgin, Ill. Strickler's revision included this claim: "In 1824 there were fifty communicants in Cape [Girardeau] County, Missouri. . . . These brethren washed feet after supper and before the communion. The sisters broke the bread and passed the cup of communion the same as the brethren" (p. 719). However, the type-written version of the longer manuscript—presumably made by J. H. Moore in 1908—does not mention that the sisters broke bread and passed the cup. Did Strickler make this addition in the version he prepared for *The Brethren's Family Almanac* or did Moore for some reason strike this reference? Unfortunately, the original manuscript has been lost. Perhaps Gibson and Strickler, relying on memory, other

documents, and family tradition, concluded that some churches among the Far Western Brethren permitted the sisters to break bread. Or perhaps they presumed that because the Far Western Brethren differed with the practice of other Brethren in regard to the method of feet-washing, they also differed in regard to sisters and communion. The evidence now available does not provide a final answer.

11. *Brethren at Work*, May 1883.
12. *Gospel Messenger*, June 23, 1883.
13. See Notes, chapter 2, note 18.
14. *Proceedings of the Annual Meeting of the Brethren*, 1885, p. 97.
15. *Proceedings of the Annual Meeting of the Brethren*, 1891, p. 23.
16. I am deeply indebted to the article by Marlene Moats Neher "The Woman Who Wanted to Break Bread," in *Messenger*, June 1976, for this account of Julia Gilbert's life.
17. Quoted in Neher, "The Woman Who Wanted to Break Bread," p. 21.
18. Quoted in Neher, "The Woman Who Wanted to Break Bread," p. 23.
19. *Minutes of the Annual Meetings, (1909)*, 1899, Number 1.
20. *Minutes of the Annual Meetings, (1909)*, 1900, Number 3.
21. Brumbaugh, *A History of the German Baptist Brethren*, p. 543.
22. Willoughby, *Counting the Cost*, p. 134.
23. *Chronicon Ephratense*, p. 241.
24. The descriptions of some non-Brethren observers are helpful at this point. Morgan Edwards account (1770) of the Brethren love feast (Durnbaugh, *The Brethren in Colonial America*, pp. 173-75) does not make note of a difference in practice between men and women. He did note the presence of both deacons and deaconesses in the church. A later account (1899) by Julius Sasche (*The German Sectarians of Pennsylvania, Volume I*, pp. 108-9) does note the difference in practice between women and men during communion. So a change may have taken place during this time. I have yet to discover another denomination which has a different practice for women and men in receiving communion. In the medieval Catholic Church and the early German Lutheran Church, the custom was for men to be served before women; but both went forward to have the elements administered to them by a priest (Helmut Lehman, *Meaning and Practice of the Lord's Supper*, pp. 83, 109). The sixteenth century Swiss Brethren distributed the bread and cup among themselves, with no distinction noted between women and men (George Williams, *The Radical Reformation*, p. 123). The seventeenth century English Baptists held a love feast and communion with feetwashing in the evenings (Horton Davies, *Worship and Theology in England, 1602-1690*, pp. 491, 504). The bread and cup were passed "from hand to hand" among the communicants (Theodore Tappert, *The Lord's Supper: Past and Present Practices*, pp. 47-48). The Brethren distinction in practice between women and men thus seems to be a form they uniquely developed.
25. *Minutes of the Annual Meetings, (1909)*, 1906, Number 5.
26. *Minutes of the Annual Meetings, (1909)*, 1906, Number 5.
27. *Proceedings of the Annual Meeting of the Brethren*, 1910, p. 104.

28. *Proceedings of the Annual Meeting of the Brethren,* 1910, pp. 104-5.
29. *Proceedings of the Annual Meeting of the Brethren,* 1910, pp. 105-6.
30. *Proceedings of the Annual Meeting of the Brethren,* 1910, pp. 106-7.
31. *Proceedings of the Annual Meeting of the Brethren,* 1910, pp. 109-110. Julia had also spoken the previous year during Annual Meeting debate.
32. *Proceedings of the Annual Meeting of the Brethren,* 1910, p. 110.
33. A few women have reported to me that in their congregations the previous practice of the bread being broken to the sisters was retained after 1910. One report came from a congregation in the Southern Pennsylvania District, where a change in practice was not made until the 1930s when an older sister who had opposed any change died. Another report came from eastern Pennsylvania (Atlantic Northeast District). These women were not sure when or why the practice changed, but they remember having the bread broken to them as late as the 1950s.

Chapter 5. Early Organizations

1. For an account of this division, see chapter 2. The "old orders" were concerned that in undertaking these new endeavors, the church was conforming to the world rather than following the teachings of scripture. Other denominations and secular groups were emphasizing publications, education, and foreign missions. The progressives believed there were scriptural grounds for these endeavors.
2. *The Brethren Encyclopedia,* p. 561.
3. *The Brethren Encyclopedia,* pp. 818-19.
4. *The Brethren Encyclopedia,* p. 2.
5. *Gospel Visitor,* February 1863, p. 51.
6. *The Brethren Encyclopedia,* pp. 425-28.
7. *The Brethren Encyclopedia,* pp. 678-89; Annual Bulletins of Juniata College in the Juniata College Archives.
8. *The Brethren Encyclopedia,* p. 231; Address by Earl C. Kaylor, Jr. for the Centennial of the Stone Church of the Brethren, in the Juniata College Archives.
9. The sources for this account are Grace Quinter Holsopple, "Founding of Women's Work," *Gospel Messenger,* December 28, 1935, pp. 6-12 (a special Women's Work issue celebrating the 50th anniversary of women's organizations), and articles on the history of the Sister's Aid Society in *Gospel Messenger,* September 25, 1920, and October 13, 1928.
10. *Gospel Messenger* 1885, p. 250.
11. *Gospel Messenger,* June, 1885.
12. "Founding of Women's Work," p. 11. (In this and subsequent references to this article, the page numbers pertain to a pamphlet reproduction from the *Gospel Messenger,* June 16, 1885).
13. "Program Booklet of the One Hundredth Anniversary Sunday of the First Church of the Brethren, Altoona, Pa.," pp. 10-11; and the *District*

Echo, August 1931, pp. 13-14; both from the Juniata College Archives.

14. "Founding of Women's Work," p. 18.
15. *The Brethren Encyclopedia,* p. 220; the *District Echo,* May 1934, p. 3.
16. *Gospel Messenger,* May 25, 1886.
17. "Founding of Women's Work," p. 13.
18. *Gospel Messenger,* June 8, 1886, p. 357.
19. *Full Report of the Annual Meeting,* 1886, pp. 29-30.
20. *Full Report of the Annual Meeting,* 1886, p. 31.
21. *Full Report of the Annual Meeting,* 1887, pp. 75ff.
22. *Full Report of the Annual Meeting,* 1895, pp. 64-67.
23. *Gospel Messenger,* February 18, 1939.
24. *History of Women's Work in the Eastern District of Maryland,* p. 2.
25. *The Brethren Encyclopedia,,* p. 217.
26. Minutes of the Sisters' Aid Society, in Brethren Historical Library and Archives (hereafter cited as BHLA).
27. *The Brethren Encyclopedia,* p. 1077.
28. *The Brethren Encyclopedia,* p. 308; correspondence from Nancy H. Morris.
29. *Minutes of Annual Conference,* 1930, p. 68.
30. *Gospel Messenger,* October 13, 1928.
31. The sources for Van Dyke and the Mothers and Daughters' Association are "A Brief History of the Mothers and Daughters' Association" (1923), in BHLA; Long, *Faces Among the Faithful,* pp. 88-94; Minutes of the Mothers and Daughters' Association, in BHLA; and *The Brethren Encyclopedia,* pp. 878, 1302.
32. *Gospel Messenger,* September 25, 1920.
33. The Council of Boards consisted of the members of all general boards responsible to the Annual Conference such as the General Mission Board, the Board of Religious Education, the General Ministerial Board, and permanent committees meeting in joint session. The council, which began meeting in 1928, prepared a joint budget to be brought to Annual Conference and attempted to avoid duplication of programs. It was a predecessor to the General Brotherhood Board, which was organized in 1947. *The Brethren Encyclopedia,* p. 346.
34. *Minutes of Annual Conference,* 1930, pp. 68-70.
35. *Gospel Messenger,* October 13, 1928.

Chapter 6. Unified Women's Work

1. *Gospel Messenger,* 1930.
2. *The Brethren Encyclopedia,* p. 897; Long, *Faces Among the Faithful,* pp. 122-28.
3. *Gospel Messenger,* December 20, 1928.
4. *Gospel Messenger,* April 16, 1938.
5. *Our Women in Service,* in BHLA.

6. *Gospel Messenger*, March 16, 1935.
7. *Gospel Messenger*, March 30, 1935.
8. R. Pierce Beaver, *American Protestant Women in World Mission*, pp. 153-63.
9. *Gospel Messenger*, February 4, 1933.
10. *The Brethren Encyclopedia*, p. 890.
11. *Women's Work Manual*, 1931, in BHLA.
12. *Gospel Messenger*, February 25, 1933.
13. *Gospel Messenger*, January 11, 1941.
14. *Women's Work in Africa*, in BHLA.
15. *Brethren Sisters Around the World*, 1952, in BHLA.
16. Paula J. Stanley, "A String of Pearls," *Brethren Life and Thought*, January 1985. Stanley is quoting from an interview with Lucille West Rupel.
17. *Gospel Messenger*, August 22, 1931.
18. *Gospel Messenger*, August 11, 1937.
19. *NCWW Minutes*, 1939, in BHLA.
20. *NCWW Minutes*, November 5, 1945, in BHLA.
21. *The Brethren Encyclopedia*, p. 816.
22. *The Brethren Encyclopedia*, p. 1689.
23. Stanley, "A String of Pearls" p. 6.
24. *NCWW Minutes*, April 26, 1945 in BHLA.
25. *NCWW Minutes*.
26. *The Brethren Encyclopedia*, p. 1180; Biographical File, BHLA.
27. *Women's Work Manual*, 1950, in BHLA.
28. *NCWW Minutes*, November, 1955, in BHLA.
29. *NCWW Minutes*, January, 1957, in BHLA.
30. *Minutes of Annual Conference*, 1953, p. 25.
31. Correspondence from Pearl Murray, October, 1983.
32. Correspondence with Fern Mohler, October, 1983.
33. *NCWW Minutes*, June 16, 1959, in BHLA.
34. *Yesterday, Today, and Tomorrow*, 1960, in BHLA.
35. Irene F. Bittinger was nominated for inclusion in this volume by her daughter Pattie Bittinger Stern, and also by the San Diego (Calif.) Church of the Brethren. They furnished the information for this sketch.
36. *The Brethren Encyclopedia*, p. 1319; *Messenger*, March 1979, pp. 18-21; interview with Anna Warstler in October of 1981.
37. *Minutes of Annual Conference*, 1965, pp. 31-34. The committee members were Curtis Dubble, Eleanor Painter, and Jack Kough. Many district and local women's fellowships continued to have active organizations. The La Verne (Calif.) Ladies' Aid Society celebrated their 85th anniversary in 1981. This group was formed just after the sanction of Annual Meeting. Many groups which began after the national organization of Sisters' Aid Society in 1910 are still active. The Sebring (Fla.) group was organized by Phoebe Brower Moore (Mrs. J. H.) in 1916, just after the Sebring Church was organized. Many societies were organized in 1916 and 1917 in eastern Pennsylvania. District women's meetings and women's camps are still held in several districts by CBWF.

Chapter 7. Women and Missions

1. *The Brethren Encyclopedia*, p. 36l. Quoted in *Founding of Women's Work*, pp. 7-8 (see Notes, chapter 5, n. 11).
2. Quoted in *Founding of Women's Work*, p. 8; letter from Abraham H. Cassel in the *Primitive Christian*, May 2, 1876.
3. Quoted in *Founding of Women's Work*, p. 9.
4. *The Brethren Encyclopedia*, pp. 204, 206. Foreign missions was one of the issues leading to the schism of 1881-82. The "old orders" were afraid that a program of church extension would lead to a salaried ministry, which they believed was not scriptural.
5. *The Brethren Encyclopedia*, pp. 858-89.
6. *The Brethren Encyclopedia*, p. 1177. Bertha Ryan was nominated for inclusion in this volume by Rachel Ziegler, former missionary to India.
7. *The Brethren Encyclopedia*, pp. 1226-27; Long, *Faces Among the Faithful*, pp. 53-60.
8. *The Brethren Encyclopedia*, p. 630.
9. *The Brethren Encyclopedia*, p. 606.
10. *The Brethren Encyclopedia*, p. 354; Long, *Faces Among the Faithful*, pp. 68-74.
11. Adalaine Hohf Beery, "The Work of Women" in *Two Centuries of the Church of the Brethren*, pp. 229-237.
12. *Full Report of the Annual Meeting*, 1910.
13. *Full Report of the Annual Meeting*, 1890, pp. 40-41.
14. *The Brethren Encyclopedia*, p. 217; Minutes of the General Mission Board, November 21, 1911, in BHLA.
15. *The Brethren Encyclopedia*, p. 345.
16. *The Brethren Encyclopedia*, p. 936.
17. *Meet Your Missionaries*, p. 16.
18. *The Brethren Encyclopedia*, p. 209.
19. *The Missionary Letters of Minnie Flory Bright*, pp. 43-44.
20. *The Brethren Encyclopedia*, p. 277; *History of the Chruch of the Brethren in Michigan*, pp. 285-87. Nettie Senger was nominated for inclusion in this volume by the Beacon Heights Church of the Brethren in Indiana, of which she was a charter member. Mary Schaeffer was another significant missionary, evangelist, and educator in China; see Long, *Faces Among the Faithful*, pp. 95-100.
21. *The Brethren Encyclopedia*, pp. 201-499.
22. "Girls' Schools in Africa, China, and India," *A Missionary Education Program of Women's Work*, p. 3.
23. *Meet Your Missionaries*, p. 23; *The Brethren Encyclopedia*, p. 697; personal interview with Kathryn Kiracofe, August, 1984. Kathryn was the author's heroine in the 1950s, her mother's cousin, and partially sponsored on the mission field by her home congregation. Ida Shumaker was another significant missionary educator and evangelist in India. See Long, *Faces Among the Faithful*, pp. 82-87.
24. "Motibai—Helper in Village Work" in *Brethren Sisters Around the World*, pp. 16-17.

25. *The Brethren Encyclopedia*, pp. 708-9; Long, *Faces Among the Faithful*, pp. 109-15.
26. *The Brethren Encyclopedia*, p. 585. Clara Harper was nominated for inclusion in this volume by Mary Eikenberry, retired missionary to Nigeria.
27. "Mayoksa, The First Christian Leper," written by Desmond Bittinger; also the *District Echo*, Volume 4, number 4 (November 1931), pp. 4-5.
28. *The Brethren Encyclopedia*, p. 230. Marguerite Burke was nominated by Naomi Waggy.
29. *The Brethren Encyclopedia*, p. 550; Long, *Faces Among the Faithful*, pp. 46-52.
30. *The Brethren Encyclopedia*, pp. 857-60, 1295-96.
31. *Chicago Sunday School Extension*, pp. 34-37.
32. *The Brethren Encyclopedia*, p. 533; *History of the Church of the Brethren in Eastern Pennsylvania*, pp. 141-42. Mary Schwenk Geiger was a prominent philanthropist who supported Brethren colleges, orphanges, mission programs, and Brethren church building funds.
33. *Brethren in Eastern Pennsylvania*, pp. 142-52.
34. *Brethren in Eastern Pennsylvania*, p. 152.
35. *The Brethren Encyclopedia*, p. 1083.
36. *The Brethren Encyclopedia*, pp. 849-51.
37. Nelie Wampler was nominated for inclusion in this volume by Nancy H. Morris, who also wrote this sketch. See, *The Brethren Encyclopedia*, pp. 664-65, 1317.
38. *The Brethren Encyclopedia*, p. 841; Long, *Faces Among the Faithful*, pp. 147-53.
39. Laura Moyer was nominated for inclusion in this volume by Phill Carlos Archbold and the Brooklyn congregation (New York). The Archbolds prepared a biography from which this sketch is drawn. See also *The Brethren Encyclopedia*, pp. 211-12, 892.
40. "Precious Jade," *Brethren Sisters Around the World*, (1952), p. 20.
41. *Church of the Brethren Yearbook*, 1928, p. 41.
42. *The Brethren Encyclopedia*,, pp. 859-60.
43. From the 'Scrapbook of the Peace Caravan,' 1930, in BHLA.
44. *The Brethren Encyclopedia*, pp. 199-200, 708.
45. Correspondence from Alma Moyers Long, July, 1984.
46. *Brethren of the Southern Plains*, p. 84.

Chapter 8. Women and Ministry

1. Durnbaugh, *European Origins*, p. 151.
2. Kurtz, *The Brethren's Encyclopedia*, p. 181.
3. Kurtz, quoted in *History of the Church of the Brethren in Southern Pennsylvania*, p. 22.
4. Elizabeth M. Barnet, "Grandmother's Church—Our Church," *Gospel Messenger*, May 19, 1916, p. 290.
5. *The Brethren Encyclopedia*, p. 1053.

6. *Minutes of the Annual Meetings, (1909)*, p. 200.

7. *Minutes of the Annual Meetings, (1909)*, p. 539.

8. This report was written by Modena Minnich Studebaker, Garkida, Africa, January 2, 1935.

9. The question of Sunday schools was one of the issues in the 1881-82 schism. See *The Brethren Encyclopedia*, pp. 1237-39, and Elizabeth Meyer, "The Growth of the Sunday-School Movement in the Brethren Church," in *Two Centuries of the Church of the Brethren.*

10. *History of the Church of the Brethren—Eastern Pennsylvania, 1915-65*, pp. 317-20.

11. From material submitted by the Battle Creek Church of the Brethren (Mich.).

12. *History of the Church of the Brethren of the District of Southern Ohio*, pp. 495-96.

13. Quoted in *History of the Church of the Brethren of the Eastern District of Pennsylvania, 1708-1915*, p. 322.

14. Quoted in *History of the Church of the Brethren of the Eastern District of Pennsylvania*, p. 324.

15. *Report of the Proceedings of the Annual Meeting of the Brethren, 1911*, p. 173.

16. *The Brethren Encyclopedia*, p. 1276.

17. *The Brethren Encyclopedia*, p. 1217; *History of the Church of the Brethren in Indiana (1952)*, p. 407.

18. *The Brethren Encyclopedia*, p. 933. See also pp. 101-8 in Long, *Faces Among the Faithful.*

19. *The Brethren Encyclopedia*, p. 1329; *Gospel Messenger*, December 1935. The author can remember her great-grandmother Cora reciting this poem to her when she was a child.

20. Myrtle Porter was nominated for inclusion in this volume by her daughter-in-law, Betty Ann Porter. Her obituary was published in *The Gove County Advocate*, January 4, 1962.

21. Correspondence from Ruth Lehman, October 1983, who was nominated by Pearl Murray.

22. Anna Warstler, *Brethren Sisters Around the World*, 1952, pp. 18-19.

23. Quoted from a letter from Inez Long responding to questions from the author, August 14, 1984.

24. Elva Bowman was nominated by her granddaughter Rae Ann Masterson Frantz, who furnished this sketch of her.

25. Rowena Peters was nominated by Pearl Murray of Kansas. The biographical sketch was provided by Mrs. Peters's daughter, Lina Catherine Baldwin.

26. *The Brethren Encyclopedia*, p. 893. The personal reflections on Gladdys Muir are those of Wanda Will Button from a 1984 interview.

27. Submitted by the Brethren Women's Fellowship of the Froid (Mont.) congregation to the "She Will Be Remembered For This" project.

28. Ethel Masters was nominated for inclusion in this volume by the women of the Mill Creek congregation (N.C.), who sent biographical information about her.

29. Florence Gibble was nominated by her grandson James's wife, Elaine, who never met her but heard much about her from other women.
30. Ada Burd was nominated by her granddaughter, Wendy Jo Campbell, who provided this sketch in a letter to the author, October 21, 1980.
31. Elizabeth Roller was nominated by her son, Robert. The sketch is from an interview, June 26, 1981.
32. Eva Meiser was nominated by Brenda Good and the women of the Prescott church.
33. Mary Elizabeth Petty was nominated by the Broadwater Women's Fellowship, who provided this sketch.
34. *Minutes of Annual Conference, 1945-54,* pp. 185-89.
35. Mary Etta Sanger was nominated by her deceased daughter's husband, Edward K. Ziegler. Desmond's description comes from the card he and his wife, Irene, submitted to the "She Will Be Remembered For This" project.
36. Vinna Helstern was nominated by her daughter Mary Sue, who also nominated her sister Joy. This sketch is taken from a joint interview with these three women in February of 1982.
37. Estelle Mohler was nominated by Salome M. Baile, who provided this sketch in a letter to the author, November 24, 1980.
38. Darlene Bucher was nominated by her husband, Gordon, who was "happy to do this without her knowledge," September 11, 1980.
39. The information from this sketch was drawn from an interview in October, 1981.
40. Mary Eikenberry furnished this biography of Nganu Gamece; also *Southern Ohio Herald,* July-August, 1983.

Chapter 9. Women and Set-Apart Ministry

1. *The Brethren Encyclopedia,* p. 368.
2. *The Brethren Encyclopedia,* p. 374.
3. Durnbaugh, *The Brethren in Colonial America,* pp. 597-607. These women are numbers 121, 172, and 173 on Mack's list.
4. *The Brethren Encyclopedia,* p. 750.
5. An abridged version of this letter was reprinted by the National Council of Women's Work in 1935 in a pamphlet "Founding of Women's Work in the Church of the Brethren." The full text was published in *Messenger,* April 1975, pp. 20-21.
6. "Sister Sarah Major," *Brethren's Family Almanac, 1901,* p. 5.
7. *Monthly Gospel-Visiter,* February 1852, pp. 175- 77.
8. *Gospel Visitor,* August 1858, pp. 245-46.
9. *Gospel Messenger,* October 7, 1884.
10. *Gospel Messenger,* January 10, 1903, p. 25.
11. Bertha Miller Neher was nominated for inclusion in this volume by her daughter Viola Neher Whitehead. A sketch of her is in the *History of the Church of the Brethren in Indiana,* (1917), pp. 405-6. The 1952 Indiana history indicates she was given license to preach at Milford in

1908. However, her name did not occur on the Brethren ministerial list as a licensed sister until 1925. She may have been given authority to preach in 1908, as was Mattie Lear in 1897 (*Brethren in Northern Illinois and Wisconsin,* 1941, p. 193) by the local church but not recognized by the district until later. These dates are based on recollections of Bertha's and Mattie's daughters, who speak of licensing and ordination. These terms were not used until later so it is difficult to establish just what official acknowledgment these women received of their ministries.

12. Important sources for this sketch are Mildred Grimley, "No Sound of Trumpet," *Messenger,* January 1976, pp. 16-20; *History of the Church of the Brethren of the District of Southern Ohio,* pp. 430-32; and *The Brethren Encyclopedia,* 395.

13. *Report of the Proceedings of the Annual Meeting of the Brethren, 1922,* pp. 99-107 is the source for this debate.

14. Bittinger, *The Brethren in West Virginia,,* pp. 168-69; *Messenger,* September 1980, p. 3. Pastor Waybright was nominated by Desmond Bittinger.

15. *The Brethren Encyclopedia,* p. 340.

16. *History of the Church of the Brethren in Middle Pennsylvania,* pp. 515-16.

17. *History of the Church of the Brethren of the District of Southern Ohio,* pp. 120, 490-91; *The History of the Church of the Brethren in Michigan,* p. 253.

18. Pastor Keller was nominated for inclusion in this volume by Pauline Domer Jones of Canton, Ohio. Mrs. Jones worked as a housekeeper for Mrs. Keller so that she would have more time to devote to her ministerial work.

19. *The Brethren Encyclopedia,* p. 1286; Frantz, *History of the Church of the Brethren in Colorado,* p. 180.

20. Pastor Broughman was nominated for inclusion in this volume by Berwyn L. Oltman and Muriel Casper, Mrs. Broughman's daughter. Various biographical materials were provided by them.

21. Frantz, *Colorado,* p. 180.

22. *Annual Conference Minutes, 1935,* pp. 113-16.

23. *Minutes of Annual Conference, 1945-54,,* pp. 185-89. The source for the debate is a tape recording of the session in the BHLA.

24. Correspondence from Edward K. Ziegler to the author, 1983.

25. *Minutes of Annual Conference, 1956,* pp. 12-14.

26. *Minutes of Annual Conference, 1958,* and the tape recording of the session, in BHLA.

27. *History of the Northern Plains Church of the Brethren, 1844-1977,* p. 21.

28. This sketch is based on the article in *The Brethren Encyclopedia,* p. 890 and Long, *Faces Among the Faithful,* pp. 141-46. See also her biography, *Sister Anna,* by Dorothy G. Murray (1983).

29. *History of the Church of the Brethren in Indiana,* p. 468; also an interview with Opal Pence Nees in June of 1984.

30. Interview with Calvert Ellis, April 7, 1982.

31. Interview with Eleanor Painter in June of 1984; her profile from the January 1985 issue of *Brethren Life and Thought.*
32. Interview with Connie Burkholder in June of 1983.

Chapter 10. Toward Full Participation

1. In the 1952 report on "The Role of Women in the Church," *Minutes of Annual Conference,* 1952.
2. *Minutes of Annual Conference,* 1945-54, pp. 52-82.
3. The sources for the names and dates of all those who held denominational offices are the *Minutes of Annual Conference* and a 1977 presentation on "The Participation of Women" by Hazel Peters, from the personal files of the author.
4. *The Brethren Encyclopedia,* p. 32.
5. The term "proportional representation" was used in the report on "The Role of Women in the Church," *Minutes of Annual Conference,* 1952.
6. *Minutes of Annual Conference,* 1970.
7. "General Board Paper on Equality for Women," personal files of the author.
8. The primary sources for the history of Womaen's Caucus are two brochures produced by the caucus, the personal files of the author, and *The Brethren Encyclopedia,* p. 1359.
9. *The Brethren Encyclopedia,* p. 492; interview by the author in January of 1982. Virginia was nominated for inclusion in this volume by Edward K. Ziegler.
10. *Messenger,* December 1981, pp. 10-14.
11. These remarks were made during the 1952 Conference debate on "The Role of Women in the Church." Eva was a member of the committee that prepared the paper. Recording of the Conference debate is in BHLA.
12. Womaen's Caucus brochure.
13. This sketch of Naomi Hartzler is drawn from a biography she prepared for inclusion in the scrapbook for the 10th anniversary of Womaen's Caucus in 1983. Shirley Kirkwood suggested its use in this volume.
14. *Messenger,* March 1974, p. 2; interview in June of 1984. Many other women have served on General Board in recent years. Each has made contributions that could be noted. Carmen Boaz brought a Hispanic woman's perspective to the Board from 1972 to 1975. Karen Spohr Carter, a former Berliner, brought an international perspective on peace. The stories of these and other women may be found in the pages of *Messenger* and *Femailings.*
15. Personal files of the author.
16. *Minutes of Annual Conference,* 1977.
17. *Messenger,* August 1979, p. 21.
18. These reports are drawn from summary sheets distributed at the two conferences, from the personal files of the author.
19. This information is from brochures and newsletters printed by the Global

Women's Project in the personal files of the author.

20. *Messenger*, January, 1980, p. 10.

21. *Messenger*, January 1980, p. 13.

22. National Council of Women's Work Minutes, January 17-30, 1958, p. 9, in BHLA.

23. From "Call for Equality of Representation on Annual Conference Ballots," an exhibit to the agenda for the General Board, March, 1983, author's files.

24. From the "Equality for Women in the Church of the Brethren" paper, Church of the Brethren Annual Conference, June 1977, p. 3. The committee which prepared this paper claimed that such affirmation already existed. Interviews the author has conducted as well as her own experience indicate that it is still a vision to be realized.

EPILOGUE

1. Padma Gallup, "Doing Theology—An Asian Feminist Perspective," *CTC Bulletin*, December 1983, p. 21.

2. "Sisters' Aid Society," *Church of the Brethren Yearbook*, 1929, p. 38.

BIBLIOGRAPHY

BOOKS

Ankrum, Freeman, *Sidelights in Brethren History*. Elgin, Illinois: The Brethren Press, 1962.

Bittinger, Foster Melvin. *A History of the Church of the Brehren in the First District of West Virginia*. Elgin, Illinois: Brethren Publishing House, 1945.

The Brethren Encyclopedia. Philadelphia: Brethren Encyclopedia, Inc., 1984.

Bright, Calvin, compiler. *The Missionary Letters of Minnie Flory Bright*. New York: Vantage Press, 1973.

Brumbaugh, Martin Grove. *A History of The German Baptist Brethren in Europe and America*. Mount Morris, Illinois: Brethren Publishing House, 1899.

Buckingham, Minnie S. *Church of the Brethren in Southern Illinois*. Elgin, Illinois: Brethren Publishing House, 1950.

Chronicon Ephratense: A History of the Community of Seventh Day Baptists at Ephrata. Lancaster, Pennsylvania: S. H. Zahm and Company, 1899.

Church of the Brethren in India. *Fifty Years in India*. Elgin, Illinois: Brethren Publishing House, 1945.

Durnbaugh, Donald, editor. *The Church of the Brethren Past and Present*. Elgin, Illinois: The Brethren Press, 1971.

Durnbaugh, Donald. *European Origins of the Brethren*. Elgin, Illinois: The Brethren Press, 1967.

Durnbaugh, Donald. *The Brethren in Colonial America*. Elgin, Illinois: The Brethren Press, 1958.

Fisher, Virginia Showalter. *The Story of the Brethren*. Elgin, Illinois: Brethren Publishing House, 1957.

Frantz, Blanche. *A History of the Church of the Brethren in Colorado, 1874-1957*. N.p., 1963.

Garst, Jesse O. and others. *History of the Church of the Brethren of the District of Southern Ohio*. Dayton, Ohio: The Otterbein Press, 1920.

Gleim, Elmer. *Change and Challenge: A History of the Church of the Brethren in the Southern District of Pennsylvania, 1940-72*. Harrisburg, Pennsylvania: Triangle Press, 1973.

Hamer, Maryanna; Fruth, Glenn; and Oltman, Berwyn. *History of the*

Northern Plains Church of the Brethren, 1844-1977. N.p., 1977.

Harris, Ethel S., ed. *Brethren on the Southern Plains.* Jennings, Louisiana: Advanced Printing Company, 1976.

Heckman, John, and Miller, J. E. *Brethren in Northern Illinois and Wisconsin.* Elgin, Illinois: Brethren Publishing House, 1941.

Helman, Harley, ed. *Church of the Brethren in Southern Ohio.* Elgin, Illinois: Brethren Publishing House, 1955.

History of the Church of the Brethren in Indiana. Winona Lake, Indiana: Light and Life Press, 1952.

History of the Church of the Brethren of the Eastern District of Pennsylvania, 1708-1915. Lancaster, Pennsylvania: New Era Printing Company, 1915.

Kaylor, Earl, Jr. *Out of the Wilderness: The Brethren and Two Centuries of Life in Central Pennsylvania.* New York: Cornwall Books, 1981.

Klein, Walter. *Johann Conrad Beissel: Mystic and Martinet.* Philadelphia: University of Pennsylvania Press, 1942.

Kurtz, Henry, ed. *The Brethren's Encyclopedia.* Published by the editor at Columbiana, Ohio, 1867.

Long, Inez. *Faces Among the Faithful.* Elgin, Illinois: The Brethren Press, 1962.

Mallott, Floyd. *Studies in Brethren History.* Elgin, Illinois: Brethren Publishing House, 1954.

Moherman, Tully S., ed. *A History of the Church of the Brethren, Northeastern Ohio.* Elgin, Illinois: Brethren Publishing House, 1914.

Moyer, Elgin S. *Brethren in Florida and Puerto Rico.* Elgin, Illinois: The Brethren Press, 1975.

Muir, Gladdys. *Settlement of the Brethren on the Pacific Slope.* Elgin, Illinois: Brethren Publishing House, 1939.

Royer, Galen B. and others. *History of the Church of the Brethren in the Middle District of Pennsylvania, 1781-1925.* N.p., 1925.

Royer, Galen B. *Thirty-Three Years of Missions in the Church of the Brethren.* Elgin, Illinois: Brethren Publishing House, 1914.

Sachse, Julius. *The German Sectarians of Pennsylvania: A Critical and Legendary History of the Ephrata Cloisters and the Dunkers.* Philadelphia: P. C. Stockhausen, 1900.

Sappington, Roger. *The Brethren Along the Snake River.* Elgin, Illinois: The Brethren Press, 1966.

Sappington, Roger. *The Brethren in the Carolinas.* N.p., 1971.

Sappington, Roger. *The Brethren in the New Nation.* Elgin, Illinois: The Brethren Press, 1976.

Sappington, Roger. *The Brethren in Virginia.* Harrisonburg, Virginia: Park View Press, 1973.

Two Centuries of the Church of the Brethren. Elgin, Illinois: Brethren Publishing House, 1908.

Two Centuries of the Church of the Brethren in Western Pennsylvania, 1751-1950. Elgin, Illinois: Brethren Publishing House, 1953.

Willoughby, William. *Counting the Cost: The Life of Alexander Mack.* Elgin, Illinois: The Brethren Press, 1979.

Winger, Otho. *History of the Church of the Brethren in Indiana.* Elgin, Illinois: Brethren Publishing House, 1917.

Young, Walter. *The History of the Church of the Brethren in Michigan.* Elgin, Illinois: Brethren Publishing House, 1946.

PERIODICALS
The Brethren at Work.
Brethren Life and Thought.
The Brethren's Family Almanac.
The Christian Family Companion.
The Golden Dawn. Juniata College Library.
The Gospel Messenger.
The Monthly Gospel Visitor.
The Progressive Christian.

OTHER SOURCES
All of these materials may be found in the Brethren Historical Library and Archives, Elgin, Illinois.

Biographical File.
Church of the Brethren Yearbooks.
Clingingsmith, Elder John. "Short Historical Sketch of the Far Western Brethren of the Dunkard Church . . . to the year 1885," unpublished typescript.
Full Report of the Proceedings of the Annual Conference of the Church of the Brethren, 1890-1930.
Miller, W. R. and others. *Chicago Sunday School Extension.* Elgin, Illinois: Brethren Publishing House, 1904. Pages 34-37.
Minutes of the Annual Conferences of the Church of the Brethren.
Minutes of the Christian Education Commission.
Minutes of the General Mission Board.
Minutes of the Mothers and Daughters' Association.
Minutes of the Sisters' Aid Society.
NCWW Minutes.
Rupel, Esther. "An Investigation of the Origin, Significance, and Demise of the Prescribed Dress Worn by Members of the Church of the Brethren" Ph.D. dissertation, University of Minnesota, 1971.
Scrapbook of the Peace Caravan, 1930.
Stanley, Paula J. "A String of Pearls." *Brethren Life and Thought* (January 1985).
Women's Fellowship Materials.

SECONDARY SOURCES
Beaver, R. Pierce. *American Protestant Women in World Mission.* Grand Rapids, Michigan: William B. Eerdmans Publishing Company, 1968.
Bliss, Kathleen. *The Service and Status of Women in the Churches.* London: SCM Press Ltd., 1952.
Boulding, Elise. *The Underside of History: A View of Women Through*

Time. Boulder, Colorado: Westview Press, 1976.

Cavert, Inez M. *Women in American Church Life*. N.p., 1948.

Community of Women and Men in the Church: US Section Final Report. National Council of Churches, 1983.

Davies, Horton. *Worship and Theology in England, 1603-1690*. Princeton, New Jersey: Princeton University Press, 1975.

Griffis, W. E. "The Anabaptists" *The New World* (December 1895).

Irwin, Joyce. *Womanhood in Radical Protestantism: 1525-1675*. New York: The Edwin Mellen Press, 1979.

James, Janet Wilson, editor. *Women in American Religion*. Philadelphia: University of Pennsylvania Press, 1980.

Lehman, Helmut, editor. *Meaning and Practice of the Lord's Supper*. Philadelphia: Muhlenberg Press, 1961.

Revised Interim Report of a Study on the *Life and Work of Women in the Church*. Geneva: World Council of Churches, 1948.

Rothman, Sheila. *Woman's Proper Place: A History of Changing Ideals and Practices, 1870 to the Present*. New York: Basic Books, 1978.

Ruether, Rosemary Radford, and Keller, Rosemary Skinner, eds. *Women and Religion in America: A Documentary History, Vol. 2*. San Francisco: Harper and Row, 1983.

Schussler, Elisabeth Fiorenza. *In Memory of Her: A Feminist Theological Reconstruction of Christian Origins*. New York: Crossroad, 1983.

Tappert, Theodore. *The Lord's Supper: Past and Present Practices*. Philadelphia: Muhlenberg Press, 1961.

Williams, George. *The Radical Reformation*. Philadelphia: Westminster Press, 1962.

INDEX

Names of Persons

Names of Subjects and Places